B80C [illegible]

Information from Data and Models

Prepared for the B800 Course Team by Richard Wheatcroft,
Rob Paton, Richard Mole, Alan Parkinson,
Clare Spencer and Graham Francis

MBA

Foundations of Senior Management

COURSE TEAM

Authoring team

Rob Paton, Course Team Chair and Co-Chair, People Block
Greg Clark, Co-Chair, People Block
Richard Wheatcroft, Chair, Finance Block
Geoff Jones, Chair, Marketing Block
Jenny Lewis, Chair, Organizations Block
Patricia McCarthy, Course Manager
Wendy Crane, Course Manager

External contributors

Professor Stephen Watson, External Assessor
Professor Martin Hilb, European Adviser
Josep Artola Ortiz
George Bell
Indira Biswas-Benbow
Ann Caro
Brian Cartwright
Luis Fernando Conde Berne
Nelarine Cornelius
Nicolas Cudre-Maroux
Michael Dempsey
Nancy Finley
John Laxton
Michael Lovitt
Ohanes Missirillian
Tim Nightingale
Virginia Novarra
Maggie Parker
Serge Rosenberg
Peter Russell
Eberhard Schaumann
Tom Scott
Adam Spielman
David Stewart
Tom Walls
Barbara Waters

Production team

Linda Smith, Project Control
Susan Tilley, Project Control
Helen Thompson, Software Quality Assurance
Colin Thomas, Software Design
Laury Melton, Computer Conferencing
Jenny Edwards, Product Quality Assistant
Richard Mole, Director of Production (OUBS)
Riz Sharma, Secretary
Sally Baker, Liaison Librarian
Amanda Smith, Editor
Mark Goodwin, Editor
Ruth Drage, Graphic Designer
Roy Lawrance, Graphic Artist
Robert Gibson, Text Processing Services
Tina Cogdell, Print Production Co-ordinator
Jan Bright, BBC Series Producer
Natasha Soma, BBC Series Production Assistant

Other contributors

Jon Billsberry
Sheila Cameron
Professor Leslie de Chernatony
Tim Clark
Chris Cornforth
Kevin Daniels
Charles Edwards
Graham Francis
Jan Gadella
Jacky Holloway
Aude Leonetti
Chris Mabey
Geoff Mallory
David Mercer
John Moss-Jones
Sue Pearce
Paul Quintas
Gilly Salmon
Clare Spencer
Rosie Thomson
Amanda Waring
Jane Whiting

This text draws on material from the following Open University courses: B752 *Managing Resources for the Market* and B600 *The Capable Manager*.

The Open University
Walton Hall, Milton Keynes MK7 6AA

First published 1996. Second edition 1996. Third edition 1998. Fourth edition 1999. Reprinted 2000

Edited, designed and typeset by The Open University.

Printed in the United Kingdom by Thanet Press Limited, Margate, Kent.

ISBN 0 7492 9276 8

For further information on Open University Business School short courses and the Certificate, Diploma and MBA programmes, please contact the Customer Service Department, The Open University, PO Box 481, Walton Hall, Milton Keynes MK7 6BN (Tel.: 01908 653473).

4.2

11001C/b800b8fini4.2

CONTENTS

INTRODUCTION TO BOOK 8

This final book in the Finance Block has a broader remit than its predecessors. Even Book 7, which widened significantly the scope of the discussion, kept within the general field of finance and accounting. Here we are concerned with three subjects which are included in this block rather than elsewhere principally on the grounds that they, too, involve a significant (although, we hope, not excessive) quantitative element.

These topics are:

- computer financial modelling (Session 1)
- managerial statistics (Sessions 2 and 3)
- operations management (Sessions 4, 5 and 6).

Session 1 continues your studies in Books 3, 4 and 7 by introducing the techniques used for modelling in a financial context. As you are probably anticipating, these days this means using a spreadsheet, a tool of great flexibility but one which is sometimes misunderstood and so not used as effectively as it could be. Since 'Visicalc' was first written for the Apple II computer at the end of the 1970s, spreadsheet programs have been continually expanding the range of financial questions which ordinary managers can analyse for themselves without resorting to specialists, which was always a slow and expensive route to information. One of the nice things about working with spreadsheets is that, while the size and complexity can vary incredibly, the principles and 'good habits' can be demonstrated and practised within a small and comprehensible example. I once looked at a spreadsheet file that covered 120 pages of tiny lettering when printed out (it was modelling the building of a motorway between Prague and České Budějovice, where the *real* Budweiser beer comes from). However, it was not conceptually much more complex than the work you will be able to tackle after studying Session 1.

Statistics is one field of endeavour devoted to drawing *information* from *data*. It is important that a modern manager has the knowledge and ability to make proper use of statistical information, and so we look into the subject in Sessions 2 and 3. We do *not* expect managers to 'crunch' the numbers themselves, so we concentrate on the *application* rather than the *production* of statistical methods and measures. However, it is often not really possible to fully understand a statistic without some knowledge of how it is created, so these sessions have some mathematics in them.

As well as having general relevance for your MBA studies, this statistics material will prove important for the Marketing Block. As a subject, marketing makes major use of market research techniques and results, and statistical analysis underlies almost all forms of market research.

This book and this block conclude with three sessions on operations management. In a perfect world all MBA graduates would know a great deal about this subject (and many other subjects too!), but given the constraints on your study time we cover topic areas from the operations management field that represent the essential knowledge that would be expected from any MBA graduate of a good business school. Session 4 looks at *designing* operations, and Session 5 goes on to consider their *planning* and *control*. While much of the operations subject is, not unnaturally, concerned with manufacturing, the design, planning and control aspects are applicable to any and all forms of business operation. Thus, they are topics with which all MBA graduates need to be familiar. This is especially true of *project management*, which is usually a significant element in most managers' work, even when they do not think of themselves as project managers. This is why we have devoted the whole of Session 6 to the topic.

Given the broad range covered by Book 8, we cannot give an overall set of aims here. Each session or subject will state its own objectives in the appropriate place. Nevertheless, one theme runs through the whole book: the construction and use of models to extract meaningful information from data, of whatever sort. A manager's decision-making can be informed only by information, and this is the common theme of this book.

FINANCIAL SPREADSHEETS

SESSION **1**

Contents

1.1 Introduction

This session is about ways to harness the power and flexibility of PC spreadsheets to manage financial information. After reading about the scope and potential of this approach in Section 1.2, you will have the opportunity to implement simple financial models on your spreadsheet. The aim is to build up your spreadsheet skills in a progressive manner. After an investigation of a particular spreadsheet that illustrates the general points in Section 1.2, two spreadsheet exercises for managing personal finance are presented in Section 1.3 in the following way:

- You will be provided with enough information, and a few hints, to help you to sketch out a possible solution on paper.
- We then provide print-outs of a spreadsheet – this is not a uniquely 'correct' answer. The print-outs show what we expect you to produce because they were produced by managers who helped develop the course materials.
- You are then expected to produce your own spreadsheet. In case you find this difficult, there are helpful hints and advice.
- Finally, you will customize your spreadsheet to reflect your individual circumstances – your personal household budget and your income tax assessment.

This leads on to two more spreadsheet exercises for flexible budgeting and break-even analysis in Section 1.4. There are three further opportunities to develop your spreadsheet skills in Section 1.5 – for cash planning, profit planning and balance sheet planning. Section 1.6 is based on a video activity to help you set your new spreadsheet skills in a wider context. We then consider internal audit and system checks and controls in Section 1.7, before completing the session with the discounted cash flow (DCF) tableau in Section 1.8.

Be sure to print out documents when instructed, and to save your work using a suitable file name in a suitable directory. You are recommended to make frequent saves under a suitable series of names (NAME1.WKS, NAME2.WKS, or NAME1.XLS, NAME2.XLS, etc.) so that you can trace your development work. Then, if you suddenly start to experience difficulties, you can check back and discover which modification brought about the difficulty.

Depending on your software, you will have file names XLS for Excel or WKS for Works.

1.2 Models and spreadsheet modelling

Note that here we are talking mainly about a manager's departmental or informal information. It is much less common for people to be allowed to 'tinker with' the main accounting or records programs – for obvious reasons!

Until relatively recently, accountants designed and controlled financial information systems in the UK and managers tended to rely on accountants for guidance in the management of financial information. The arrival of the PC rapidly changed this pattern because at last managers were in a position to use and even design their own small-scale information and decision-support systems. The spreadsheet provided a 'user-friendly programming environment' for financial modelling.

Models and modelling

A model may be defined as 'a representation of reality' and certainly any financial model must be regarded in that sense; but we shall also be extending this definition to include means of simulating the financial affairs of an organization. The following definition of a model is helpful:

> ... a specification of the interrelationships of the parts of a system, in verbal or mathematical terms, sufficiently explicit to enable us to study its behaviour under a variety of circumstances and, in particular, to control it and predict its future.
>
> (Kendall and Stuart, 1979)

When the underlying structure of a problem has been established, a model may be built and manipulated in order to suggest possible outcomes. There are many advantages to this approach, as long as the model is a reasonable reflection of reality. Models can be manipulated and analysed more easily than any real system and invaluable insights may be gained from sensitivity (or 'What if?') analysis. Sensitivity studies enable the manager to see the effects of deviations from some commonly assumed base conditions, and to assess the validity of different models.

We must acknowledge that not all problems are amenable to this type of computer-modelling – witness some of the ideas of 'messy problems' that you met in Book 1.

Identifying and defining the problem

The first step in the construction of a model is to identify and define the problem as clearly and completely as possible so that the most significant factors are not overlooked. Unless we know precisely what problem we are addressing, we cannot hope to reflect its features in a realistic model. The description of a problem may include simple mathematical formulae, such as the basic accounting equation:

Assets = Liabilities + Capital

It may include rather more complex relationships, for example between the return on capital employed and the level of sales. In this session we start with simple descriptive problems and then introduce causal relationships as our knowledge and experience of model building increase.

Analysing the problem

The statement of the problem should identify:

- the nature of the decision to be made
- the output information required (say, for inclusion in a management report)
- the input information required to produce the outputs
- the processing needed to convert inputs to outputs, i.e. the sequence of arithmetic, logical or other operations needed to process the inputs into the outputs.

There may be cash flow problems, for example, and we may decide never to overdraw on an account at the bank. The bank account balance is the output variable, the cash inflows and the cash outflows are the input variables, and the processing involved is the addition and subtraction of cash flows. Simple specifications such as these can be expanded to give the more detailed prescriptive processing requirements needed for solution by computer.

Programming the model

Spreadsheets provide an automatic problem-solving environment. This is not to say that the problem is automatically solved for us, but it does mean that the spreadsheet makes it easy to see the results of changing any of the assumptions built into a model, or any of the data inputs. The charting capability provides helpful charts, bar graphs and other graphical forms of presenting numerical data that can be included in reports. Spreadsheet outputs or extracts can be readily incorporated into management reports.

Testing the model

Testing is an iterative process. It involves trial and error with sample data inputs, finding and correcting errors of logic and procedure within the spreadsheet. This 'debugging' is almost inevitable because most spreadsheets, except perhaps the simplest, require repeated correction before they can be accepted as complete. There is always the very real danger of errors being left in spreadsheets even though they are considered to be complete – a result of inadequate testing.

Sensitivity and 'What if?' analyses

The technique of sensitivity analysis is quite simple. We first build a model based on assumptions that typify the most likely case. Then we change the value of each input in turn, usually by small increments, and note the effects on the output variables. We must also consider the effect of changes to combinations of inputs. In this way we simulate a wide range of likely causes and effects and try to deduce valid guides to improved decision making.

We discussed sensitivity analysis in Book 7 Session 5.7 in the context of DCF analysis. You will have a chance to try it for yourself later in this session.

When we use a spreadsheet we can alter one value and all its dependent values are changed automatically. The identification of causal relationships is thereby enhanced. (More advanced spreadsheets have a 'goal seeking' facility. It is then possible to start with some desired output and the spreadsheet software will identify the required inputs. We may, once more, have to reassess the model and, if necessary, change the structure so that the model is improved in an iterative way.)

Documenting the model

There are few who would disagree that it is essential to document the definition, analysis, specification, design, programming and testing of spreadsheet models. In practice, however, the need to tackle a problem quickly will often mean that its documentation is postponed until after it has been used, or even postponed indefinitely.

If a report is to be produced, then the documentation process is incomplete unless a full report specification is also included. Such a specification must cover not only the titles and descriptive labels, page numbers and text, but also the spreadsheet settings, column widths and formats, calculation and protection modes, and so on. A directory showing these details should be a feature of the manager's specification when commissioning modelling work from others. It is also helpful to include information that is necessary to customize a spreadsheet – for example, any special commands, input data and the other key factors required to produce the report. Other relevant information, such as any business concepts used, is also likely to help prospective users and it is particularly helpful to include a section that explains the inherent logic of the model.

Updating the model

Model construction and use should be seen as part of a continuous process. The model should be reviewed and kept up to date because models that do not reflect actual conditions sufficiently closely can lead to wrong management decisions.

Advantages and disadvantages of spreadsheet modelling

A financial model, then, consists of facts and assumptions which are related in an explicit and systematic way, and when the model is implemented as a spreadsheet model the input data (unassembled information) are accurately and speedily manipulated into useful management output. A budget is a good example of a financial model. It seeks to represent the real activities of the organization and to predict the impact of the future upon the organization. Some budgets are managed manually, others by a mainframe computer, and others by the manager's own spreadsheet software on a PC. Experience has established that spreadsheet models offer managers some significant advantages within the work place, including:

- the provision of a framework for problem solving
- a better understanding of a particular problem through the process of designing and building a model to help manage that problem
- the facility to test a wide range of possible scenarios exploring 'What if?' situations
- savings in time and money.

Spreadsheet models can offer managers a relatively simple way of managing and planning with the benefit of superior financial information. They allow managers to test out the implications of their plans well before action needs to be taken. Such an approach allows managers to establish the likely impact of their plans upon profits and surpluses, assets and liabilities, cash flow, budgets, break-even points, and so on. Managers can learn more about their organizations, reassess their targets, explore problems, search for new options – and manage financial information on a day-to-day basis. A real bonus is that, as tedious arithmetical calculations are removed, time is released for more productive activities. Modelling is often a learning process in which the current model represents our limited understanding and knowledge. It is through model building, with its repeated testing and improvement, that we seek to increase our knowledge and understanding.

Pressure often reduces the time available for planning but, conversely, the process of building financial models for planning and decision making requires an initial, and sometimes large, investment of time. Note, however, that recalculations for changed 'What if?' assumptions require only seconds.

A model can only predict and behave within its design constraints and so the output from a financial model must be treated with a degree of caution. This rather negative view should not be interpreted as a rejection of modelling but, rather, as an encouragement to learn. This is because, by learning about modelling, we learn not only about the modelling process but also about our business and the world around us. In designing and constructing financial models, we automatically import the limitations of the accounting process into the models. If we do this, and then use the models in the work place to help manage financial information – looking backwards or forwards – we must be aware of the strengths and weaknesses of the financial information we handle.

There are some other obvious disadvantages associated with spreadsheet modelling:

- There is a danger of oversimplification – crucial factors may be omitted at the design stage.
- Not every important relationship can necessarily be expressed explicitly in terms of built-in spreadsheet functions.
- The design of the spreadsheet model may be too rigid to cope with future changes.
- Users may forget that spreadsheet models produce predictions based on the programmed logic – which may be flawed.
- Some managers have a tendency to manipulate spreadsheet models to produce their desired outcomes.
- Some managers fail to recognize their own limitations and produce very badly implemented spreadsheets, while other managers may fail to recognize the limitations of the spreadsheet software and try to build over-elaborate spreadsheets on too large a scale.

Recent surveys indicate that there are mistakes in as many as 90% of spreadsheets!

To maximize the advantages and minimize the disadvantages, it is important to adopt a systematic approach to the design of a spreadsheet model that considers first the context of modelling and then the specific details of the model in question.

Starting to use spreadsheets

One manager, who tested these course materials, told us:

> I find it very hard to resist the temptation to get started on my spreadsheet before I have thought it through properly. The result is twofold. First, I waste a lot of time as I rush to set up a table, only to discover that I have not taken account of some related data or function. Secondly, I realize that I have not fully worked out how I can set up the spreadsheet to fulfil its intended function, including the reports. This may not matter, if you are the only person likely to use the spreadsheet. However, as a manager, you are more likely to pass it on to one of your staff to keep up to date, or to use for reporting future periods.
>
> To summarize – work out your model as well as you can before you start building it on the PC.

The first step, then, is to try to imagine 'the whole'. Consider the purpose of the model. Is it a 'one-off' or are you going to use it more than once – either regularly or *ad hoc*? Does it produce a report which you want to print out, or does it provide a result or data which you want to read and apply elsewhere? Are you the model user as well as the model builder, or will it be used by others? You should consider spreadsheet structure in terms of:

- the input of fresh data, such as the latest sales data
- the basic assumptions that normally remain fixed, such as taxation rates

- how the data are to be processed in order to produce the results – do they involve totals and differences in cash figures, or complex calculations, say for a tender price against a substantial invitation to contract?

Our manager also told us:

> I was very casual about this preparatory work, even though the computer package is no help at all in the preliminary stages when you are thinking through your basic approach.

Spreadsheets are very powerful and it is possible to set up extremely sophisticated and complex calculations and logical relationships. However, the spreadsheet software and the PC hardware – especially the memory – will limit the size and complexity of your model. This is unlikely to cause you any problems on this course, but it would be a mistake to assume that an entry-level spreadsheet package could or should be used for complex models. A financial model of a whole organization is far too ambitious. As a manager, you are much more likely to use your spreadsheet modelling either on a one-off basis or regularly in a relatively straightforward decision-support role. Complex financial models may require specialized software with much greater functionality than an entry-level spreadsheet, and the design and implementation will lean heavily on systems analysis skills which lie outside the scope of this course.

An example of spreadsheet modelling

At this point, we will illustrate what is meant by building and using a spreadsheet model to support a specific decision:

- First we describe a particular decision-support problem and explain how it is dealt with.
- Then we show you a print-out and ask you to use the model yourself.
- Finally, we briefly suggest a helpful development to the model.

Do not be surprised that the total for Series C in Figure 1.1 is 13, not 16. The reason is explained later in this section.

A distributor who wanted access to Open University materials, telephoned the commercial distribution subsidiary Open University Education Enterprises (OUEE). Among other things, OUEE sells the University's television programmes to overseas educational markets, and a US distributor was interested in securing rights in the television programmes from three of our undergraduate courses – a total of 36 programmes (16 in Series A, 4 in Series B and 16 in Series C). If the deal went through, the distributor would buy the master tapes of the 36 programmes (at cost) and market them in their own catalogue, paying a royalty on all sales.

OUEE has substantial marketing and administrative overheads and substantial copyright clearance costs are also payable if programmes are sold into particular market-places and for particular purposes. These 'one-off' copyright clearance costs are specific to individual programmes. Particular programmes may therefore have to be excluded from deals if they are too expensive to clear.

Negotiations with the US distributor were imminent, by telephone, and were expected to revolve around a number of points:

- the distributor's selling price – which might be non-negotiable – as our titles would be only a minor addition to their existing list
- the royalty rate based on the distributor's selling price

- the impact of clearance costs which we would have to pay – it might be advisable to exclude some programmes from the deal
- the number of sales that could be made – bearing in mind that some academic disciplines sell better than others
- the dollar exchange rate with the pound.

In the OUEE manager's judgement, it was going to be important to settle the terms straightaway if possible. It seemed, therefore, that a spreadsheet model could be a great help, provided he could build it in such a way that the effect of various possibilities could be tested as he talked on the telephone. The spreadsheet model was built and tested in less than a day. It had two parts: a top screen showing a summary of results, as in Figure 1.1, and the two screens immediately below the summary screen which contained the clearance cost schedules for all the programmes in each of three programme series, as shown in Figure 1.2 (overleaf).

This is a real example, not a contrived one. The only thing that the manager has done for this course is tidy up the spreadsheet for publication.

As you can see, the top screen summarizes the necessary information for each programme series and for the whole deal. As he negotiated the manager could:

- agree a royalty rate
- agree a price
- flex the exchange rate
- enter forecast sales
- delete specific programmes from each of the three programme series.

'Flexing' the budget is covered in Book 4.

To assess the results of excluding a programme, all the manager has to do is enter the programme number underneath the full list – in Figure 1.2 programmes 7, 10 and 24 from Series C have been withdrawn from the deal. The financial summary changes accordingly in the top screen. Every other cell in the spreadsheet was 'locked' so that the contents could not be changed by mistake in the heat of the moment.

	A	B	C	D	E	F	G	H
1	OUEE VIDEO NEGOTIATIONS; BREAK-EVEN AND PROFIT ANALYSIS							
2								
3								
4	**Flexing assumptions**							
5	Royalty rate	20% based on US price per title						
6	US price per programme	60 $						
7	Exchange rate	1.5 $ per £						
8								
9	Each series consists of a number of programmes;							
10	programmes can be deleted from the deal in the third screen (PgDn twice							
11								
12	Forecast sales are entered in the table below							
13								
14	**Financial summary**							
15		Series A		Series B		Series C		All
16	No. of titles	16		4		13		33
17	Clearance costs	£4,815		£1,780		£6,504		£13,099
18	Break-even sales	38		56		63		50
19	**Forecast sales**	100		50		100		
20	Forecast Royalty	£12,800		£1,600		£10,400		£24,800
21	Forecast contribution	£7,985		-£180		£3,896		£11,701

Figure 1.1 *Summary screen of the spreadsheet OUEEDEAL.XLS*

	A	B	C	D	E	F	G	H
25	**Clearance costs**							
26		SERIES A		SERIES B		SERIES C		All
27	Program number pn	£	pn	£	pn	£	pn	£
28	1	37.50	1	130.20	5	41.25		
29	2	0.00	3	0.00	6	36.00		
30	3	172.50	4	700.00	7	111.00		
31	4	2000.00	8	950.00	10	105.00		
32	5	30.00			11	52.50		
33	6	300.00			12	45.00		
34	7	0.00			13	45.00		
35	8	5.25			14	75.00		
36	9	72.00			15	45.00		
37	10	1500.00			17	63.00		
38	11	10.50			18	3000.00		
39	12	0.00			19	52.50		
40	13	61.98			21	2500.00		
41	14	0.00			22	48.75		
42	15	439.90			23	500.00		
43	16	185.00			24	20.00		
44	**TOTALS**							
45	16	4814.63	4	1780.20	16	6740.00	36	13334.83
46								
47								
48	**Flexing; programmes that could be deleted from the deal**							
49								
50	Enter programme numbers in cells A51:A55, C51:C55 and E51:E55 below							
51		0.00		0.00	7	111.00		
52		0.00		0.00	10	105.00		
53		0.00		0.00	24	20.00		
54		0.00		0.00		0.00		
55		0.00		0.00		0.00		
56	**NET TOTALS**							
57	16	4814.63	4	1780.20	13	6504.00	33	13098.83
58								
59								
60	**Breakeven calculation**							
61		37.6		55.6		62.5		49.6

Figure 1.2 *Lower part of the spreadsheet OUEEDEAL.XLS*

Depending on your software, you will have file names:

- WPS for Works
- DOC for Word.

ACTIVITY 1.1

Load the word-processing file **OUEEDEAL.WPS** or **OUEEDEAL.DOC** and follow the instructions carefully.

The model shown in Figure 1.2 is as the OUEE manager prepared it for his telephone negotiation without adding any further frills. It was a useful workaday spreadsheet that gave him increased confidence in the discussions and negotiations. As he said afterwards:

> I had to remember to test every different calculation. I also checked a number of the calculations which were simply copies of other calculations (where I had used Copy/Fill Right or Copy/Fill Down). Then I did a set of manual calculations on certain parts of the model. When I had corrected all my mistakes, I tested the model by changing the assumptions, having worked out with my pocket calculator (although I could have used the calculator in Works itself) what the answer should be. I tried to do these checks really thoroughly, even working under severe time pressure, because I realized the potential for disastrous results if I failed to spot an error in the model!
>
> Of course, the model does not cover all contingencies. I realized later that I could not easily check on the effect of deleting an entire programme series from the deal. Nevertheless, this spreadsheet 'decision-support tool' amply repaid the few hours spent on developing it.

1.3 Two spreadsheets for managing personal finance

A personal income and expenditure spreadsheet

A spreadsheet that details personal income and expenditure is an example of a cash flow model – it is, in fact, a simple financial model, which captures personal flows of finance and predicts an end-of-year surplus or deficit.

How do you manage your personal income and expenditure? Most of us need to keep a close watch on how things are going. Although some months are easy for most people, with no special items of expenditure, other months, such as those around birthdays and public festivals, have heavy additional costs and there are large quarterly electricity and telephone bills – the monthly salary then stands no chance of covering everything. Personal cash has to be managed and what is needed is an income and expenditure budget.

It is not necessary to compare actual against budget – that would be far too painful! What is needed is a table which would show month-by-month the estimated, or budgeted, income and expenditure. Any month-end surpluses or deficits must be carried forward to the next month. At the end of the year, there should be something in hand, but if there is a deficit then expenditure must be trimmed back.

The data below were offered by a critical reader during the development of the course materials. The estimated income for our critical reader for next year is:

Salary	£1200 per month which should increase in April by 2%. Salary is paid in the middle of each month.
Salary (partner)	£200 per month in a part-time job and £360 per quarter from fees in other jobs (March, June, September and December). Salaries are paid in the middle of the month.
Dividends	Dividends are paid in January (£100), March (£150), July (£100) and November (£200).
Bank interest	The bank pays interest on deposit accounts in September (£325).

The total income for the full year looks as if it will be £19,331 from:

Salary	£14,616
Partner's salary and fees	£3,840
Dividends	£550
Bank interest	£325

There are several expenditure headings detailed below and there is a final category called 'Sundry Unforeseen Bills' or SUBs – since they attack you underwater and can torpedo your best-laid plans. Our critical reader does not even try to put these into the budget directly but plans for a surplus over the year, either to build up savings or to pay the SUBs.

Regular monthly payments:

Housekeeping – food, etc.	£300
House mortgage payments	£275
Local Authority tax	£75
Water bills	£25
Car purchase instalments	£250
Personal expenditure	£50
Personal expenditure (partner)	£50
Car running costs	£200

Quarterly payments:

Gas	£250 in March, £100 in June and September, £250 in December
Electricity	£80 in March, June, September, December
Telephone	£70 in April, July, October, January

Irregular additional items:

Car: tax and repairs	£100 in March and £200 in September
Insurance (house and car)	£1000 in December
Television licence	£90 in September
Holiday expenditure	£1400 in August

The expenditure for the year totals £18,790 which would leave a surplus £541 for all those SUBs, such as house repairs, the furniture fund and contingencies.

ACTIVITY 1.2

Sketch out the shape of a suitable personal income and expenditure spreadsheet.

A simple table is perfectly adequate – using one column for each month and one row for each item of expenditure or income. Individual expenditure items are better shown first, then a total monthly expenditure category, followed by income items and total monthly income. Then a simple subtraction yields the monthly surpluses or deficits. It is equally straightforward to include the cumulative total each month.

The critical reader's spreadsheet is shown in Figure 1.3. Remember that this is not the only 'correct' approach, simply the way one person prepared it.

ACTIVITY 1.3

Load the word-processing file **MONEY.WPS** or **MONEY.DOC** and follow the instructions carefully.

	A	B	C	D	E	F	G	H	I	J	K	L	M	N	O	P
1			**BUDGET OF MONTHLY INCOME & EXPENDITURE**													
2																
3	EXPENDITURE:		January	February	March	April	May	June	July	August	September	October	November	December		TOTAL
4																
5																
6	Housekeeping		300	300	300	300	300	300	300	300	300	300	300	300		3,600
7	Mortgage		275	275	275	275	275	275	275	275	275	275	275	275		3,300
8	Local Authority tax		75	75	75	75	75	75	75	75	75	75	75	75		900
9	Water		25	25	25	25	25	25	25	25	25	25	25	25		300
10	Car purchase		250	250	250	250	250	250	250	250	250	250	250	250		3,000
11	Car Petrol/repairs		200	200	300	200	200	200	200	200	400	200	200	200		2,700
12	Gas				250			100			100			250		700
13	Electricity				80			80			80			80		320
14	Telephone		70			70			70			70				280
15	Insurance													1,000		1,000
16	TV Licence										90					90
17	Holiday									1,400						1,400
18	Personal		50	50	50	50	50	50	50	50	50	50	50	50		600
19	Personal (partner)		50	50	50	50	50	50	50	50	50	50	50	50		600
20																
21																
22	TOTAL Expenditure		1,295	1,225	1,655	1,295	1,225	1,405	1,295	2,625	1,695	1,295	1,225	2,555		18,790
23																
24																
25	INCOME		January	February	March	April	May	June	July	August	September	October	November	December		TOTAL
26																
27																
28	Salary		1,200	1,200	1,200	1,224	1,224	1,224	1,224	1,224	1,224	1,224	1,224	1,224		14,616
29	Salary (partner)		200	200	200	200	200	200	200	200	200	200	200	200		2,400
30	Fees (partner)				360			360			360			360		1,440
31	Dividends		100		150				100				200			550
32	Bank interest										325					325
33																
34																
35	TOTAL Income		1,500	1,400	1,910	1,424	1,424	1,784	1,524	1,424	2,109	1,424	1,624	1,784		19,331
36																
37		c/f														
38	SURPLUS/(DEFICIT):		205	175	255	129	199	379	229	-1,201	414	129	399	-771		541
39																
40	CUMULATIVE	0	205	380	635	764	963	1,342	1,571	370	784	913	1,312	541		

Figure 1.3 *The critical reader's spreadsheet for an annual income and expenditure budget*

A personal income tax spreadsheet

In this section you will develop a model that calculates liability for UK personal income tax. It is based on UK tax law and principles as they applied in 1993/4 but, irrespective of when you read this or whether you live in another country, your work on this model will help you to develop your spreadsheet skills. If you so wish, you could develop a spreadsheet model for your current situation and circumstances.

It is because taxation rules are exceedingly long and complicated in most countries that many people resort to employing tax experts to help them through the maze of legislation. However, calculating your own tax liability is easy in the UK when your income and your allowances are fairly straightforward. The objective of this exercise is to let you practise using spreadsheets rather than to understand tax law.

The UK tax year runs from 6 April to 5 April of the following year so that for the 1993/4 tax year we need to collect all the income and allowable expenses together for the year ending on 5 April 1994. We will assume that Olive Asch has a taxable salary in 1993/4 of £28,000, which is the bulk of her salary once her contributions to her employer's pension scheme, which are tax-free, have been deducted. A total of £6454 in tax has been deducted from her monthly salary payments during the year. She has two other sources of income in the form of share dividends and interest from deposits with a bank, which she receives after tax has been deducted at the standard rate of 25%. These other sources of taxed income are:

- Dividend from ABC plc of £750 tax paid – £1000 less tax of 25%.
- Dividend from High Dividends plc of £1125 tax paid – £1500 less tax of 25%.
- Dividend from Blue Chip plc of £900 tax paid – £1200 less tax of 25%.
- Interest of £900 tax paid – £1200 less tax of 25% from the bank.

Thus, Olive's pre-tax income totals £32,900 from which tax of £7679 has already been deducted at source. Before calculating her tax liability, she is given a number of allowances:

1 She is given a personal allowance of £3445.
2 She can claim an additional allowance of £1720 because she is married.
3 She is a member of a professional association and the tax authorities allow her to deduct her annual subscription of £150.

The total of these allowable deductions is £5315 and thus some £27,585 is taxable income (£32,900 less £5315).

The total tax payable is worked out from her taxable income and the following tax bands:

1 The first £2000 of taxable income is charged at 20% 'reduced rate' – the tax liability is £400.
2 The next £21,700 is charged at 25% 'standard rate' – the tax liability is £5425.
3 Anything over that amount is charged at 40% 'higher rate' – the tax liability on the £3885 taxable income that falls within this tax band is £1554.

Finally, from this total tax payable of £7379 Olive may subtract the tax of £7679 which was deducted at source. The balance is either a 'net tax due' by

Olive or 'net tax overpaid' by her. Happily for Olive, we calculate that she had overpaid by £300 (£7679 – £7379) and was due a refund.

It would be useful for Olive to have a separate table to list the dividend income because she is required to list dividend income separately on her tax return form, which must be sent to the tax office each year. It would also be helpful to show the three tax rates and the tax bands separately so that if the bands change it will be an easy matter to update the spreadsheet, and this will also be helpful to anyone who needs to see or check the calculations.

ACTIVITY 1.4

Sketch out the shape of a suitable personal income tax spreadsheet. Think carefully about the presentation of the computations and make it as clear and intelligible as possible.

How did you get on? Compare your version with ours in Figure 1.4. Which do you feel is preferable?

	A	B	C	D	E	F
1	UK PERSONAL INCOME TAX COMPUTATION				TAX YEAR:1993/4	
2						
3						
4				Gross	Tax	Net
5				Income	Paid	Income
6				----------	----------	----------
7	INCOME SUMMARY					
8	Salary			£28,000	£6,454	£21,546
9	Dividends (see below)			£3,700	£925	£2,775
10	Bank Interest			£1,200	£300	£900
11				----------	----------	----------
12				£32,900	£7,679	£25,221
13				==========	==========	==========
14						
15	DIVIDENDS					
16	ABC plc			£1,000	£250	£750
17	High Dividends PLC			£1,500	£375	£1,125
18	Blue Chip plc			£1,200	£300	£900
19				----------	----------	----------
20				£3,700	£925	£2,775
21				==========	==========	==========
22						
23						
24		Less Tax Allowances:				
25						
26		Personal	£3,445			
27		Married	£1,720			
28		Prof. Fees	£150			
29		----------	----------			
30		Total	£5,315			
31		----------	----------			
32	TAXABLE INCOME			£27,585		
33	==========	==========	==========	==========		
34						
35	TAX PAYABLE:	Tax	Tax	Income	Tax	
36		Rate	Band	in band	payable	
37						
38	Reduced Rate	20%	£2,000	£2,000	£400	
39	Standard Rate	25%	£21,700	£21,700	£5,425	
40	Higher Rate	40%	unlimited	£3,885	£1,554	
41					----------	
42				Total	£7,379	
43		Less: Tax deducted at source			£7,679	
44					----------	
45		Net Tax due/(overpaid)			-£300	
46					==========	

Figure 1.4 *Spreadsheet for personal income tax calculations*

ACTIVITY 1.5

Load the word-processing file **TAX.WPS** or **TAX.DOC** and follow the instructions carefully.

1.4 Spreadsheets for flexible budgeting and break-even analysis

Fixed and flexible budgets

As you know, some organizations produce a series of budgets for different levels of activity. Such budgets take account of likely variations and may provide the only practicable means for retaining control. An effective alternative is to have a fixed budget for a low level of activity and a second fixed budget for a high level of activity. The low and high budgets will then bracket the expected range of activity. A flexed budget for some intermediate level of activity can be derived from the low and high budgets if the extra costs are assumed to vary directly with the extra level of activity.

Two budgets have been prepared for a particular department as shown in Table 1.1. The first budget assumes that 8000 hours will be worked, which corresponds to the lowest level of activity. The second budget assumes 12,000 hours of working and this corresponds to the highest level of activity. The flexed budget of 10,000 hours is the mid-point of the low and high budgets.

Table 1.1 Fixed budgets for low and high levels of activity

	Low	*High*	*Flexed*
Hours of work	8,000	12,000	10,000
Costs:	(£)	(£)	(£)
Supervision	10,000	17,200	13,600
Depreciation	16,000	22,500	19,250
Consumables	9,600	14,400	12,000
Heat and light	1,800	2,200	2,000
Power	12,000	18,000	15,000
Cleaning	1,200	1,600	1,400
Repairs	4,000	7,000	5,500
Indirect wages	16,000	24,000	20,000
Rent and rates	7,200	7,200	7,200
Total	77,800	114,100	95,950

Assuming that the increase in costs between these levels of activity is solely due to variable cost, the variable cost per hour will be the difference between the high and low budgeted costs divided by the extra 4000 hours' work-load. For example, the variable costs of supervision per hour would be £17,200 minus £10,000, divided by 4000, or £1.80 per hour.

The flexed budget for working hours anywhere in the range 8000 to 12,000 can be calculated by applying the variable costs in each cost category to the hours worked in excess of 8000 hours, plus the budgeted costs for 8000 hours of work. For example, the supervision costs for 10,000 hours of working will be

2000 hours at £1.80 per hour plus £10,000, which is £13,600. Again, the supervision costs for 9000 hours will be 1000 hours at £1.80 per hour plus £10,000, which is £11,800.

ACTIVITY 1.6

Load the word-processing file **FIX&FLEX.WPS** or **FIX&FLEX.DOC** and follow the instructions carefully.

Break-even and profit–volume analysis

The requirement here is to establish the relationships between costs, revenues and profits at different levels of activity. Suppose that you have the summary of results shown in Table 1.2 for a particular organization. At first sight it may seem impossible to generate all the cost and profit interrelationships, as well as the break-even sales and the margin of safety for each year. Yet, there is sufficient information here to do so.

Break-even and profit–volume analysis are described in Book 3.

Table 1.2 Summary of results

	Year 1 (£)	*Year 2* (£)	*Increases* (£)
Sales revenue	100,000	150,000	50,000
Total costs	90,000	130,000	40,000
Profit	10,000	20,000	10,000

We make the reasonable assumption that the fixed costs have not changed from the end of Year 1 to the end of Year 2. On this basis, the increase in total costs can only be due to the increased variable costs associated with the increased sales revenue. Thus, the variable cost per pound of sales revenue must be £40,000 divided by £50,000, or £0.80.

Knowing the variable cost per pound of sales revenue, we can calculate the variable costs for each year because we know the sales revenue each year. In Year 1, for example, the sales revenue is £100,000 and so we can easily calculate that the variable costs must be £80,000, given that the variable costs are £0.80 per pound of sales revenue.

Furthermore, the fixed costs can be obtained by subtracting the variable costs that we have just calculated from the total costs. The results are shown in Table 1.3.

Having established the cost structure for the organization, we can analyse its profitability structure. The contribution, for example, is obtained by adding the fixed costs to the profit (Table 1.4). We are now in a position to calculate the contribution as a percentage of sales as shown in Table 1.5.

Table 1.3 Calculation of fixed costs

	Year 1 (£)	*Year 2* (£)
Total costs	90,000	130,000
Less variable costs	80,000	120,000
Fixed costs	10,000	10,000

Table 1.4 Contribution

	Year 1 (£)	*Year 2* (£)
Profit	10,000	20,000
Plus fixed costs	10,000	10,000
Contribution	20,000	30,000

Table 1.5 Contribution as a percentage of sales

	Year 1	*Year 2*
Contribution	£20,000	£30,000
Sales	£100,000	£150,000
Contribution as a percentage of sales	20%	20%

It is reassuring that the contribution percentage calculated for Year 1 is the same as that for Year 2 – if there had been a difference then an error must have been made!

Since 20% of sales is the contribution and this equals the fixed costs at break-even, it follows that:

Break-even sales = Fixed costs ÷ 20% = £50,000.

It is then a simple matter of determining the margin of safety as shown in Table 1.6. Table 1.7 summarizes all this information.

Table 1.6 Margin of safety

	Year 1 (£)	*Year 2* (£)
Sales	100,000	150,000
Less break-even sales	50,000	50,000
Margin of safety	50,000	100,000

The analysis relies on an underlying proportional relationship between sales and variable costs. It also assumes that the fixed costs are constant. Clearly, these assumptions may not apply over wide ranges of activity – all costs are variable in the long term or over large activity ranges. However, in the short term and within a narrow range of activity levels, it is not unreasonable to make these assumptions.

The analysis is complicated and you are not expected to be able to remember all the stages, although the principles should be clear enough. You may be relieved to know that the following PC activity provides step-by-step instructions for constructing a spreadsheet for break-even analysis.

ACTIVITY 1.7

Load the word-processing file **B-EVEN.WPS** or **B-EVEN.DOC** and follow the instructions carefully.

Table 1.7 Summary figures

	Year 1 (£)	*Year 2* (£)	*Increases* (£)
Sales revenue	100,000	150,000	50,000
Total costs	90,000	130,000	40,000
Profit	10,000	20,000	10,000
Variable costs	80,000	120,000	
Fixed costs	10,000	10,000	
Contribution	20,000	30,000	
Contribution as percentage of sales	20%	20%	
Break-even sales	50,000	50,000	
Margin of safety	50,000	100,000	

1.5 Three interlinked spreadsheets for financial planning

Planning is a crucial management activity. In this section you will develop spreadsheet models to help Tresham Manufacturing's management to plan ahead. There are three spreadsheets for projecting the three master budgets you saw in Book 4, Session 1.3 – the profit and loss account, the cash flow forecast, and the balance sheet of Tresham. The relevant figure from Book 4 is reproduced here as Figure 1.5. You will find that all the details are provided in the associated word-processing files that you are required to use in the PC activities in this section.

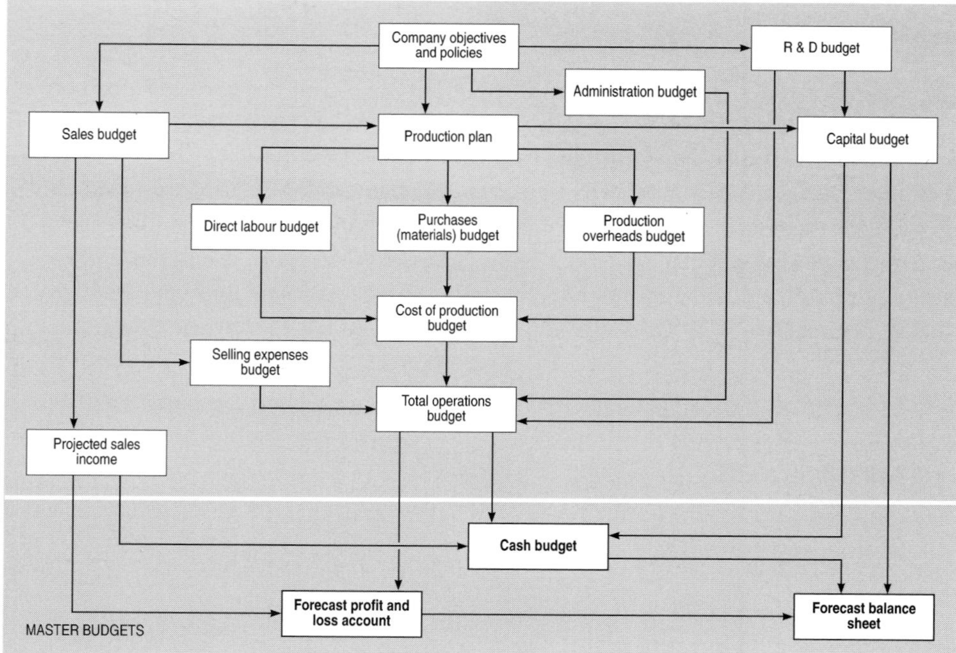

Figure 1.5 *Tresham's budgeting structure*

Profit planning

The following activity will give you practice in constructing larger-scale spreadsheets.

ACTIVITY 1.8

Load the word-processing file **PROFIT.WPS** or **PROFIT.DOC** and follow the instructions on the first screen.

Cash planning

Earlier in the Finance Block you saw the need for businesses to ensure that they are not only profitable but also solvent. Many profitable businesses have failed because they have had cash flow problems. A cash flow model can indicate the possible need for extra funds and can help in any funding decision – such as whether to use short-term sources, such as bank overdrafts and loans, or whether to obtain long-term loans or additional share capital. The projected cash flow forecast differs from the profit and loss account in that the latter:

- includes the accrued (unpaid) expenses but excludes pre-paid expenses related to subsequent trading periods
- excludes *capital expenditure* and instead includes an annual depreciation charge
- projects profits as opposed to cash surpluses/deficits.

ACTIVITY 1.9

Load the word-processing file **CASH.WPS** or **CASH.DOC** and follow the instructions carefully.

The output includes both capital and revenue items. A bank manager would need to see projections like these when considering a proposal for a business loan.

Balance sheet planning

We have examined various aspects of planning and come now to the ultimate planning document – the forecast balance sheet. It is essentially a summary statement covering perhaps the previous five years and the next five. It summarizes the details of the fixed assets and the capital expenditure budget. It projects the trading operations and their effects on working capital. It is concerned with liquidity, solvency and profitability. Finally, it considers the sources of finance and the balance between long-term loans and shareholders' funds. Its purpose is both to provide an overall plan for the business, a statement of intent, and to present to those concerned a blueprint for future strategy.

ACTIVITY 1.10

Load the word-processing file **BALSHT.WPS** or **BALSHT.DOC** and follow the instructions carefully.

The spreadsheet models in this session were selected to give you as comprehensive an introduction to financial modelling as possible within the time available. We hope that you have enjoyed using your spreadsheet software and that you will develop and use spreadsheets for your own purposes.

1.6 Modelling in action

The following video activity shows how financial modelling can be put to effective use.

ACTIVITY 1.11

In 'Making models work' we visit a charity in Dublin, a leisure centre in Potters Bar, a broadcasting company in Dublin and a financial services organization in Jersey. As you watch the video you should note the scope for financial modelling, and for using spreadsheets in particular.

Watch sequence 5 'Making models work' on Video-cassette 2 and write down your comments below.

The scope for financial spreadsheets

Area *Comments*

The managers in the video identified the following areas where spreadsheets could be applied:

- *general financial control*
- *budgetary control*
- *flexible budgeting for control*
- *break-even and contribution (profit–volume) analyses*
- *decision making in the light of scarce resources*
- *managing working capital.*

We hope that the following review is helpful as a reminder of the context in which financial spreadsheets can be used.

Financial models – a contextual review

General financial control

Broadly speaking, the development of accounting has passed through three stages:

- keeping records of actual expenditure and revenue (the 'stewardship reporting' aspects)
- making detailed costings of existing activities
- management accounting – the development of planning and control mechanisms to improve the effectiveness of business operations and to provide information for decision making.

Accounting records were originally kept solely to record the inflow and outflow of the funds of the business, and there is still a primary emphasis on historic accounting systems for stewardship reporting. But with the increasing complexity of business organizations, the actual expenditure records have been found to be insufficient for most useful purposes, and cost accounting grew out of the need for a deeper analysis of costs. The emphasis has shifted from historical accounts to planning and budgeting for future profits and costs. This entails the control of costs as and when they occur, by comparing them with planned costs.

Management accounting, in particular, is concerned with how the information in the management accounts might be used to achieve more effective control. Models for budgeting, costing and the control of working capital may be developed to help managers exercise control and take responsibility.

Budgetary control

The essence of management control lies in the corrective action that can be taken in response to information about significant departures from predetermined targets or standards. Control implies that certain managers have the power or the right to take action that may affect others in the same organization. To be effective, therefore, a control system should be an integral part of the organizational structure. Budgetary control provides such a system. The setting of departmental budgets links the responsibilities of executives to their policies. Detailed plans, and the actions that give them effect, are expressed in financial terms.

Revenues and costs can be controlled by identifying deviations, either from the original budget or from some revised version. Reports are required if there are significant deviations or where discrepancies exceed a predetermined level so that corrective action is needed. Such cost and revenue control statements must be designed to compare the actual expenditure incurred or the actual revenues received with the levels of costs and revenues that should have been incurred or received for the actual level of operations achieved. This is the essence of budgetary control.

Flexible budgeting for control

A flexible budget is designed to change in accordance with the level of activity attained. Many of the advantages of using budgets for control are lost if, through no fault of the person responsible, the budgeted figures become unrealistic, or if explanations of the variances between the actual and the planned level of costs become too complicated.

The budget is normally fixed on the basis of a level of activity that can be achieved during a particular period. If activities are to be increased for any reason during the course of the budget period, then the manager responsible must be permitted to incur additional expense to make this possible. Similarly, if the level of operations is reduced, the relevant budget must be reduced to prevent overspending. It is necessary to determine new levels of allowed expenditure when activity levels change. Some costs change with changes in the level of activity whereas others remain fixed. While allowing variable costs to change with the level of sales or other measure of activity, it is also essential that management monitors this variability so as to ensure that the spending remains within recognized control limits.

Clearly it is necessary to have an accounting system that permits the collection and allocation of expenses into fixed, variable and semi-variable costs. Fixed costs are perhaps better defined as 'period' or 'policy' costs. This distinguishes between the periodic fixed costs, which are inevitable if the business continues to operate, and policy costs, which are only inevitable as long as the policy is in force. Variable costs vary directly with the levels of activity attained, while semi-variable costs are stepped costs, usually increasing in unequal increments as activity increases. Even if a full system of integrated budgetary control is not installed, the distinction between fixed and variable costs and the preparation of flexible budget statements at different levels of activity will help management to determine future operational policy.

Break-even and contribution (profit–volume) analyses

The three factors price, cost and volume are fundamental to almost every business activity and every business decision. In both profit–volume and break-even analyses, we are concerned with the study of fixed costs, variable costs, selling price and the effect of changes in sales volume on overall profit.

All costs are variable in the long term. Fixed costs, for example, are incurred to provide additional capacity and can be reduced or avoided by forgoing this additional capacity. In the short term, however, fixed costs are incurred irrespective of the level of activity attained. Nevertheless, this analysis makes a significant contribution to our understanding of financial change. In break-even analysis we are particularly concerned with that level of sales at which neither a profit nor a loss is made. This is the point at which the fixed costs are fully recovered. Above this point, profit is generated and below it a loss is incurred. The objective in profit–volume analysis is to summarize the effect of change in sales volume on profits, to indicate the margin of safety above the break-even point, and to evaluate the implications of alternative courses of action.

Decision making in the light of scarce resources

The expected level of sales will often be the factor that constrains budgeted activity, but at times the shortage of any of the factors of production, such as labour, materials, manufacturing capacity or cash, may provide the limiting constraint. The rational decision-maker must therefore choose the course of action that yields the highest contribution per unit of limiting factor and thus maximize total contribution. Of course, management action should be devoted to removing limiting factors.

Managing working capital

The management and control of working capital is so important that it is not surprising that the earliest applications of computers were concerned with these aspects of management and that PC-based systems are now readily available. The accountant will assist in the control of the assets and liabilities of the business and help to ensure that the management information systems and records provide the necessary control information. Systems of stock control and storekeeping, of credit control and, most importantly, of cash control are prerequisites for effective and efficient management. Stock control is usually achieved by calculating reorder quantities and by setting maximum, minimum and reorder stock levels. Most businesses with substantial stock levels will have computerized systems.

Account sales can be an expensive drain on a company's resources. Direct costs may be incurred on borrowing money in order to finance these credit sales, or in *factoring* book debts. In addition, there will be administrative costs incurred in recording and collecting debts, and the possibility of bad debts. Therefore, an

Factoring is the sale of debts – a specialist provider of finance will take over book debts and supply immediate finance in return.

Just think how you feel when asked for immediate payment of an account that you know you have already paid!

efficient system of credit control should be in operation and database software is often used for this purpose. The accounting system must provide an efficient procedure for invoicing customers and for preparing statements. There must also be an efficient collection system for bad payers. Customers' accounts must show their true state at all times. Inadequate records are not only wasteful and costly but also may cause inconvenience and annoyance to customers who are prompt payers. A system of 'age of debts' analysis would highlight overdue accounts and sort them into priority order for legal processing.

1.7 Checks and controls

Properly designed, implemented and operated, a financial model should save time, effort and money in the future. Such savings, however, will fail to materialize if the checks and controls that were built into the model are inadequate or inappropriate. Therefore, we conclude this session with a more detailed review of the need for checks and controls. The discussion may seem excessive as far as the individual manager's use of spreadsheets is concerned but it is, in fact, most important that managers appreciate the requirements for internal audit and control.

Internal audit and control

Internal audit and control can be defined here as the methods and measures established by management to safeguard assets, ensure the reliability of records and promote operational efficiency. Whereas internal audit consists of company staff checking the adequacy of office systems and procedures, internal control is exercised through requiring staff to conform to these standard procedures. An external audit is conducted by an independent outside firm of auditors, but any auditor, whether internal or external, is concerned to ensure that an efficient system of internal control exists.

Audit procedures should be based on an appropriate series of tests designed to satisfy the external auditors that the internal control system is properly operated and effective. The accounting records may then be regarded as a reliable source of data for decision making. The type of tests should complement the internal checks that should already exist. The main tests and controls are described below along with the accounting controls that are generally considered to be necessary in any computer-based system or model.

The audit trail

The International Federation of Accountants publishes Exposure Drafts as a basis for the harmonization of accounting standards throughout the world.

Computer systems and models that provide information for management decision making will affect the work of both internal and external auditors, and so they will need to be subject to audit and control procedures. In the International Federation of Accountants Exposure Draft No. 25, three components of audit risk are defined:

A material error is one which would affect the view of the organization presented by the financial statements.

- inherent risk (the risk that material errors will occur)
- control risk (the risk that the organization's system of internal control will not prevent or correct such errors)
- detection risk (the risk that any remaining material errors will not be detected by the auditor).

An audit trail is one of the main methods used to minimize these risks. It involves:

> … the preparation and retention within an organisation (a) for an adequate period, (b) in a reasonably accessible form, and (c) in enough detail to satisfy the auditors, of records which allow each detailed element of any transaction to be tracked from its source through each intermediate stage to its final disposition (or dispositions); and vice versa – that is, the facility to use records to trace back in detail from the final outcome (or outcomes) through the intermediate stages back to the initial source (or sources) of the transaction.
>
> (Chambers, 1981, p. 13)

However, before we consider the methods and procedures that are required when auditing PC modelling systems, study the following list of some of the problems and difficulties that may arise.

- The usual principles of internal check may not apply. They are based on the separation of functions to avoid collusion and fraudulent intent. This includes the separation of data origination, control of input by means of 'batch totals' (some measure that identifies groups or batches of material for processing), data preparation and processing, systems and programming. Such segregation of duties may not be possible or may be impractical in PC-based systems.
- There may be open access to machines, no password control and no log of computer usage. There may not even be procedures for regularly backing up the systems files, thus increasing the risk of losing vital data.
- Data and information that are stored on floppy disks are particularly vulnerable. Unless strict control procedures are exercised, the disks are easily corrupted and may be easily lost or stolen.
- There may be little or no documentation. Systems and models may have evolved piecemeal, with little or no attempt to document the inputs, outputs and processing involved.
- There may be little or no provision for ensuring that systems and models are regularly updated.
- The validity checks on data and/or programs may be inadequate.
- Sequence checking, to ensure that records in a database are in the correct order, may be poor.
- There may be substandard filing systems for original documents such as invoices and purchase orders.

These difficulties and problems arise because of the lack of effective management control, and should be the subject of management reviews.

One common method of providing an audit trail in larger systems is to maintain detailed records of the users. The user log then forms part of the audit trail, and if something goes wrong it can help reconstruct where, when, how and by whose hand the system became corrupted. This does necessitate the use of passwords. Most large systems use password protection to ensure that only bona fide users have access to the system. Smaller systems should also have a list of authorized users. This list of users' passwords needs to be carefully controlled because systems are particularly vulnerable when control is slipshod.

Software checks and controls

Typically, software such as spreadsheet models is 'almost complete' or needs 'only minor modifications'. Often, the quality and completeness of software are unknown until the 'systems test' which may be the first time that anyone reviews the total processing logic. Inadequate attention may be paid to procedures that validate inputs, outputs or processing logic, and there may be no in-built programming controls, and no specific accounting controls. The usual problem areas are:

- completeness of input
- accuracy of input
- authorization of input
- updating controls
- maintenance controls.

Completeness of input

In large systems, the control techniques include one-to-one checks for standing data, such as direct debits or standing orders on bank accounts or salaries and wage rates, and batch totals for transactions data. There are often no such controls on PC-based systems.

In 'one-to-one' checks, named people are made responsible for checking the accuracy of particular entries.

Where documents such as invoices are entered in batches, their totals are pre-listed on an adding machine and checked against the computer-produced totals.

Hash totals have no purpose other than to indicate lost or corrupted data. For example, the total of reference numbers of a batch of invoices would be compared before data entry, after entry and after processing.

Accuracy of input

Batch totals may also confirm the accuracy and validity of the input data. Sometimes 'hash totals' are used in large systems as a safeguard against data being lost or corrupted during processing. If hash totals fall outside pre-specified limits then an appropriate warning and action will result.

Authorization of input

Password protection usually ensures that only authorized users have the power to input data but, as noted above, this can lead to vulnerability in the system. In addition, data verification may be required whereby input by one person is checked by another person before being processed.

Updating controls

Where control accounts are maintained there is a check on the validity of transaction processing. But in the absence of such control accounts the only effective controls may be the pre-lists, control totals and hash totals. Alternatively, the system can process 'test packs' of predetermined transactions that have been independently validated and compare the results with the validated calculations.

Maintenance controls

Usually only authorized people can update software since unauthorized amendments can create spurious information. It is essential that standing data and programs are correctly maintained.

Individual managers producing spreadsheets for their own use may not need such elaborate processes. But all these matters should certainly be considered when a manager requires another member of staff to operate software.

ACTIVITY 1.12

List the checks and controls, if any, to which staff are, or would be, subjected when using a financial spreadsheet in your organization.

What additional checks and controls would you instigate voluntarily?

1.8 The DCF tableau

In the last section of this session, we move on from the essentially 'accounting' based models you have been constructing until now to the key 'finance' topic you studied in Book 7: discounted cash flow. In Sessions 4 and 5 of that book, you saw the typical layout used when working with DCF methods, be they NPV or IRR. In this section, you will create such a tableau for yourself.

For most managers who are not accounting specialists, the DCF tableau is typically the most common form of spreadsheet model they find themselves creating or using; it, therefore, seems the appropriate choice for you to 'fly solo'. Whereas the preceding activities have led you through the relevant model creation, to a greater or lesser extent, this time you will be asked to work from scratch on a suitable scenario.

However, you are not going to be forced to work without any guidance; you will have the computer version of the Budalarms case to look at as a template. In this section we explain some of the reasons behind the methods used in its construction, plus a few other points that did not arise with that example. These, we believe, show examples of good practice *but are not the only way to achieve the required result*. Thus, the tableau which we have constructed as our answer to the question posed in the 'solo flight' scenario is unlikely to be identical to yours, but the similarities should be obvious – the final NPV and IRR will, we hope, be identical.

ACTIVITY 1.13

Load the file **BUDALARM.WKS** or **BUDALARM.XLS** into your spreadsheet program. Compare the tableau with those in Session 5 of Book 7; the spreadsheet should be a direct computer analogue of the printed version.

Having confirmed that the overall spreadsheet is the same as in Book 7, look at the actual formulae used in the construction; as you should remember by now, you do this by highlighting the relevant cell and then the formula is displayed – in Microsoft Works or Excel the 'formula line' is at the top of the screen, but your spreadsheet program may show it somewhere else. Most of the points about building a DCF tableau were covered in Book 7, for example continuing the time columns (or rows, if you prefer) until all relevant cash flows have been included.

However, one general tip that was not discussed in Book 7 is to *make the machine do as much of the work as possible.* By this we mean that you should design the spreadsheet so that you input or change figures that are as close to 'raw data' as possible, and let the computer do the calculations. In our Budalarms example this is demonstrated in the 'Sales revenue' row. The figures there are not put in by the user but are *calculated* from the 'Sales volume' and 'Unit price' data. This means that, when one comes to undertake sensitivity or scenario analysis, one can vary either of the two parameters independently, and the machine then recalculates the results automatically.

While mentioning changes to input variables, it is worth noting that the Budalarms spreadsheet uses one method: change only the variable in the cell(s) that is (are) highlighted. Thus, if one thought that sales in Year 1 would be only 4000, one would change only the appropriate cell, leaving volume in subsequent years unaltered. But sometimes one wants to consider changes to a variable for *all* time periods, for example 'price increased by 5%'. Implementing this in the spreadsheet as presently constructed is rather laborious; an alternative method is to arrange it so that changes to, say, Year 1 are copied across to later periods as well. If you scroll down to row 30 and below in the Budalarms spreadsheet, you can see this method in use; the basic tableau looks unchanged, but the formulae for volume, price and cost in Years 2–5 are now referenced to Year 1. Changing 'Unit price' from £25.00 to £26.25 in Year 1 will now automatically make the same change in subsequent years. Neither method is 'better', they are both useful but typically for different situations, and depending on the type of analysis you intend to do.

You will also notice that the spreadsheet does not use the built-in NPV function, but goes back to the basic equation. The reason for this is given in Book 7, but it can be summarized by saying it ensures the spreadsheet does what its creator intends, rather than what the program assumes is wanted. In a similar vein, I personally do not normally use the built-in IRR function, preferring to alter manually the discount rate until the NPV = 0. It takes around one minute and avoids any difficulties which might be caused by the built-in function operating differently to what I am expecting – for example, the computer assuming that the first figure is Year 1, when I want it to be Year 0 (this is a problem with most spreadsheets' IRR functions, at the time of writing).

In the relatively straightforward Budalarms case, tax is, in effect, calculated on the annual net *cash flow*. While this is a reasonable simplification to make in the first presentation of DCF methods, reality is not usually that simple; in most investment appraisal situations, the annual *taxable profit* is not the same as the annual *cash flow*, complicating the spreadsheet a little. This is typically dealt with by working out the taxable profit in a 'sub-calculation', often just beneath the main tableau. This may involve depreciation, 'capital allowances', stock relief – whatever adjustments to the figures are required by the tax authorities. Once the correct taxable profit has been worked out, the tax *cash flow* is inserted in the right place in the main tableau; you will have the opportunity to try this out in your own spreadsheet in the following Activity. It is now time for you to create your own DCF analysis.

ACTIVITY 1.14

Following extensive consumer research, Reginald Iolanthe of the marketing department of SoftKing Enterprises' ice-cream division has concluded that the time has come to resurrect the old 'exotic ices' project. The product line would be launched with a range including flavours such as 'walnut and lychee ripple', 'mango and prune Neapolitan' and the like.

The project would require an initial outlay for plant and equipment of £1,250,000 and it is expected that an upgrade and expansion programme in Year 3 would cost a further £75,000 in terms of today's money. For assessment purposes, the project can be treated as to be terminated at the end of Year 6, at which time the remaining equipment should realize £350,000.

Sales are estimated at 4,000,000 litres in Years 1–3 and 6,500,000 litres for Years 4–6, i.e. after the Year 3 expansion has been completed. The average ex-factory selling price is estimated at £0.88 per litre in today's money. Materials cost £0.47 per litre, and direct labour £0.18 per litre. Incremental fixed costs are estimated at £400,000 per year and general company overhead allocation at £150,000 per year. All figures are given in terms of today's money.

Tax is payable at 25% of taxable profit, paid one year in arrears. For tax purposes, plant and equipment create a tax-deductible notional expense as if depreciated on a four-year straight-line basis.

(a) Using a 12% required real rate of return, and working in real terms, create a spreadsheet that calculates the NPV of this project.

(b) What is the IRR of this project?

(c) If sales in Years 1 and 2 are only 2,000,000 and 3,000,000 litres respectively, what would be the new NPV?

*Our tableau for the answer to this case is given in **PERRIN.WKS** or **PERRIN.XLS** for you to compare with your spreadsheet. Good luck!*

1.9 Summary

Financial spreadsheet models can be of real use to managers in the work place, removing tedious arithmetic and leaving time for more productive work. When creating them, however, it is sensible to think them out carefully in advance before setting digits to keyboard; it usually produces a more effective model and may actually save time in the long run. Testing and debugging are key steps in producing a computer model, and a vital activity which is sometimes skimped is *documenting* the model. Always assume that someone else will have to use your model without your assistance – in fact, that someone may turn out to be you long after you have forgotten how you built the spreadsheet!

Finally, be ready to update your models or develop them further. A manager's world is not static, nor should his or her computer models be.

Objectives

After studying this session you should be able to:

- Recognize the potential applications of financial models and spreadsheets in relation to your own work and organization.
- Design, construct and use a simple financial spreadsheet.
- Understand the situations in which financial models are most likely to prove effective.
- Appreciate the limitations as well as the benefits of models, and the need for appropriate checks and controls on a continuing basis.

SESSION 2 INTRODUCTORY STATISTICS

Contents

2.1 Introduction

Information is data that have been processed in some way so as to be useful to the recipient. In this session we examine some of the ways in which data can be converted into information. You may, for instance, be confronted with a mass of figures you have to interpret, or you may want to challenge someone else's interpretation. Quantitative data – which is what we will be dealing with in this session – can, quite legitimately, be interpreted in different ways according to the circumstances. You need to be aware of the potential for different interpretations. Take, for example, an apparently authoritative statement such as 'The average waiting time for an appointment is three days.' What does this mean? What kind of average has been used? As we shall see, there are three main measures that are all 'averages' – the mean, the mode and the median.

Whatever your job, you are likely to be required to summarize data relating to the performance of your department for higher levels of management or for outside bodies. Perhaps you need to provide summarized data as part of an audit. Summary figures make the data easier to digest and can also be used as a basis for comparison with other departments or for making tactical or strategic decisions about future policy. This session explores ways in which data can be arranged and analysed in such a way as to make them useful. To keep the calculations simple, we shall be looking at small-scale examples and concentrating on developing skills in analysis and presentation which any manager can use. The techniques remain the same, however, even on a larger scale, and regardless of whether you are using the back of an envelope or a sophisticated software package to turn your raw data into usable information.

We start this theme of converting data into useful information by looking at how you can represent data using graphs and charts. Section 2.2 covers the different types of graphs and charts, starting with simple bar charts and progressing to more complex diagrams.

It is often not possible to see any kind of pattern in a mass of raw data but drawing a graph – even a rough and ready one, simply for your own purposes – can be the best way to tease out the salient points and to identify trends or areas of concern. Once these have been identified, you may have to analyse the figures further before you can reach a decision.

The easiest way to draw graphs and charts is to enter your figures into a computer spreadsheet and let it do the work for you. There are now many spreadsheet and graphics packages which can produce a wide range of graphs and charts; this has made the production of high quality material much easier than it used to be and thereby transformed the exchange of graphical information. In this session you will be asked to do a number of computer activities using the Microsoft Excel or Works spreadsheet to produce several of the graphs and charts discussed. Nevertheless, even if you let the computer do the work you still need to understand the underlying principles.

In some cases it is not enough to just represent the original data; a statistical measure such as the average of the data may be required. In Section 2.3 we show you how to calculate the three different forms of average – the *mean*, the *mode* and the *median*. We go on to explain how averages are calculated from frequency distributions. Measures of spread in Section 2.4 looks at another useful way of taking meaning from data – analysing something about how much the readings differ from each other. Two of these measures will be described: the *range* and the *standard deviation*.

You have probably come across claims in books or the media such as:

- Research has found that there is a strong negative correlation between raw material quality and production line wastage rates.
- Smoking causes lung cancer.
- Poverty is an important factor in the health of the population.

These kinds of claims should only be made after a large data collection exercise followed by careful analysis of the results. Sometimes you may suspect that there is a pattern to the data you are analysing, perhaps after you have seen them displayed in graphical form. We conclude this session by providing some important and powerful techniques for identifying and qualifying possible relationships between data. These may be historical data, found by monitoring how something alters over time, or consist of survey results where a number of factors have been recorded and you are trying to identify possible relationships. In either case, the aim is to establish whether there really is a discernible pattern that is unlikely to be mere coincidence and, if so, to represent it mathematically.

Therefore, the aims of this session are to look at how to present data, how to analyse data by calculating averages and measures of dispersion and how to identify possible relationships between sets of data. We start by looking at how to present data.

2.2 Charts, graphs and diagrams

In order to present data in an accessible form it is often useful to put it into some form of chart, diagram or graph. The choice will depend on the type of data you are given and also the relationships you are trying to demonstrate.

Bar chart

In its simplest form, a bar chart consists of a number of separate bars whose heights correspond to the sizes of each of the groups being illustrated. An example is shown in Figure 2.1.

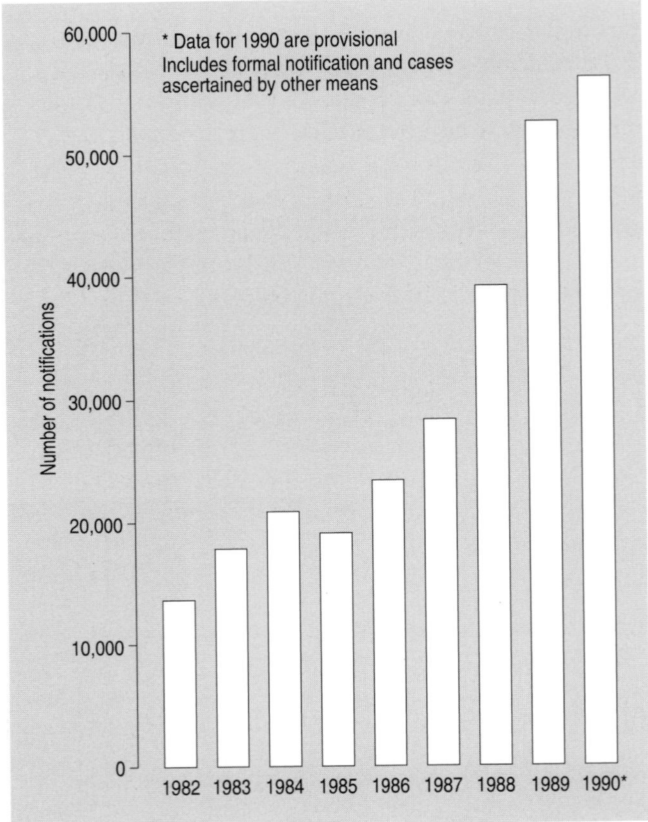

Figure 2.1 *Notification of food poisoning in England and Wales, 1982–90 (Source: Department of Health, 1991)*

ACTIVITY 2.1

What information does Figure 2.1 give you?

Apart from a slight fall in 1985, there has been a steady increase in the number of notifications of food poisoning, with more pronounced rises in 1988 and 1989. What you cannot tell from this graph, of course, is whether an increasing number of people are getting food poisoning or if more people are contacting their doctors; increased publicity could be a contributing factor to the high jumps in reports in the two years mentioned. The graph gives the impression that the increase tailed off in 1990, but these are only provisional figures (the report was published in 1991). The scale on the vertical axis allows you to estimate the number of cases in any given year to about the nearest thousand but you would not be able to ascertain the exact number of reports from this graph. The purpose of the graph is simply to give an overall impression of the incidence of reported food poisoning.

The component, or stacked, bar chart

A more complicated type of bar chart is the *component bar chart* or *stacked bar chart*, which allows an extra dimension of the data to be shown. The sizes of the various components that make up a bar are illustrated using different colours or shading and the components are always stacked in the same order. The components of the bars that represent the same item are always shaded or coloured in the same way so that they can be easily compared.

Look at the data shown in Table 2.1. A good way to examine any patterns that emerge from the data would be to draw a stacked bar chart (Figure 2.2). One thing to keep in mind is that there is usually considerable flexibility about the way graphs and charts are presented – it is very much a creative process. By actually drawing some graphs for yourself, you will get a feel for some of the choices involved and this will make you more aware of how people can, for instance, choose their scales to paint their figures in the most favourable light.

Table 2.1 Time use in a typical week: by employment status and sex, 1992–93

	Full-time employees				*Retired*	
	Males	*Females*	*Part-time female employees*	*Housewives*	*Males*	*Females*
Weekly hours spent on:						
Employment and travel[1]	47.1	42.2	20.8	0.4	0.5	0.6
Essential cooking, shopping and housework	13.0	25.5	32.5	38.1	17.0	33.0
Essential childcare, personal hygiene and other shopping	13.2	20.0	25.2	29.4	10.0	14.0
Sleep[2]	49.0	49.0	49.0	49.0	49.0	49.0
Free time	45.7	31.4	40.6	51.1	91.5	71.4

[1] Travel to and from place of work
[2] Seven hours per night

(Source: The Henley Centre for Forecasting, 1993)

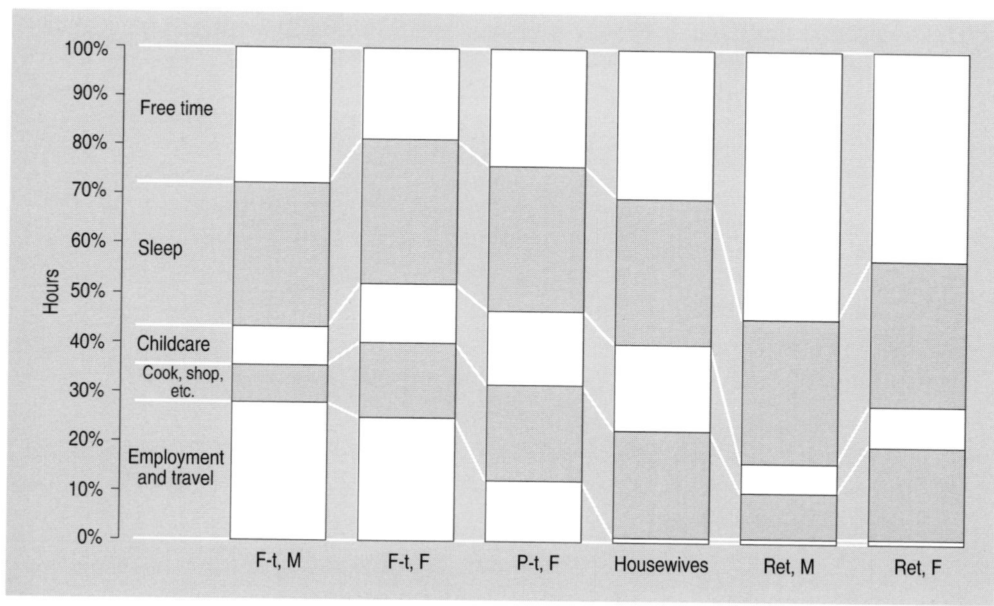

Figure 2.2 *A stacked bar chart of Table 2.1*

The features of the various types of component bar charts can be summarized as follows.

- Straightforward component bar charts are used particularly when class totals need to be represented; however, it is not easy to compare the components across the bars.

- Percentage bar charts are used when relative comparisons between the components are important; however, the actual figures (including the class totals) are lost.
- Multiple bar charts are useful for comparing components both within and across classes, since each bar is drawn from a fixed base; however, the class totals are not easy to assimilate and they can be unwieldy if there are a large number of classes.

Line diagrams

Line diagrams are another class of graphs that can be used to help identify patterns and trends in data. Line diagrams often have time as the horizontal axis and illustrate the development of a chosen variable over time. The data are plotted as points and then these points are joined to form a continuous line. The technical name for a graph like this is a *time series* or *historigram*. If required, more than one line can be superimposed on the same axis; this is called a *multiple line diagram*. Since these graphs show how the variable has behaved in the past, they are often used to attempt to predict what is likely to happen in the future by identifying underlying trends. This is covered in more detail in Session 3.

The historigram in Figure 2.3 shows the number of measles notifications between 1940 and 1990 in England and Wales; the slope of the line shows whether the number of notifications (the variable) is rising or falling. We can see from this graph that it fluctuated wildly from year to year until 1968, when the measles vaccine was introduced. The number still fluctuated a little after that date but continued the overall decline that had begun around 1960. This type of graph makes it much easier to pick out underlying trends than if you are faced with the original figures in a table.

Figure 2.3 has a time-scale covering 50 years but you will come across other time series that have much shorter time-scales. In Figure 2.4, for instance, each line covers just a single year. However, it shows two time series – one for 1982/3 and one for 1992/3.

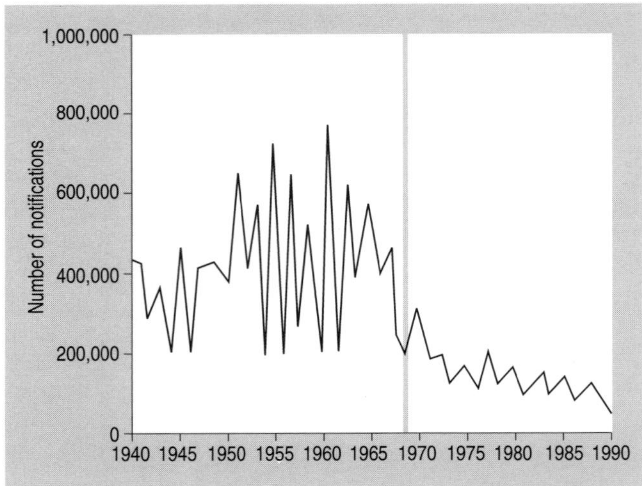

Figure 2.3 *Measles notifications in England and Wales, 1940–90 (Source: Department of Health, 1991)*

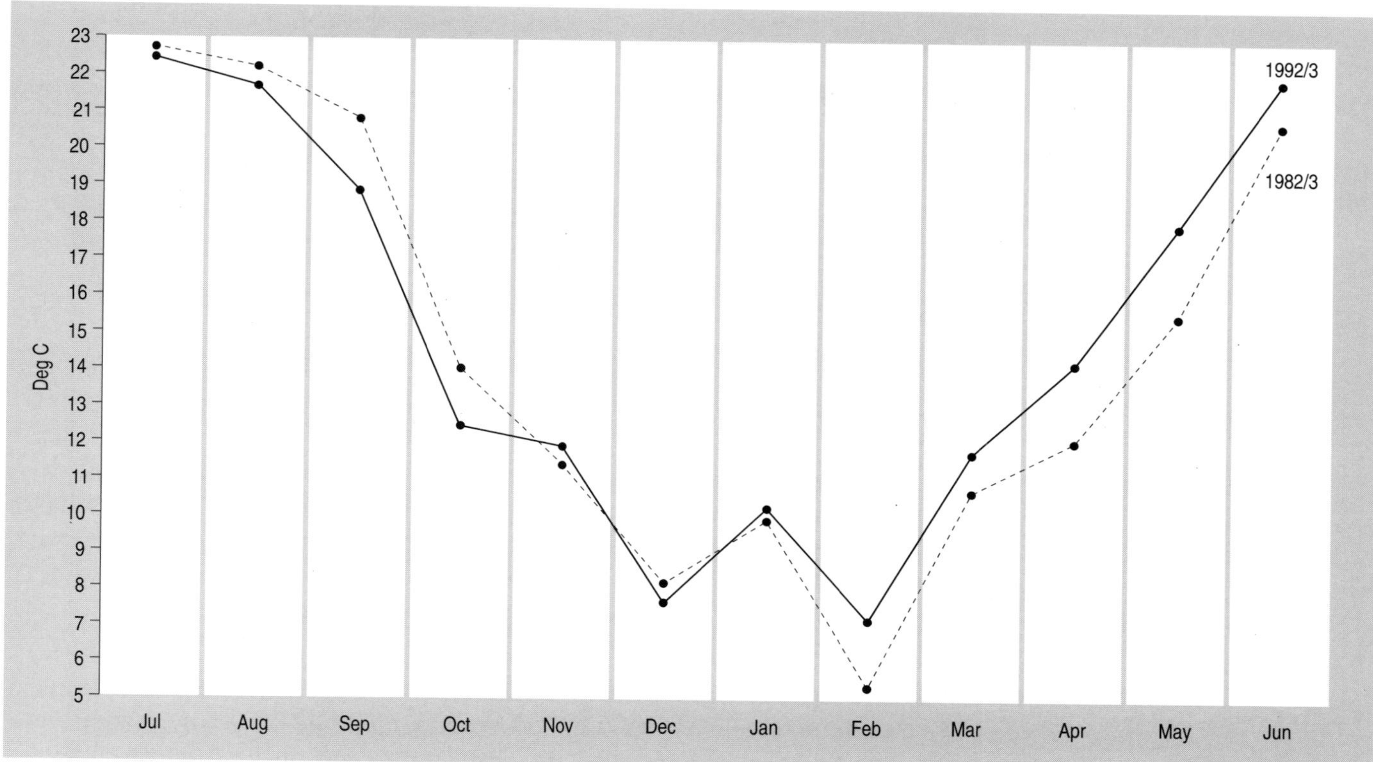

Figure 2.4 *Monthly mean temperature*

ACTIVITY 2.2

If these two years of data were being used to look for evidence of climate change over the 10-year gap, do they indicate any significant change?

No, the variations are too small to be regarded as showing any climatic change; the differences look to be within normal levels of annual variability.

It is often sensible to scale a line graph – or, indeed, a bar chart – by comparing all the readings with that for a particular 'benchmark'. This is called *indexation*. You are probably familiar with the retail price index (RPI), which compares the costs of a whole range of goods and services with a base value of 100. The RPI was last re-referenced on 13 January 1987. The cost of all the items in the index (which includes food, travel, household expenditure, etc.) was given a value of 100 on that day. The index for June 1991 was 134.1 which indicates that prices had risen by just over 34 per cent since January 1987. Indexing is a very useful technique when you are illustrating comparisons between variables, and it is looked at in more detail in Session 3.

Box 2.1 Working with index numbers

In June 1994 the RPI stood at 144.7, indicating prices were 44.7 per cent higher than in January 1987. Does this mean they were 10.6 per cent higher in June 1994 than in June 1991 (i.e. 144.7 – 134.1)? No, to see the percentage change over the three years one must divide the later number by the earlier. So the change from June 1991 to June 1994 was 144.7/134.1 = 1.079, or 7.9 per cent.

The main features of line diagrams can be summarized as follows:

Advantages	*Disadvantages*
They are easy to construct and understand.	They can be confusing if too many lines with similar values share the same axes.
They are an ideal medium for making direct comparisons.	On multiple line diagrams, there is no provision for total figures.

Strata charts

One of the disadvantages of line diagrams is that there is no provision to display totals. This shortfall is overcome by strata charts, which are also known as *cumulative line diagrams* or *area graphs*.

A strata chart is, in effect, a collection of line graphs stacked on top of one another with the area between the lines shaded in (Figure 2.5). They are similar in this respect to component bar charts and show how the various components of a total vary over time. It is important to shade the regions between the lines to distinguish this type of chart from a multiple line diagram.

You can see that strata charts are an effective way of getting a message across, but they can be difficult to interpret in detail. The main use for this type of graph is to show how proportions of a whole change over time; they are intended to give an instant visual impression rather than a reference point from which to read pertinent figures. Sometimes the vertical axis of a strata chart will be given in percentages rather than total numbers, just as with percentage bar charts.

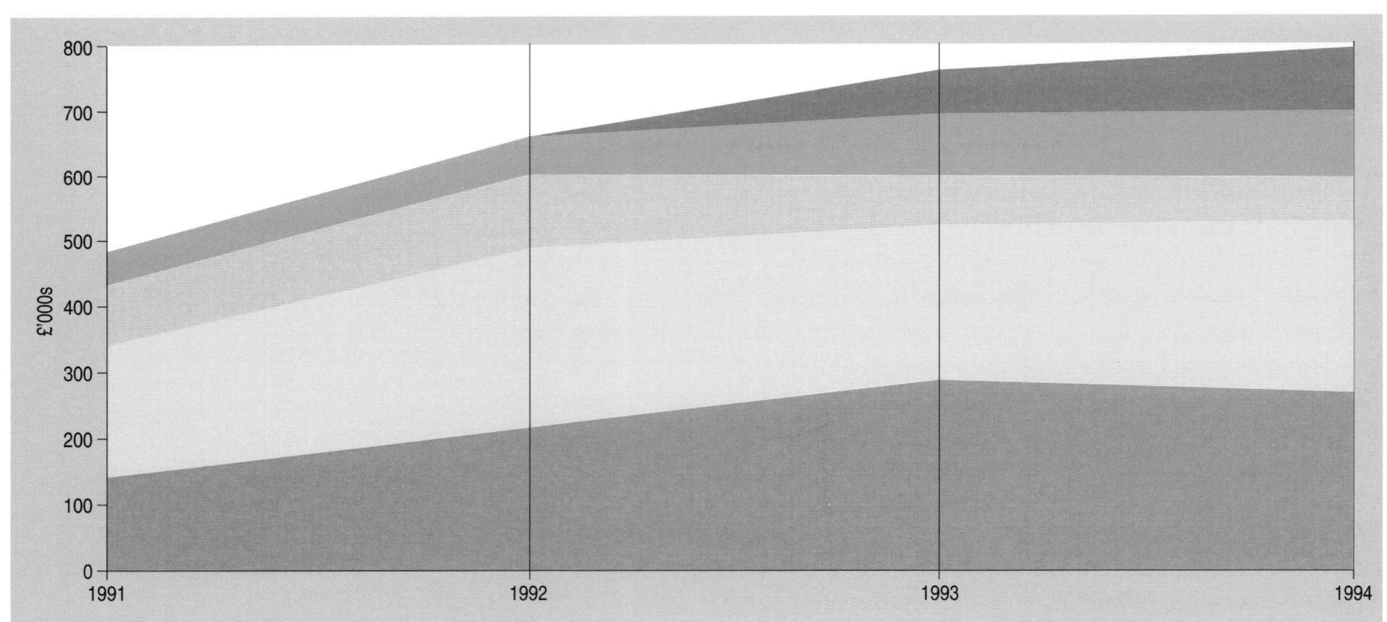

Figure 2.5 *Strata chart of SoftKing CDs Ltd area sales (the shaded areas represent different regions of the UK)*

Pie charts

You will probably have seen pie charts like the one shown in Figure 2.6. They are extremely useful for displaying the proportions that go to make up a whole. An important feature of Figure 2.6 is that the percentages are written on this pie chart; this is helpful when there are several classes with almost identical totals.

Many spreadsheet packages provide facilities for drawing pie charts.

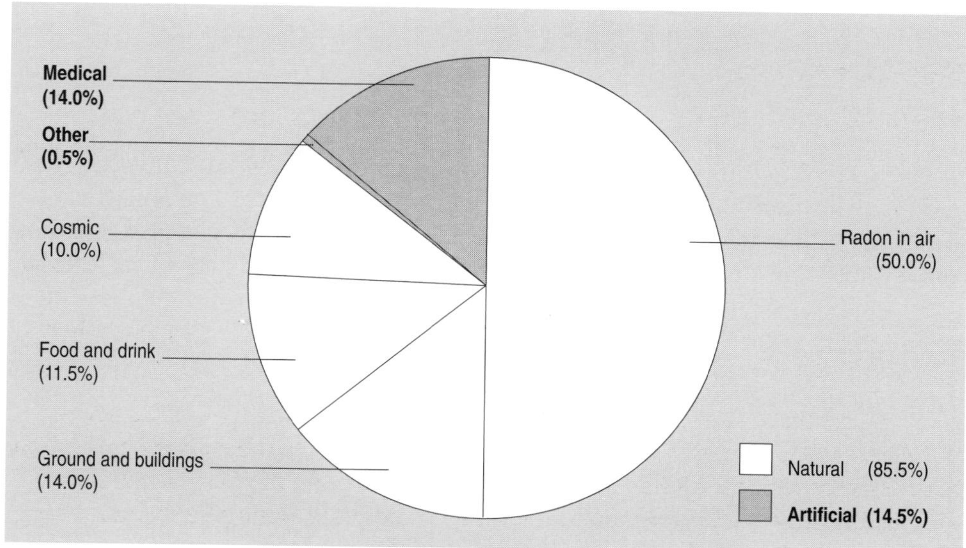

Figure 2.6 *Radiation exposure of the population: by source, 1991 (Source: National Radiological Protection Board)*

Presentation of data

The choice of the style of presentation for data can radically alter the impression it creates. Particular care must be taken when using pictograms to convey information.

Consider the mythical republic of Gawcotia. The UK average weekly wage is twice that of its Gawcotian counterpart. This could be represented in an attractive way using a pile of money-bags – see Figure 2.7.

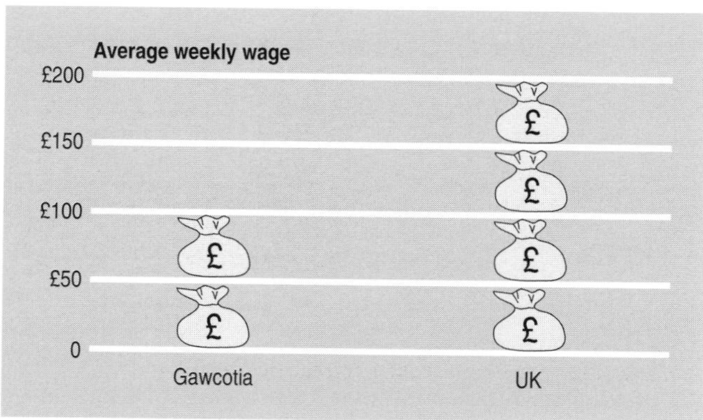

Figure 2.7 *A pictorial histogram*

But can we make the picture even more immediate? Perhaps we could replace the piles with one money-bag each, scaled so that their heights are in the ratio 1:2. This has been done in Figure 2.8.

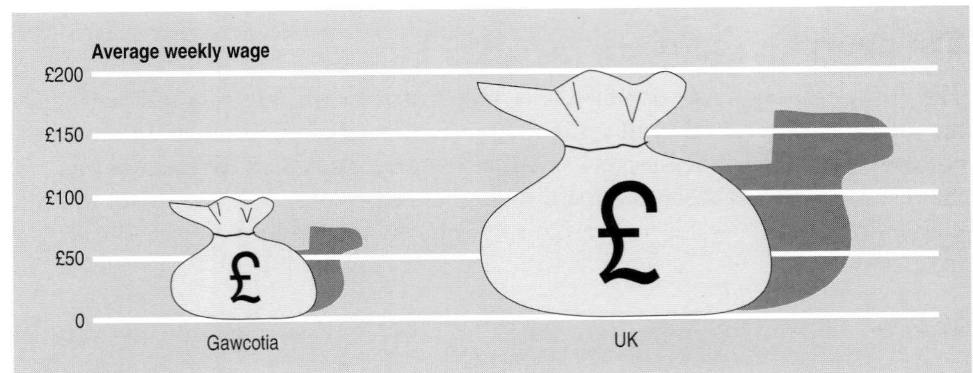

Figure 2.8 *A pictogram*

It gives a striking image, but look at the message this pictogram conveys. The icon is twice as high but also twice as wide. It therefore shows an area four times the size of its fellow. If it is perceived as representing a physical object in three dimensions, one might believe it to be eight times the 'size' of its fellow.

ACTIVITY 2.3

Load the file **STATS2.WPS** or **STATS2.DOC** into your word-processor.

Print the file. It contains instructions for spreadsheet exercises on bar charts (simple and multiple), stacked bar charts, strata and line charts. Now work through the exercises as described in **STATS2.WPS** or **STATS2.DOC**.

2.3 Averaging

What is the average of 60, 30, 20 and 10?

The chances are your answer was 30, which you arrived at by totalling all the figures (the values) and dividing by 4, the number of items. This is what most people understand by 'the average' but it is actually called the *mean* or, more correctly, the arithmetic mean. However, this is only one of several different kinds of common summary statistics that are all referred to as 'averages'. Each has its own advantages and disadvantages, but it is not always clear which method has been used to calculate the statistic given – and knowing this can be very important to one's understanding of the information. When you are presented with 'the average' of a particular set of data, you need to know what kind of average it is that is being referred to.

Why should you want to look at averages anyway? Consider a few examples:

- A bank manager may want to know how long a typical customer waits before being served by a cashier.
- The bank might also want to know the average amount per transaction withdrawn from its ATM (Automatic Teller Machine).
- A specialist bakery might want to know how many rolls, on average, were bought by relevant customers (i.e. those who came in for rolls).

Consider these examples as you read about the mean, mode and median. We shall return to them at the end of the section.

The arithmetic mean

The arithmetic *mean* is calculated by adding up all the values and dividing by the number of items. We will just call this 'the mean' from here on. Let us consider data from a sickness and absence reporting system. We want to find the mean length of absences during July. To do this we would add up the number of days that each person had been absent and then divide the total by the number of people. Assume the data for July were as follows:

Mick Brandon	1	Norman Richards	16
Sam Cassimally	0	Peter Stevenson	0
Sheila Holdsworth	2	Mae Wong	1
Ruby Papario	0		

The total number of days of sickness is therefore:

$$1 + 0 + 2 + 0 + 16 + 0 + 1 = 20$$

The number of people is 7.

So the mean length of absence due to sickness is:

$$20 \div 7 = 2.86 \text{ days}$$

This highlights a distinctive feature of the mean: it often gives a value that is not typical of the data from which it was calculated – no one had actually had 2.86 days of sickness. In the reporting system there are only complete days of absence, yet the average time is not a whole number. This is the case for the mean number of children per family in the United Kingdom, currently 1.8, which conjures up absurd visions of families with bits of children.

Another problem with the mean is that a potentially misleading value can be obtained if the data contain extreme values. In the above example, one person (Norman) has a far higher sickness rate than anybody else because of a car accident. Let us see what happens to the mean if we do not include Norman in our calculation. The mean for the remaining people in the department is 0.67 days (4 days' absence divided between 6 people). By including the atypical data for Norman, our mean was nearly three days' absence per person, as opposed to about two-thirds of a day when he was not included. You can see that this can make an important difference. Suppose a sales manager is averaging the waiting time between receiving an order and delivery; he or she would certainly not want to include the occasional customer who orders two weeks in advance for delivery after their summer holiday shutdown.

The mode

The *mode* is the data item that occurs most frequently. It is a boon for people who dislike mathematics as it hardly requires any calculation at all!

In the example we are using, the most common number of days' absence is 0, so the mode is 0. Therefore, if you use the mode as your average, you could say, hand on heart: 'The average number of days' sickness in my department is zero.' This is, arguably, a fairer indication of the true pattern of attendance by the seven people in the department over the period observed; most of them have, indeed, had no absence from work through sickness and the figure is then not distorted by Norman's prolonged absence. The mode also gives a typical value, unlike the mean which came up with an atypical fractional number of days. Furthermore, the mode is very easy to find; you just have to look for the most commonly occurring figure, which is easier than the calculations required for the mean. Sometimes, quick and simple solutions are best if you are just trying to get a feel for something and do not have time for an in-depth analysis.

Of course, in this example, finding the most commonly occurring value was easy as there were not many observations. If you had a much greater amount of data, you could find the mode by constructing a tally chart to keep a count of how many times each value occurred. A possible layout is shown in Table 2.2. The row with the largest count is the mode or modal value. Note that the mode is the *value* in the row with the largest count rather than the size of the largest count itself. Thus, in Table 2.2, the mode is 0 days' sickness, because it has the largest tally of 3 occurrences.

Table 2.2 A tally count to find the mode

Number of days' sickness	*Tally*	*Count*
0	I I I, totalling:	3
1	I I	2
2	I	1
3		0
4		0
5 etc.		0

A limitation of the mode is that it only records one value, the most popular; no other values are taken into account in its derivation, unlike the mean which includes all of the data in its calculation. However, an advantage of the mode is that it can be used to give the average of 'category variables'; these are variables which are not numbers but descriptions, such as 'married', 'divorced', 'widowed'. Other examples would be 'fuel types', or 'pet types' – cat, dog, gerbil, etc. Since the variables are not numbers, it would be meaningless to calculate the 'mean' but it is possible to give the most frequently occurring category. Incidentally, a set of data can have two or even more modes if there are several items that occur with equal frequency. A set of data with two 'most popular' classes is called *bimodal*, one with three classes would be *trimodal*, and so on.

The median

The *median* is calculated by arranging all the recorded values in order of magnitude and taking the middle value. In the case of the sickness figures we are working with, rearranged in order of size, they are:

0, 0, 0, 1, 1, 2, 16

There are seven figures so the middle one is the fourth value which, in this case, is 1. So using the median as an average, you could say that the average number of days' sickness in the department is 1. Again, this seems a reasonable figure since a couple of people did have one day's sickness and most of the others had either none or two. Like the mode, the median is unaffected by extreme values such as Norman's 16 days off, which distorted the mean. Similarly, it (usually) gives a typical value, since you are actually picking one of the data items to use as a representative.

Box 2.2 An even median is not an odd idea

As the calculation of the median relies on picking the middle value of the list, you may be wondering what you do if there is an even number of data items and, consequently, no one 'middle' item. In this case, the median is the mean of the two middle items, i.e. you add them together and divide by two. To find the middle value in a long sequence:

- Add 1 to the number of items in the sequence.
- Divide this number by 2.
- If the answer is a whole number, then take the value of this item in the list as the median.
- If the answer is not a whole number, then the median is the mean of the two numbers either side of this item.

For example, for seven items:

- Add 1 to the seven items in the sequence = 8.
- Divide 8 by 2 to give 4, which is a whole number.
- The median is the value of the fourth item in the sequence of data items written in ascending order of size.

For eight items:

- Add 1 to 8 items = 9.
- Divide 9 by 2 to give 4.5 so the median is the mean of the fourth and fifth items.

Review of averages

There are three commonly used averages: the arithmetic mean, the median and the mode. For the data shown, they have all produced different results, although they can each legitimately be quoted as the average of the data:

	Mean	*Mode*	*Median*
Value	2.86	0	1

ACTIVITY 2.4

List the advantages of each type of average.

Mean:

Mode:

Median:

Mean

- *Can be used in further analysis.*
- *Takes account of all items of data.*

Mode

- *No calculation needed.*
- *Not affected by extreme values.*
- *Always gives a typical data value.*

Median

- *Easy to calculate.*
- *Not affected by extreme values.*
- *Usually gives values which are typical of the data from which it was derived.*

This section has introduced you to (or reminded you of) the different kinds of average you may come across in written reports. Since the results of each of them are different, you can see that you need to maintain a healthy scepticism and ask yourself what the author is trying to convey. Perhaps the figures have been 'massaged' to portray a particular point of view.

Consider the following question: 'What is the average waiting time of clients waiting to see their solicitor?'. If someone were to carry out a survey and come up with a figure for the average time, what would it mean? Say it was discovered that the mean waiting time was 9.5 minutes. Would anybody actually wait that long? Could I reliably turn up 9.5 minutes late for my appointment and know I would be seen immediately? How long do most people wait?

ACTIVITY 2.5

How appropriate is the use of the mean in this situation? What, if anything, does it tell you about how long clients would have to wait?

Although the mean waiting time is 9.5 minutes, people may have to wait anything from no time at all to perhaps half an hour or more. However, you cannot assess that from the information you have been given. It might have been more useful to know the modal waiting time, as this represents the most common waiting time and, therefore, tells you how long people are most likely to have to wait.

Referring back to the three examples mentioned at the beginning of this sub-section, what would be the appropriate average for us in each case?

The first example – typical waiting time in a bank branch – is essentially the same as the solicitor question in Activity 2.5, and so the *mode* is probably the most suitable measure to use.

When considering the ATM question, it is likely that the *mean* will be the most useful, because one can combine it with knowledge of the expected number of customers for each day to decide on how much cash to load into the machine. It seems likely that, while the number of customers may well differ depending on the day of the week (for example, Monday, Friday and Saturday might be high and Tuesday and Wednesday low), the average amount withdrawn per transaction will be quite stable from day to day.

With the third example – rolls from a bakery – the *median* may be quite sufficient, being easy to calculate and yet almost certainly giving a whole number of rolls per customer as the result.

To end this discussion, do remember to make clear what measure you are using; use the relevant, precise term – arithmetic mean, mode or median – instead of the vaguer word 'average'. But always bear in mind when using other people's statistics that they may not be as scrupulous in their language as you would have been!

ACTIVITY 2.6

Examine critically some of the summarized management data you come across in your work.

Where data have been averaged, identify (if possible) which kind of average has been used. Is it appropriate? What would be the effect of using a different kind of average? How might the choice of average influence your interpretation of the data?

2.4 Measures of spread

The mean, mode and median give us useful information – when interpreted correctly – but alone they are often not enough to give a real 'feel' for the underlying data. Averages – strictly speaking the mean or median – tell us something about the 'middle' of the data, but we do not know much about the *spread* of outcomes around this 'middle'. Such detail can prove to be very informative and we often look at *measures of spread* to help us gain a better understanding of the data.

We will consider two main measures of spread: *range* and *standard deviation*. As a sub-set of the 'range' measure we will also consider *quartiles*.

Range

If we look at the two diagrams in Figure 2.9, it is clear that the data set represented in (b) is more spread out than that in (a). Note that both have the same mean of 50; the distributions are just examples and do not represent any set of real data.

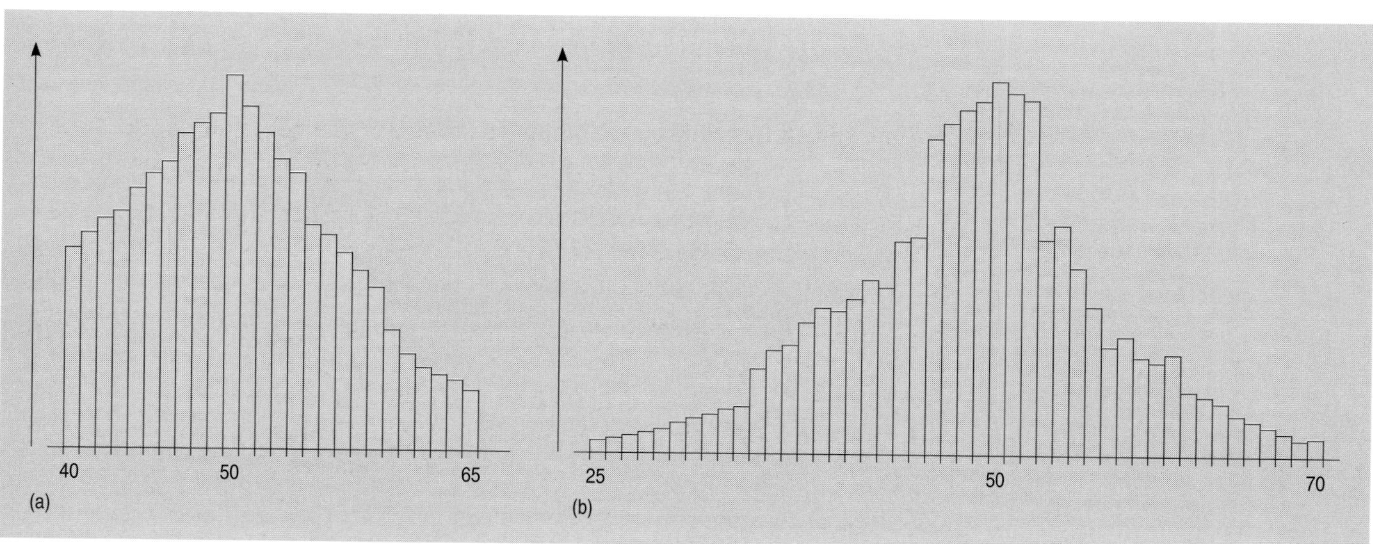

Figure 2.9 Same mean, different range

The *range* of (a) is 40–65, that of (b) is 25–70. We thus know that all the results recorded were between the relevant extreme points. This often helps to give us some idea of the variability of the activity that the data represent, which is clearly sometimes important. It also has the benefit of being extremely easy to calculate – you just look for the highest and lowest items in the data! On the other hand, it is not very descriptive of the data; to show this a little more clearly, Figure 2.10 shows three very different distributions that all have a mean of 50 and a range of 30–70.

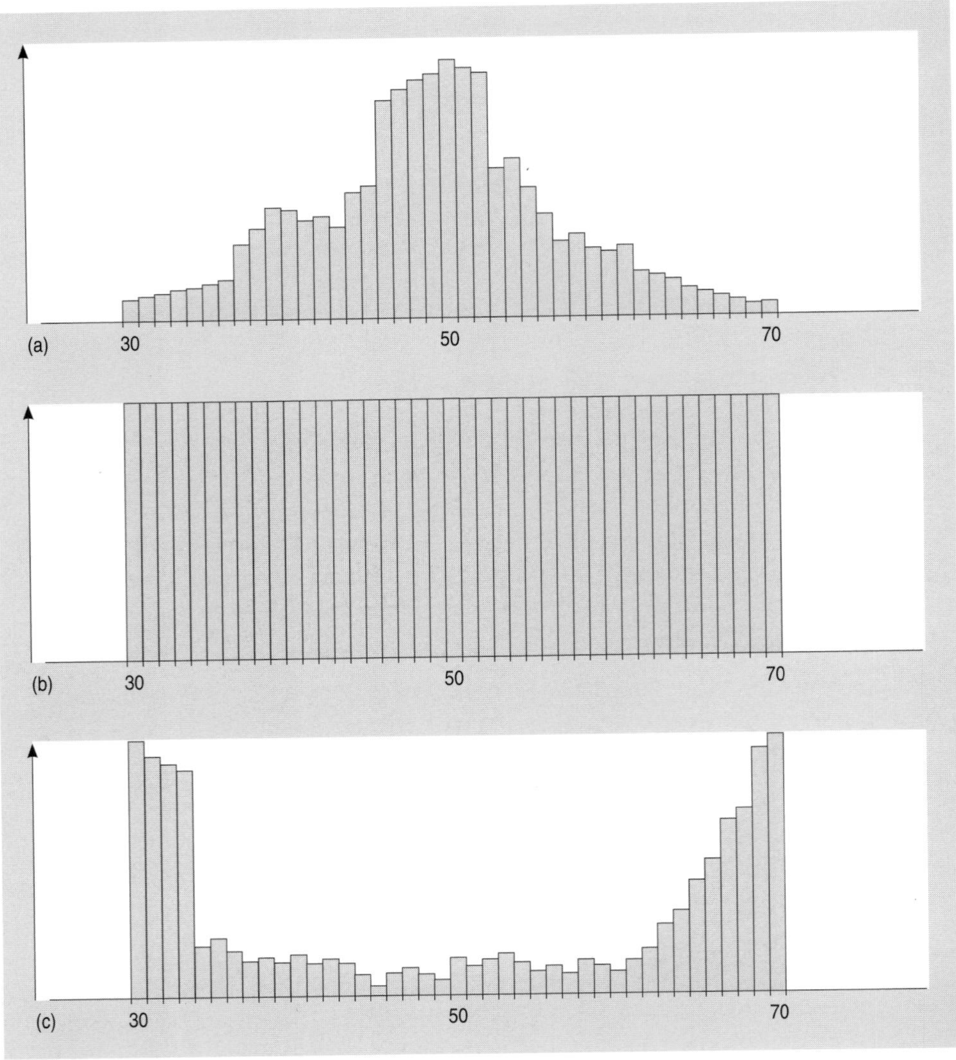

Figure 2.10 *Range does not define shape*

To an extent, this lack of distinctiveness can be ameliorated by calculating the standard deviation, and we will consider this shortly.

Before that, however, we should consider another potential problem with using a 'raw' range measure: namely, that of *outliers*. Sometimes a range measure is distorted by including extreme, unrepresentative items of data. In Figure 2.11, both distributions have, again, a mean of 50; (a) has a range of 20–80 and (b) a range of 30–70. But, just by looking at the two diagrams, it is clear that, in a practical sense, (b) is actually more dispersed than (a). The range measure is biased by the very few readings well away from the mean. Indeed, it is quite possible that they are actually misreadings, anyway. One way to get round this problem in a quite straightforward way is to divide the distribution into

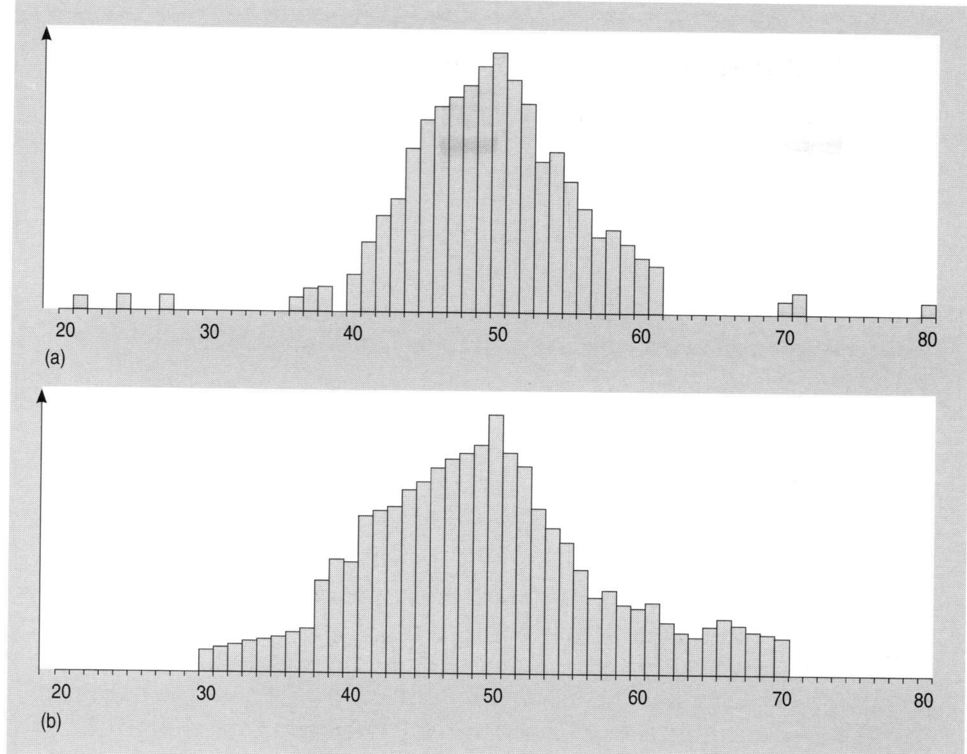

Figure 2.11 *Ranges and outliers*

quartiles (that is, quarters), and then only to consider the span of the middle two quarters. This is known as calculating the *inter-quartile range* (or IQR); in the example from Figure 2.11, the inter-quartile ranges are 44–55 for (a) and 39–64 for (b), which fits better with our visual impression that the latter is more spread out than the former.

The inter-quartile range can be useful, but it can also be misleading. Perhaps this was temperature data which was accurately recorded – any temperature over 75 is dangerous and should be avoided at all costs. It is true that distribution (a) clusters more closely about 50 than does (b), but it also shows the occasional event above the danger level. Often, IQR gives a very helpful measure, as long as one remembers to be cautious.

Standard deviation

You may well have come across the term *standard deviation* which is a very useful measure of how spread out the data are from the mean; the larger the standard deviation, the more spread out the data and the more they vary from the mean. (See Box 2.3 overleaf.)

For example, consider waiting times at solicitors' firms. The mean for Firm 1 shown in Table 2.3 is 9.5 minutes and the standard deviation is 5.3 minutes. This fact is fairly meaningless on its own but it does allow comparison between sets of data. Imagine that a second law firm, Firm 2, has also collected figures for its waiting times and has found that its mean is also 9.5 minutes but that its standard deviation is 1.3 minutes. What this tells us is that, although the average waiting times are the same at both firms, there is far more variation at the first. This is confirmed by a glance at Figure 2.12.

Box 2.3 Standard deviation – calculation and meaning

The formula for calculating standard deviation, *s*, is:

$$s = \sqrt{\frac{1}{n}\sum (x - \bar{x})^2}$$

where

$\bar{x}$ is the mean of the *x* readings.

This equation can be rewritten in a form that sometimes makes calculation easier:

$$s = \sqrt{\frac{1}{n}\sum x^2 - \bar{x}^2}$$

The two forms are algebraically the same, so use whichever is more convenient.

If we look at the bracket in the first version, we see that we are taking the square of the *difference* between a particular reading and the mean (squaring is a typical mathematical way of getting rid of pluses or minuses when it is only the difference itself that is needed). We then add up all the squared differences and divide by the number of readings. (More sophisticated analysis would divide by (n–1) instead of n, but that is a technicality beyond the needs of this course. Where there are many readings, the replacement of n by (n–1) produces an insignificant change in the standard deviation.) We then take the (positive) square root. In effect, we have calculated an 'average difference' of a reading from the mean, which gives us an idea of how spread out the readings are around the mean.

Table 2.3 Waiting times in two solicitors' firms

Firm 1 waiting time (minutes)	*Firm 2 waiting time (minutes)*	*Firm 1 waiting time (minutes)*	*Firm 2 waiting time (minutes)*
10	8.5	10	9.5
9.5	9	10.5	8
26	10	12	9
8	11	8.5	10
12.5	9.5	7.5	12
11	9	12	11
9	8	6	8.5
2	10	3	10
21	13	14	8
16	12	11	7.5
6	7	2	9.5
3	10	1.5	10
15	9	8.5	8.5
4.5	8.5	8	10
8	9.5	9	9

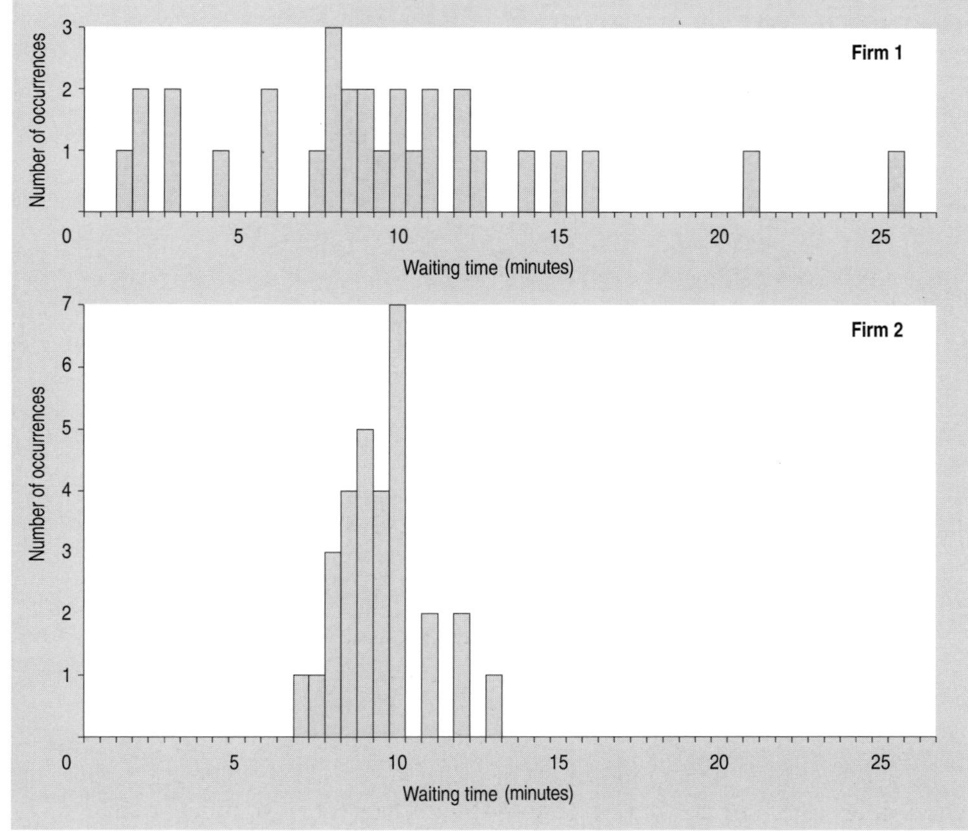

Figure 2.12 *Distributions of waiting times from Table 2.3*

If you look at the figures for both firms shown in Table 2.3, you will see that those for Firm 1 fluctuate much more wildly from the mean figure of 9.5 minutes than do those for Firm 2. Consequently, the mean waiting time for Firm 1 is a far less reliable guide to how long you will actually have to wait to see the solicitor than for Firm 2.

You may be wondering why there needs to be a measure like the standard deviation when you can work out for yourself which data set shows the most variation simply by looking at the figures. Remember, however, that you may not have access to the original data and there may well be far too many of them so you would have to rely on a measure like the standard deviation to tell you.

ACTIVITY 2.7

Load the file **STATS1.WPS** or **STATS1.DOC** into your word-processor and print it. It contains instructions for spreadsheet exercises on the mean, mode, median and standard deviation.

Now work through the spreadsheet exercises as described in **STATS1.WPS** or **STATS1.DOC**.

2.5 Correlation

Durham Family Health Services Authority carried out a random survey of 18,000 people in its area to discover their perceptions of their standards of health. The purpose of this research was to establish a base-line against which to evaluate health standards in the future. Surveys like this can investigate whether there are any links between different elements of people's lifestyles – such as poverty – and health problems, or between working conditions and absenteeism. There are many examples of researchers aiming to prove a connection between two different factors and you may become involved in such research yourself.

Imagine that you have done a survey among your employees which included the following two questions.

	Very poorly	*Poorly*	*Same*	*Well*	*Very well*
How well do you think your salary compares with that for similar jobs in industry?	1	2	3	4	5
	Very poor	*Poor*	*OK*	*Good*	*Very good*
How would you rate your job satisfaction?	1	2	3	4	5

You may want to test the theory that low pay and low job satisfaction and, similarly, high pay and high job satisfaction, are linked. If the two factors – pay and job satisfaction – are connected, you would expect to find that a particular rating for one question would result in a predictable rating in the other. When a relationship exists between the factors in which an increase in one variable gives a corresponding increase in the other, this is known as *positive correlation*. This is not the only kind of link that variables can exhibit; sometimes you will come across examples where high values of one variable correspond to low values of the other and vice versa. This type of relationship is known as *negative correlation*. An example of negative correlation would be the number of sightings of sharks near a beach and the number of bathers!

Whichever type of relationship you believe may exist between two variables, the purpose of correlation analysis is to establish how likely it is that there really is a link of some sort and, if so, how strong it is. One way of doing this is to draw a scatter diagram. This type of graph has one variable on each axis with the data plotted correspondingly; it is often a good idea to make both axes of equal length so that the scatter diagram can be enclosed in a square (although this is not always appropriate).

When trying to establish a link between two variables, you will often have an idea that one of them *depends* on the other. In our example, we want to see whether job satisfaction *depends* on pay. If you have a clear idea that the dependency is a particular way round, then it is usual to plot the *dependent* variable – in this case, job satisfaction – on the vertical axis, while the *independent* variable is plotted on the horizontal axis.

Often, it is not possible to make any assumption about which variable depends on which. Consider the height and weight of children. Does height depend on weight or does weight depend on height? In this case, which variable you chose to allocate to which axis would be quite arbitrary.

A scatter diagram is plotted by making a small mark at the intersection of the readings on the horizontal axis and the vertical axis. The data in Table 2.4 on the height and age of children are shown as a scatter diagram in Figure 2.13. By plotting the points in this way we can often see, sometimes quite easily, whether there is a pattern.

Table 2.4 Heights and ages of children

Age (years)	*Height (cm)*
2	75
3	81
4	96
4	102
5	90
5	120
6	106
6	122

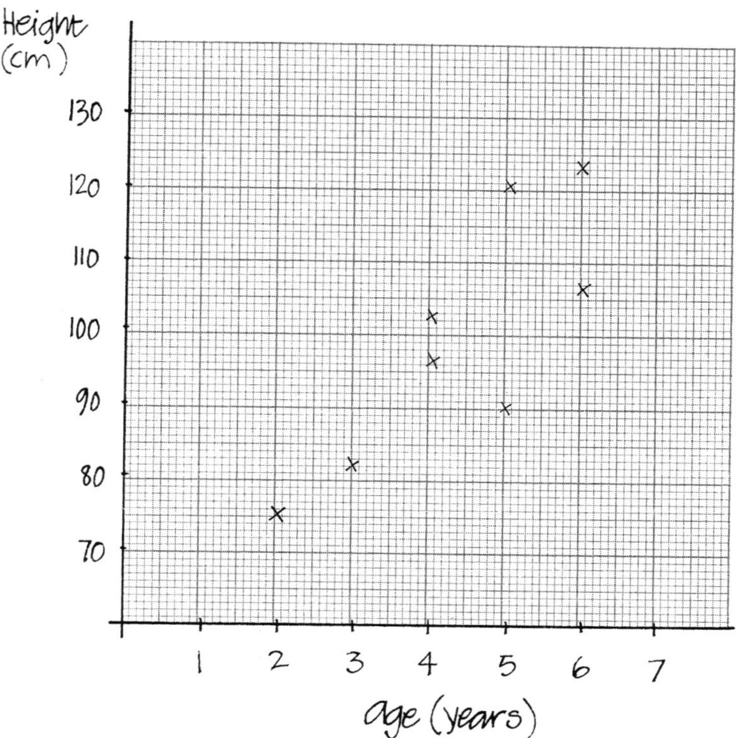

Figure 2.13 Scatter diagram for ages and heights of children

Drawing round the points marked in Figure 2.13 roughly forms a sausage shape, as shown in Figure 2.14.

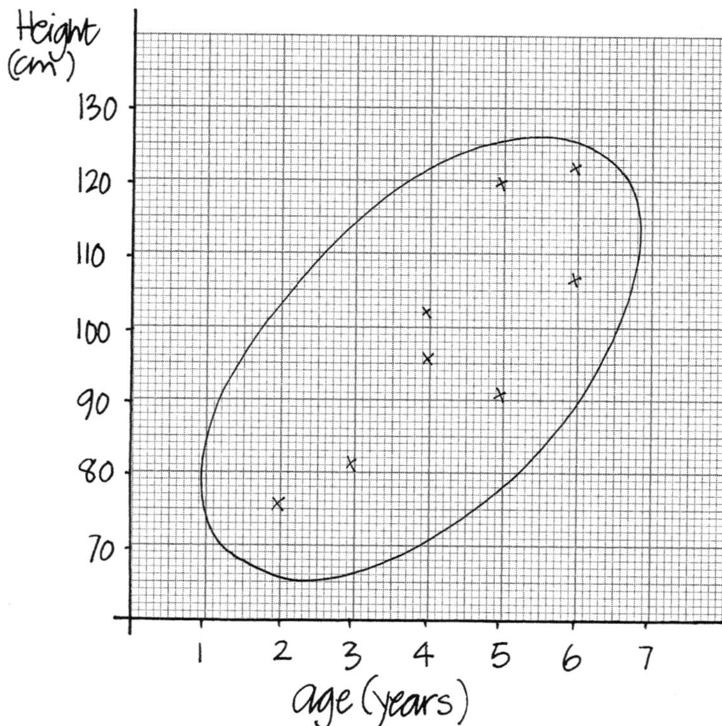

Figure 2.14 *Scatter diagram indicating positive correlation*

As mentioned earlier, if a scatter diagram gives an obvious sausage shape, or the points are more or less in a straight line as opposed to scattered widely in a kind of cloud, then the variables are changing together and are said to be *correlated*. If the sausage shape is angled as it is in Figure 2.14 (i.e. bottom left to top right), the variables are *positively correlated*. This simply means that an increase in one variable will be associated with an increase in the other variable by a roughly predictable amount.

If, however, the scatter diagram looks more like the one in Figure 2.15 – top left to bottom right – the variables are still related but, this time, they are *negatively correlated*. This means that as one variable increases, the other will decrease and vice versa. An example of two variables which are negatively correlated is the age of a car and its value. As a car gets older, i.e. the age gets bigger, its value usually decreases – although this can change if the vehicle survives long enough to achieve classic and rarity status!

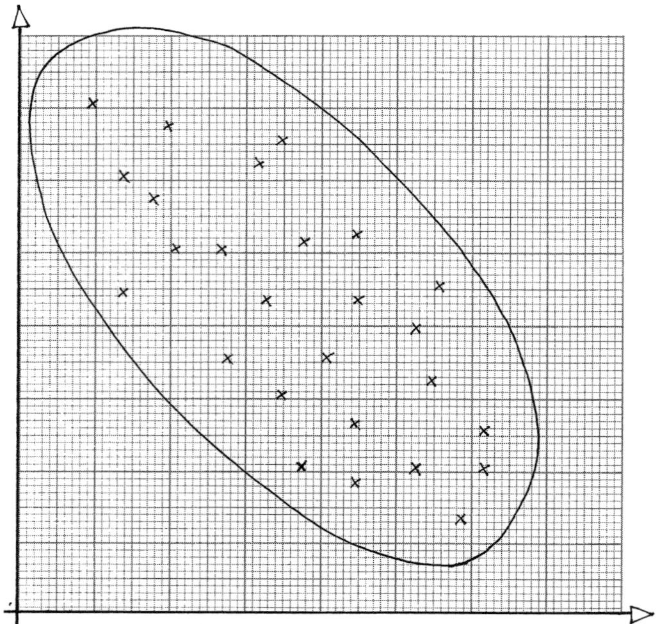

Figure 2.15 *Scatter diagram indicating negative correlation*

ACTIVITY 2.8

If you were going to illustrate the relationship between the age of a car and its value on a scatter diagram, which of the variables (age or value) would you put on the vertical axis?

Age ❑ Value ❑

The value depends on the age and so it is the dependent variable, while the age is the independent variable; consequently, the value would go on the vertical axis.

ACTIVITY 2.9

Plot the following figures from a used-car magazine on a scatter diagram.

Age (years)	Value (£000s)
0	10
1	8.5
2	7.9
3	7.1
4	6.1
5	5.9
6	5.1

What do you notice?

Keep your diagram to hand as you will need it again for a future Activity.

Your scatter diagram should look like the one in Figure 2.16. If you were to draw a 'sausage' around the crosses, it would lie top left to bottom right, which indicates a negative correlation. It would also be a much thinner sausage than for the height/age example – in fact, almost a straight line, showing a stronger correlation between the variables than for the previous example. When the two variables are strongly correlated, more of the change in the dependent variable can be associated with the change in the independent variable than if the correlation between them is weak.

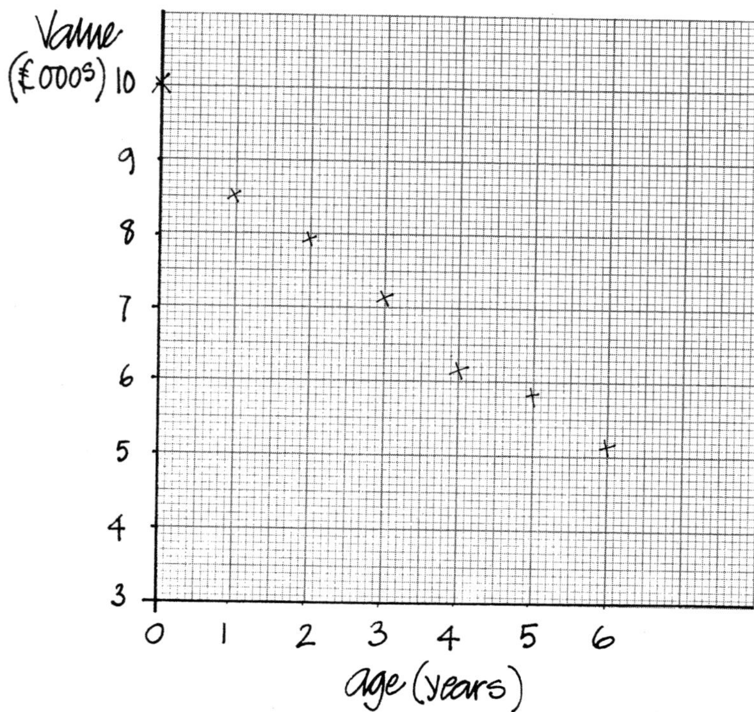

Figure 2.16 *Scatter diagram for age and value of used cars*

As well as being related to each other, the variables can be related to other factors and can also be subject to random or unpredictable influences. With perfect correlation, all the variation in the dependent variable can be matched to the variation in the independent variable.

A mathematical formula can be used to calculate the amount of association – the *correlation coefficient* – between two variables. The correlation coefficient is always a number between –1 and +1. If it is 0, there is no correlation between the variables, i.e. there is no association whatsoever between them. It is actually very rare to find pairs of variables with zero correlation, but if variables have very weak correlation (a correlation coefficient near 0), this means there is no clear tendency for a variable to move in one direction (up or down) with changes in the other variables. This idea that 'it is rare to find pairs of variables with zero correlation' should appear odd. Surely, if one chose two variables at random, for example midday temperature in Barbados and paperback book sales in Oxford, one would not expect any true correlation to appear. The key word is 'true'. While there is no real connection between these two variables, it is very possible that the two sets of readings may – by pure chance – show a weak correlation. In technical terminology, 'correlation does not automatically mean causation'. In other words, just because two variables appear connected (using the particular set of data at hand) does not necessarily mean that one caused the other. The stronger the correlation, the better the evidence that there is a real linkage between the two, but it is never certain. This is a key point about using statistical analysis: the results can only indicate a stronger or weaker likelihood of there being a real connection between the two variables. To be certain, one needs to discover the mechanism that links the two variables and statistics cannot do that for us.

Remember that a scatter diagram for variables with very weak correlation has no obvious sausage shape or straight line but just a random cloud shape. For the used car price example (Figure 2.16), there was strong negative correlation as the points on the scatter diagram lay almost in a straight line. In this case, the correlation coefficient would be near to –1; to be precise, when calculated it was –0.985. For the height and age example (Figure 2.13), there was strong positive correlation, so the correlation coefficient would be near to +1; when calculated it was +0.91.

If the two variables are strongly correlated (either negatively or positively), it implies that there is a relationship between them. When one variable changes, the other will too. The further the value of the correlation coefficient is away from 0, the stronger the correlation between the variables. It is difficult to attach labels to strengths of correlation coefficients but the following are some guidelines (the same applies to negative correlations).

	Sociological data	*Engineering/scientific data*
0 to 0.2	Very weak, negligible	Negligible
0.2 to 0.4	Weak, low	Negligible
0.4 to 0.7	Moderate	Weak
0.7 to 0.9	Strong, high, marked	Moderate to strong
0.9 to 1	Very strong, very high	Strong to very strong

Box 2.4 Correlation coefficient – calculation and meaning

In statistics books, the formula for correlation coefficient, r, is given as:

$$r = \frac{n\sum xy - \sum x \sum y}{\sqrt{[n\sum x^2 - (\sum x)^2][n\sum y^2 - (\sum y)^2]}}$$

where '$\sum x$' means the total of the figures in the x column, '$\sum x^2$' means the sum of the x figures squared, and so on, and 'n' is the total number of observations.

This seems quite complicated to calculate, but it can be divided up into manageable pieces, as you will see in the PC Activity at the end of this session.

But what is going on? In essence, we are capturing in one number, scaled between –1 and +1, information about how close the observations are to lying on a straight line – which one can think of as being the ultimate in 'sausage-shapedness'.

If the data points all lie close to a particular straight line (in which case the correlation coefficient will be close to +1 for an upward-sloping line or –1 for a downward-sloping one) then there is a quite strong indication that if we took a new x value we could predict reasonably well what the corresponding y value will be by using the straight line as our guide. Creating such a line is called *regression analysis* and we shall look at it in Section 2.6.

You will have noticed the difference in 'opinion' of what constitutes strong correlation between those dealing with sociological data, such as a market survey, and those using engineering data, for example glued joint failures measured against time allowed for setting. This does not imply that the latter are more rigorous than the former, but that the engineer usually has data better 'focused' on the matter at hand; social data are, inevitably, much 'noisier' as there are many influencing factors and the interrelationships are often very complex. Also, engineering or scientific data sets are often trying to identify direct, physical relationships that are easily measurable. We know that the chemical bonding that makes glue stick surfaces together takes time to build up strength, so we would expect a clear negative correlation between the joint failures recorded and the time allowed for the chemical bonds to form.

ACTIVITY 2.10

In the glue example, if we did *not* see a strong negative correlation, what might we deduce?

Since we are reasonably sure about the chemistry of glue bonding, we would conclude that other factors *were swamping the time effect. Perhaps the application of the glue is too variable, or the surfaces are not consistently prepared. So we may be able to gain useful information from an* absence *of correlation. As Sherlock Holmes said, sometimes the dog* not *barking in the night is what is significant!*

If you had two scatter diagrams for pairs of variables whose correlation coefficients were 0.47 and 0.58 respectively, it would be difficult, merely by looking at the diagrams, to see any difference between them. Both diagrams would display a fair degree of scatter representing a moderate degree of correlation (assuming they represented sociological data). Both would illustrate a possible, though not particularly strong, link between the two variables.

ACTIVITY 2.11

Decide whether the correlation between the following pairs of variables is likely to be positive, zero or negative.

		Positive	Zero	Negative
1	Number of miles driven and amount of fuel used	❑	❑	❑
2	Number of mortgage repossessions and number of people unemployed	❑	❑	❑
3	Ability to see in the dark and number of carrots eaten	❑	❑	❑
4	Amount of rainfall and number of people on a beach	❑	❑	❑

We think there would be:

1 positive correlation
2 positive correlation
3 effectively, zero correlation
4 negative correlation.

Remember that the fact that two variables are strongly correlated does not necessarily imply that one variable *causes* the other. There may be a cause and effect relationship between the variables or there may not: the correlation simply indicates that they both vary together. This may be because both variables change as a result of a third factor. For example, strong positive correlation has been found between the number of people owning telephones and the incidence of cancer of the colon in various countries. Does this imply that there is a *causal* relationship here? Does owning a telephone cause cancer? Common sense would suggest that it does not. It seems there is a third factor at play here: the argument may be that in more affluent countries – where there are more telephones – people also have more red meat in their diet which leads to the observed higher cancer rate. Hence, both variables are dependent on the third variable – wealth – and causality between them is not implied. Other published examples of spurious inferences from correlation include that between the salaries of clergymen and the sales of rum! Although these examples seem obvious, you need to be very careful – when the situations are less clear – about assuming a causal relationship that may not exist. Strong correlation may give evidence of a connection between the variables but it still requires other evidence to decide the significance to be placed on the result.

2.6 Regression analysis

Sometimes it is sufficient just to know that there actually is a relationship between two variables. For example, you may be researching the effect of poverty on ill health (as in the Durham study) and establishing a link between the two factors could lead you to suggest changes to health care provision in deprived areas. (Equally important is finding that there is little or no link between variables; it would be pointless to make special provision if, in fact, poverty had no effect on health.) There are other occasions, however, when being able to express the relationship between the variables in a precise way can be a great advantage. For example, if it were possible to derive a formula which related the age of a piece of monitoring equipment to its annual repair cost, you would be able to allocate funds from your budget for repairs and also make a decision on the optimal time to replace the machine.

Regression analysis is used to describe a relationship between two sets of data in terms of a mathematical equation. Although there are many kinds of relationships between data sets, we will confine ourselves to the simplest kind, the so-called *linear* relationship. This is one in which the data points would lie along a straight line if they were plotted on a scatter diagram. The used car price chart (Figure 2.16) was a good example of a nearly linear relationship between the variables as all the crosses lay just about on a straight line. If we actually drew this line, we could use it to estimate the value of any car of this model if we knew its age. What we are doing is using the observed values of cars to estimate the value of any other similar car. This is a simple case of building a mathematical 'model' which can be used to predict future cases.

We shall concentrate on *linear regression*. While this is the most common technique and sufficient for the needs of B800, you should be aware that there are other, more complex methods such as *non-linear regression* and *multivariate analysis*.

'Estimate' does not mean 'know for certain'. Individual cars have different characteristics; for example, how many high-speed crashes has the car been in?

Now let us look at how we could produce the straight line from which to make the predictions. The simplest method is to draw the line *by inspection*. The inspection method involves drawing the scatter diagram and then adding by eye a straight line that best represents the relationship. Unless the crosses are in a perfectly straight line, i.e. there is perfect correlation between them (which is highly unlikely), it is a bit 'hit and miss' how you draw the line. What you are aiming to do is to get as near as possible to as much of the data as possible. This will usually mean drawing the line so that there are the same number of crosses above the line as there are below it, with the distances of crosses from both sides of the line being about the same. The problem is that if you gave the same scatter diagram to five different people, they would probably all come up with a slightly different 'best' straight line and, hence, a slightly different relationship on which to base predictions.

ACTIVITY 2.12

Draw the 'best' straight line on to the scatter diagram you drew as part of Activity 2.9 for the used car price data (a transparent ruler might help you).

Compare your straight line with the one in Figure 2.17 (overleaf). Even if it is not exactly the same, it is probably perfectly acceptable. This just serves to illustrate the point that there is no precise 'best' line.

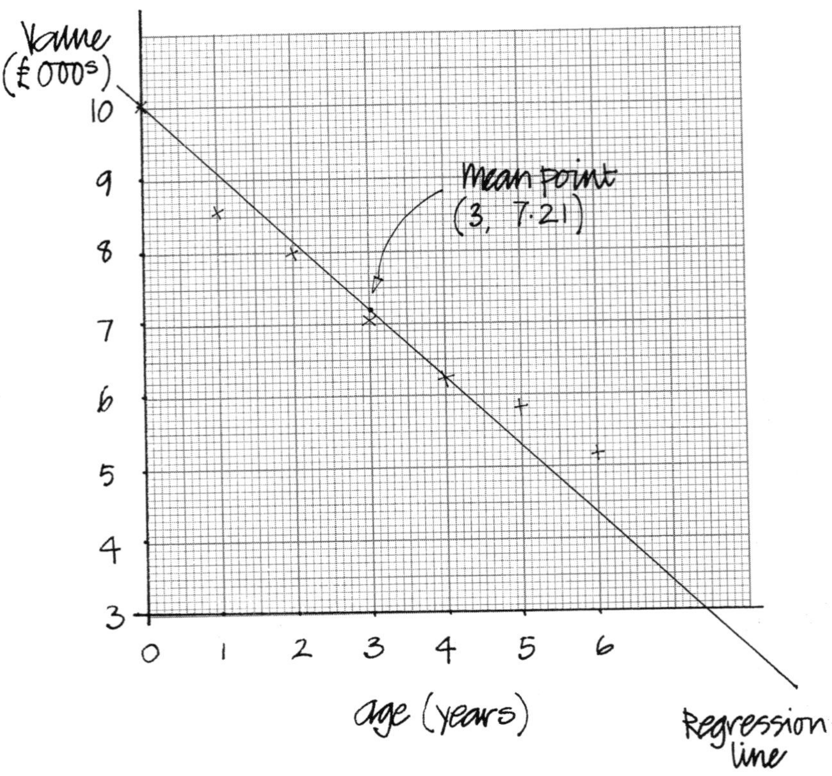

Figure 2.17 *A regression line drawn by inspection*

We drew in the regression line manually because most budget software packages do not have regression analysis functions built in. Specialized (and more expensive) spreadsheets, such as Excel, do have such facilities but the ways of using them vary considerably between programs, so we shall not discuss them here.

Actually, we cheated a bit because, before drawing the line, we plotted the *mean point* of the data. The regression line should always pass through this point. The mean point of the data is found by plotting the data pair:

(mean of first variable, mean of second variable)

In this case, the first variable is age. Remember that this is the *independent variable*. The mean of the ages is:

(0 + 1 + 2 + 3 + 4 + 5 + 6) ÷ 7 = 3 years

The second variable is value, the *dependent variable*. The mean of the values is:

(10 + 8.5 + 7.9 + 7.1 + 6.1 + 5.8 + 5.1) ÷ 7 = 7.21 (£7210)

The mean data point to plot, therefore, is (3, 7.21) and the line is then drawn so that it goes through this point. While this still leaves some flexibility as to where the line should go, it makes it a little easier to decide where to draw it.

Now that we have drawn the regression line, we can use it to make some estimates. I may have seen, for instance, a 4.5-year-old car on a garage forecourt with a price tag of £6000 and I want to know if this is a fair price to pay for a car of this age.

ACTIVITY 2.13

Carry out the above procedure on your scatter diagram. Does the car that I have seen on the forecourt represent a good buy?

I reckon that I would have to do a bit of bargaining with the salesperson as, according to the 'model', a car of that age should be worth about £5800. Remember that your estimate may vary a little from this depending on exactly where your regression line was placed. When you make an estimate like this within *the range of observed data, it is known as* interpolation.

Another type of estimation is called *extrapolation*; this is when you make estimates for values *outside* the observed range. In the case we are discussing, this would involve making predictions about the price of cars more than six years old. The estimates are made in exactly the same way as for interpolation: you read up from the horizontal axis until you reach the regression line and then read horizontally across until you reach the vertical axis.

ACTIVITY 2.14

Estimate the value of a 7-year-old car.

My calculations suggest that the 7-year-old car is worth around £3600.

The difference between interpolation and extrapolation is that it is more risky to predict behaviour outside the observed range. We have surveyed the values of cars between new and six years old, and discovered that there is a pretty good linear relationship between the ages of the cars and their values. But we have no direct experience of what happens to cars older than this. It would seem reasonable to assume that the straight line relationship continues, and the estimate you have made, assuming this to be the case, seems acceptable. But we do not know whether some other factor that we are not aware of from our observation comes into play at this age. For example, there might have been a design fault on this model of car eight years ago that rendered a car of this age virtually worthless, in which case the extrapolated straight line would be totally inappropriate. Eventually, when the car reaches, say, 30 years old, it may start rising in value if the market blesses it with the accolade of 'classic'. The message is to treat estimates based on extrapolation – which are the vast majority of estimates you will receive (including financial ones) – with a good deal of caution.

But do not continue the straight line too far, or you will end up *paying* to give away a car that was, say, 11 years old!

In the PC Activity at the end of this session, you will find that the equation of the regression line is:

$$y = 9.554 - 0.775x$$

where y is the car value (£000s) and x is the age of the car (years).

What can we use these equations for? Well, just as we could carry out interpolation and extrapolation graphically when we had found the regression line by eye, we can also make these types of estimate when we have an equation connecting the variables. It is more accurate to work from an equation, and it also means that the process can be automated if required. Let us say you wanted to repeat the estimate of the value of a 4.5-year-old car that we did graphically earlier. Remember, the equation linking the age (x) and value (y) of a car, with $x = 4.5$, is:

$$y = 9.554 - (0.775 \times 4.5) = 6.066$$

So we would expect the value of a 4.5-year-old car to be £6070, to the nearest £10. You might like to compare this figure with the one you calculated graphically in Activity 2.13; my estimate then was £5800.

Box 2.5 Regression analysis – calculation and meaning

Regression analysis calculates the coefficients a and b of the line:

$y = a + bx$

that 'best fits' the data points on a scatter diagram. We will discuss briefly what 'best fit' means later in this box.

The coefficients are calculated from the two equations:

$$b = \frac{n\sum xy - \sum x \sum y}{n\sum x^2 - (\sum x)^2}$$

$$a = \frac{\sum y}{n} - b\frac{\sum x}{n} = \bar{y} - b\bar{x}$$

where $\bar{y}$ and $\bar{x}$ are the means of y and x respectively.

If you compare the equation for b with that for the correlation coefficient, r, you will see that the top line of the equation is identical and the bottom line is the same as the contents of one of the brackets in the bottom line of the correlation formula. This emphasizes the close connection between the two ideas of *correlation* and *regression*, and also makes for quicker calculation of the 'b' coefficient if you have already calculated 'r'.

So what is this 'regression line' we have calculated? It is the straight line that minimizes the scatter of the data points around the line (see diagram below) and so is the straight line which best represents the 'cloud' of data points. The correlation coefficient indicates how good that representation is; if the points all do nearly lie on the line, r will be high (close to ±1); if there is a lot of scatter – the line, although the 'best fit', is a poor representation – the correlation coefficient, r, will be close to 0.

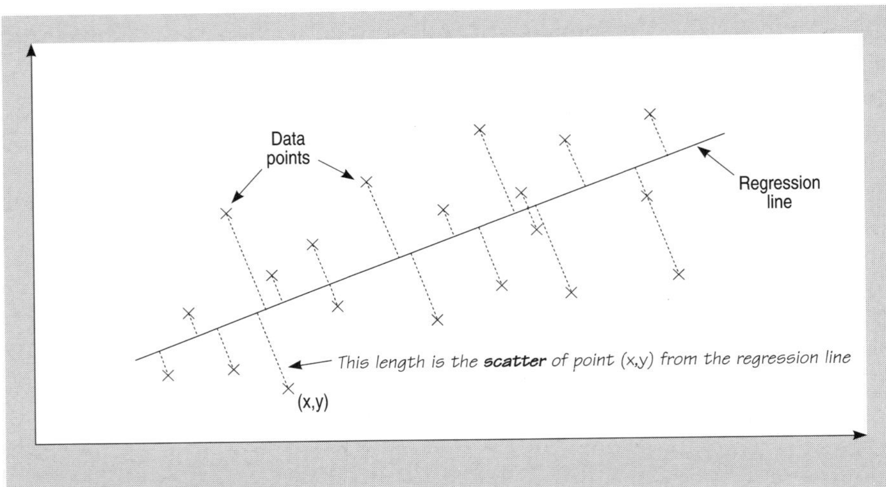

Scatter about a regression line

It is important to note that the equation you have calculated assumes that y depends on x, and that you are trying to find a value of y for a given value of x. You cannot meaningfully rearrange this equation to determine the value of x, the age of a car, given a particular value of y, the value in £000s. A car that cost £6070 might be 4.5 years old – or a newer example of a smaller model!

ACTIVITY 2.15

Use the regression equation $y = 9.554 - 0.775x$ to predict the value of a car that is 6.5 years old.

On substitution, we find: $y = 9.554 - (0.775 \times 6.5) = 4.516$

Thus a 6.5-year-old car should be worth £4520, rounding to the nearest £10.

ACTIVITY 2.16

Load the file **STATS3.WPS** or **STATS3.DOC** into your word-processor.

Print the file. It contains instructions for spreadsheet exercises on scatter diagrams, correlation coefficients and regression analysis.

Now work through the exercises as described in **STATS3.WPS** or **STATS3.DOC**.

2.7 Summary

We have seen that, in order to make effective use of data for decision making, managers need to be presented with summaries which can take the form of tables, aggregates or averages. We have looked at a range of methods for producing each of these.

Representing data visually can often be the most powerful way of making them meaningful for the recipient: it can help to show patterns and trends that may be more difficult to detect in a mass of figures. There are several types of graph and chart that can be used, each with their own special features. We have discussed those that you are most likely to come across, looked at how some of them can be drawn using a spreadsheet, and identified the situations in which each might be most effective.

This session concluded by looking at two important techniques in data analysis. First, the correlation coefficient (r), which has a value between –1 and +1, measures the likelihood of some sort of relationship between two variables. A correlation of 0 indicates no relationship. The nearer r gets to +1 or –1, the stronger the relationship. Strong correlation does not imply causality; it indicates that the variables both vary together, but one may depend on the other or they may both depend on a third factor.

Secondly, regression analysis is a technique for quantifying the relationship between two variables. The first variable is known as the independent variable and is plotted on the horizontal axis of a scatter diagram. The second variable, which depends on the first, is called the dependent variable and is plotted on the vertical axis. In linear regression, the assumed relationship is represented by a straight line on a graph, which can be derived either by eye on a scatter diagram or by calculation. Once this line is drawn (or the equation known), it can be used to predict values for the dependent variable both inside (interpolation) and outside (extrapolation) the range of observed values of the independent variable.

In concentrating on simple linear regression, we have assumed that the dependent variable depended only on one other variable and that the relationship was a straight line. Many more complicated relationships can be constructed, and if you are interested in exploring this further, you are encouraged to refer to one of the many textbooks in this field. Such methods are beyond the requirements of B800.

Correlation and regression analysis can be extremely useful in identifying and quantifying relationships between variables. However, the calculations involved can become rather tedious, so using a computer spreadsheet is a great advantage.

Objectives

You should now be able to:

- Identify a range of graphs and charts.
- Interpret graphs and charts in order to glean the appropriate information from them.
- Select an appropriate type of chart for the data that need to be presented.
- Construct a variety of graphs and charts using the Works or Excel spreadsheet – including component bar charts, line diagrams and pie charts – in order to present numerical data in an appropriate and effective way.
- Distinguish between and evaluate different kinds of average and use them appropriately.
- Understand the significance of measures of spread, such as the range or standard deviation.
- Understand the implication of a 'high' or 'low' correlation coefficient.
- Draw by hand a linear regression line.
- Calculate, manually or by computer, the correlation coefficient 'r' and the linear regression line '$y = a + bx$'.
- Describe qualitatively (i.e. not in formal mathematical or statistical terms) the connection between correlation and regression.

Contents

3.1 Introduction

In this session we shall consider what managers can do to transform data and statistics into useful and reliable information. The treatment will be kept to as non-mathematical a level as possible, and will concentrate more on the presentation and interpretation of statistics than on their calculation. Here we are looking at the statistical techniques that need to be available to a modern senior manager. There is nothing mathematical in here that you are expected to learn verbatim – what is important is that you acquire an understanding of the underlying statistical meaning.

The session introduces several statistical techniques to help you transform data into useful and reliable information. In particular, this session aims to familiarize you with:

- the Normal distribution
- time series analysis
- sampling
- testing significance.

It is often said that a little knowledge is a dangerous thing; statistics may well be a case in point. At an advanced level, statistics may be a sophisticated set of techniques that require much experience to master but, in its everyday forms, sadly you will often find that those who seek to bombard you with figures are not always masters of their trade (or, if they are, there may sometimes be an ulterior motive to their efforts).

> [He] uses statistics as a drunken man uses lamp-posts – for support rather than illumination.
>
> (Andrew Lang)

A classic small book was written by Darrell Huff in the 1950s called *How to Lie with Statistics*. He offered it as a manual 'for self-defence' and its points are as valid today as when it was first published. The check-list of questions in Section 3.8 of this session is largely based on Huff's ideas.

3.2 Summary statistics

The Normal distribution

In statistical analysis it is often possible to deduce that the data set one is faced with can be represented by one of a small group of 'typical' distributions. Members of this useful band go by exotic names such as 'Poisson', Binomial', 'Negative Exponential', 'Log Normal', but the only one that we shall discuss is called the Normal distribution. Each of these 'typical' distributions is characterized by certain key conditions, and so each has relevance in particular circumstances. For example, if you are analysing 'Yes/No' types of data, the Binomial would probably be the one to use.

Rather conveniently for us, many phenomena in the real world may be described in terms of the so-called 'Normal' or 'Gaussian' distribution. You will probably recognize the familiar bell-shaped curve in Figure 3.1.

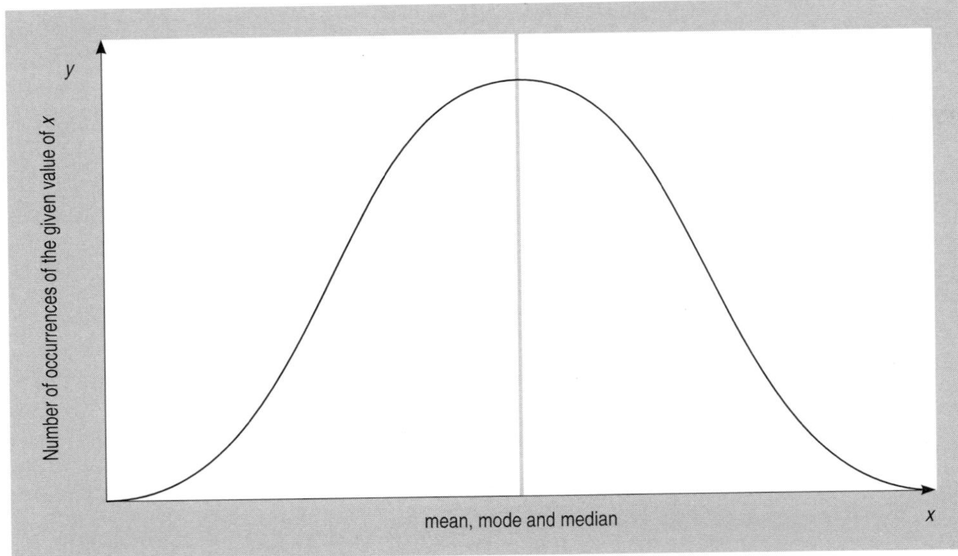

Figure 3.1 *A Normal distribution*

Obvious examples of this are large data sets where points are clustered around some central value, the classic example being the height of adult males in a population. In the case of the Normal distribution, the mean, median and mode converge on the same value.

One of the major advantages of this (and other) types of distribution is that they make the data more amenable to analysis, either by sophisticated mathematics or by more elementary description in terms of standard parameters.

One of the key benefits of using the Normal distribution is that it can be completely described using just two parameters: its mean and standard deviation. The term standard deviation (often abbreviated as σ, the lower-case Greek letter sigma) is the most widely used measure of 'spread' for a distribution, and is defined as 'the root mean square deviation from the mean'. It is more important that you should understand what are the implications of standard deviation, and how to use it, rather than get too embroiled in the basis of its derivation and calculation, which were outlined in Session 2.

The important thing to know about standard deviations is the way they divide up a Normal distribution. As Figure 3.2 shows, the $\pm 1\sigma$ points include 68.26% of the data points in the distribution, $\pm 2\sigma$ includes 95.44%, and $\pm 3\sigma$ includes 99.72%.

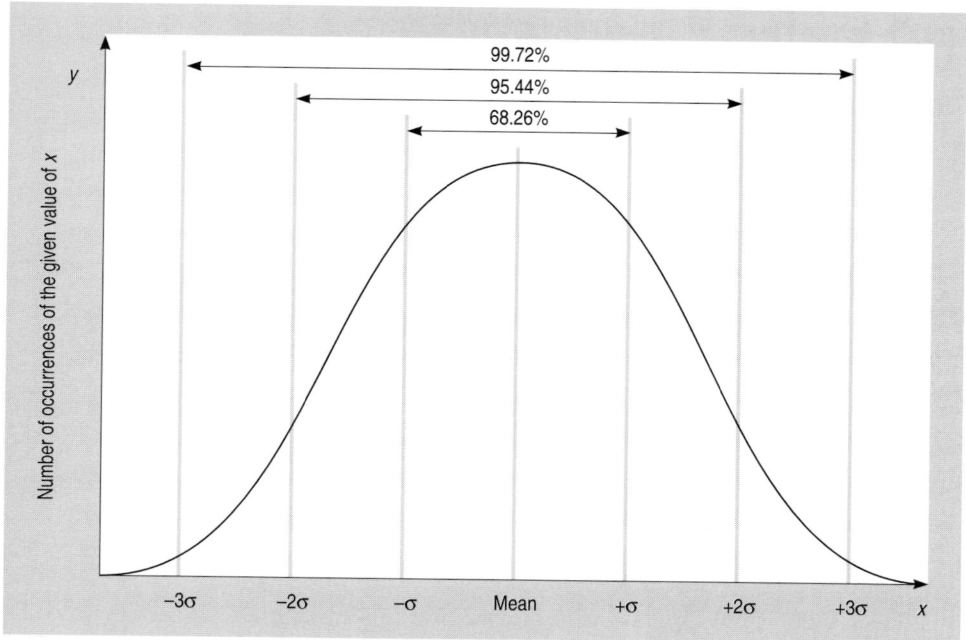

Figure 3.2 *Annotated graph of a Normal distribution to show σ, 2σ and 3σ points*

QUESTION 3.1

Use Table 3.1 (overleaf) to help you answer the following questions. If the weight of widgets is normally distributed with a mean of 500 grams (g), and a standard deviation of 25 g, what percentage of widgets weigh:

(a) More than 500 g?

(b) More than 550 g?

(c) Less than 525 g?

(d) Between 490 g and 510 g?

(e) Outside the range 440 g to 560 g?

The dispersion of a frequency distribution can also be described in terms of such things as *quartiles*. Just as a median divides up a distribution into two, so quartiles divide it into four, with equal numbers of data points in each quarter. (The rather grandiose term *semi-interquartile range* is a measure of the spread of the distribution, indicating the difference in value between the mean and the upper, or lower, quartile.) Quartiles are often seen in salary surveys; an employer may espouse a salary policy of paying at the upper quartile rate, meaning that, for a given person specification, they will try to attract and/or retain staff with a salary which is higher than three out of four comparable employers.

A refinement of this technique involves the use of *deciles*. In a given distribution, each decile (first, second, etc.) is one of the values which divide the distribution into 10 equal populations (i.e. ranges with equal numbers of data points). Similarly, where the samples are large enough to justify a higher degree of discrimination, *percentiles* are sometimes used.

Table 3.1 Table of Normal distribution

σ	*In 1 tail*	*Outside 1 tail*	*In 2 tails*	*Between 2 tails*
A	B	C	D	E
0.0	50.00	50.00	100.00	0.00
0.1	46.02	53.98	92.04	7.96
0.2	42.07	57.93	84.14	15.86
0.3	38.21	61.79	76.42	23.58
0.4	34.46	65.54	68.92	31.08
0.5	30.85	69.15	61.70	38.30
0.6	27.43	72.57	54.86	45.14
0.7	24.20	75.80	48.40	51.60
0.8	21.19	78.81	42.38	57.62
0.9	18.41	81.59	36.82	63.18
1.0	15.87	84.13	31.74	68.26
1.1	13.57	86.43	27.14	72.86
1.2	11.51	88.49	23.02	76.98
1.3	9.68	90.32	19.36	80.64
1.4	8.08	91.92	16.16	83.84
1.5	6.68	93.32	13.36	86.64
1.6	5.48	94.52	10.96	89.04
1.7	4.46	95.54	8.92	91.08
1.8	3.59	96.41	7.18	92.82
1.9	2.87	97.13	5.74	94.26
2.0	2.28	97.72	4.56	95.44
2.1	1.79	98.21	3.58	96.42
2.2	1.39	98.61	2.78	97.22
2.3	1.07	98.93	2.14	97.86
2.4	0.82	99.18	1.64	98.36
2.5	0.62	99.38	1.24	98.76
2.6	0.47	99.53	0.94	99.06
2.7	0.35	99.65	0.70	99.30
2.8	0.26	99.74	0.52	99.48
2.9	0.19	99.81	0.38	99.62
3.0	0.14	99.86	0.28	99.72

3.3 Changes over time

Change is a topic that is often covered in management texts these days, but the qualitative aspects of change are not of immediate concern in this part of the course. Rather, we will think about some of the more quantitative aspects.

The point of the exercise in Box 3.1 is to make you think about percentages. It should be obvious, but unfortunately it sometimes is not, that percentages are easily misconstrued. Given even a small lapse of concentration, it is all too easy to forget the basics.

Note the following.

In an attempt to get business moving, Bloggs of Bloggs' Emporium decides to have a sale; everything is reduced by 10%. At the end of the sale, business has picked up and so Bloggs raises his prices by 10% – and is surprised to find that he has not regained his original prices! The arithmetic is extremely simple: 10% off reduces the price of a £10.00 item to £9.00. The subsequent 10% price rise takes the £9.00 article only to £9.90. It is not our intention to insult anybody's intelligence, but it is all too easy to neglect the arithmetic and adopt a 'common sense' approach without thinking. It is surprising how often errors like Bloggs' are made in real life, and they can sometimes be serious.

Box 3.1 Percentages – some revision

Many modern calculators feature a key labelled simply '%'. What is it supposed to mean? Try the following (it may be that your calculator gives different results from ours, but that just serves to illustrate the problem):

5	÷	10	=	0.5

So far so good; this much seems perfectly logical. What about:

5	÷	10	%	50

The picture emerging is that the '%' key is used to express the answer as a percentage rather than a decimal.

5	×	10	%	0.5

This seems to suggest a different pattern, telling us that 10% of 5 is 0.5. Now if we try:

5	+	10	%	5.55555

when we might have expected to get 5.50 as (5 plus 10%).

Interestingly:

5	–	10	%	–50

so it is clear that this particular calculator at least is not especially intuitive. You might like to do a similar exercise with your own calculator.

Our particular response to the issue of calculators and percentages is to dispense with the '%' key altogether and work exclusively in real numbers, so that adding 17.5% VAT to a £42 bill requires a calculation of 42 × 1.175, or calculating a 10% discount off the same bill is achieved by 42 × 0.9 (before tax of course).

Percentage points

It is even easier to confuse percentages with percentage points.

A colleague had been doing some research into TMA scores achieved by different groups of OUBS MBA students. One day as we passed in the corridor, he announced that, in accordance with the hypothesis we had discussed earlier, group A had indeed performed better than group B, scoring on average (mean, to be precise) 10% more. Like many corridor conversations, this remark was duly acknowledged and mentally filed away for future reference. Back in my office, I reflected on what he had said. If the mean score for group B was 60%, what would be the mean score for group A?

The remark is capable of two quite different interpretations. If group A had a mean score of 66, they would indeed have amassed 10% more marks, whereas if their mean score was 70%, their mean score could be said to be 10 *percentage points* higher.

The distinction is quite clear, but our imprecision led to my being unable to answer the question with certainty.

ACTIVITY 3.1

Suppose, for the sake of simplicity, that at a recent election there were only three candidates. Their share of the vote was as follows:

Silly Party	36%
Serious Party	36%
Minority Party	28%
Votes cast:	10,000

There are quite a few ways we can discuss this result, so let us ask a question first. How much better does the Minority Party need to do to stand any chance of victory?

The first task is to recognize that the finishing post in this three-horse race is approximately 34%, assuming the Minority Party can attract votes equally from the other two parties. (In arithmetic terms it is actually 3334 votes but, for the moment, we will confine ourselves to percentages, and to whole numbers at that.) So the question becomes, how much more than 28% is 34%? The answer is of course 6 'percentage points' or just over 21% (34/28 = 1.214). Sadly, the distinction between 'percentage change' and 'percentage points difference' is often glossed over, with many people in the media in particular failing to adequately make the distinction.

Remembering for a moment Bloggs' Emporium, it is also worth emphasizing that the re-framed question 'How much more than 28% is 34%?' cannot be expected to yield the same answer as 'How much less than 34% is 28%?' Although the six percentage points *difference remains, the answer is that 28% is just under 18% less than 34%. (If you are in any doubt, convert the percentages into actual votes cast and redo the arithmetic.)*

3.4 Time series analysis

A time series is no more than a series of measurements of how a value of particular interest varies over time.

The most obvious examples are series such as production volume charts, exchange rate variations, and inflation measures. Again, the choice of a simple graph, smoothed curve or histogram is a matter for personal choice but it should reflect the *granularity* of our interest.

Granularity is an interesting concept that owes its origins to a photographic analogy. If you are content to take snapshots, and view them as postcard-sized prints, you are unlikely to be overly concerned with granularity. If, however, you have a favourite photograph enlarged to poster size, as is now commonly available, you will undoubtedly notice that, when viewed close up, the fine detail is obscured by the graininess of the process. If the whole picture is viewed from across the room, it looks as good as the postcard did at arm's length; if you look closely at the detail, there are distinct limits to what may be discerned.

Collections of data are also subject to granularity. If the daily closing value of the FTSE-100 share index were to be plotted for a whole year, it would not matter at all whether it were represented by a simple graph, smoothed curve or histogram – the net result would still look the same. If you were only concerned with a week's observations, a smoothed curve would be totally unjustifiable (you cannot interpolate, and you do not know what the behaviour was during the day, since you only have the closing value), whilst a histogram of just five data points will tend to look bland. The simple graph seems to be the most appropriate.

FTSE (pronounced 'foot-sy') stands for Financial Times/Stock Exchange and is the name given to the indices produced by the London Stock Exchange.

The concept of granularity can be extended to consider the total period over which the observations should be made in order to show us a meaningful picture. Imagine that you are in the business of selling ice-cream. Daily sales are obviously of interest to you, but you observe that, in any given week, you sell much more at the weekend than during the week. Perhaps weekly figures are more valuable – until you remember that you tend to sell rather more during the summer than during the winter. Monthly figures? Annual? What about that year when we had a really good summer?

The problem with simple time series is that most of them tend to jump about rather a lot. We can collect many data, but the interpretation is not made any easier unless we make some simplifying assumptions. Typically, we might want to smooth the data, and thereby detect any underlying trends.

Moving averages

Returning to ice-cream selling, if we plot daily sales for a month, as shown in Table 3.2, we observe that the day-to-day variations tend to conceal any underlying trend (see Figure 3.3).

Table 3.2 Table of daily sales (in £) over 28 days

	Week 1	*Week 2*	*Week 3*	*Week 4*
Monday	98	91	92	84
Tuesday	95	86	85	77
Wednesday	90	86	80	79
Thursday	76	70	78	68
Friday	109	103	97	91
Saturday	247	252	205	222
Sunday	198	176	201	154

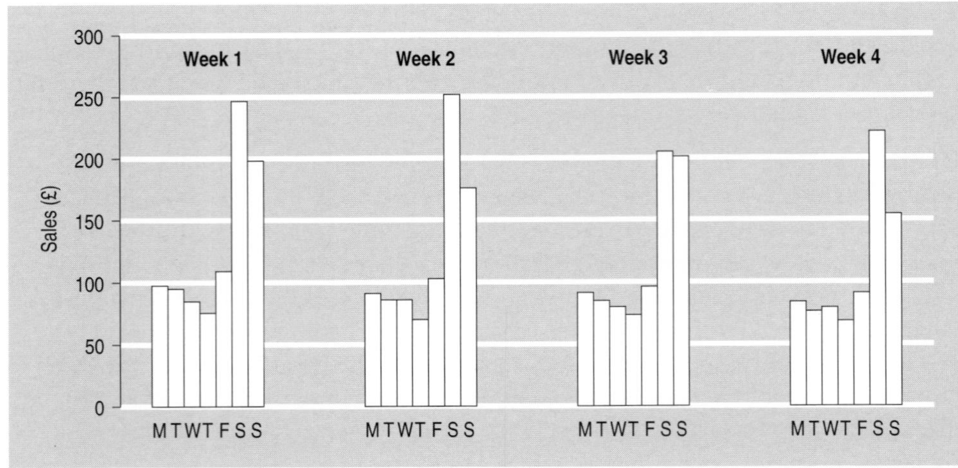

Figure 3.3 *Plot of daily sales*

Let us now examine what happens if we plot a seven-day moving average (it is actually a mean). To be exact, the seven-day moving average for Day N is the mean of the reading for Day N and the six preceding days (see Table 3.3).

Table 3.3 Value of daily sales (in £) when expressed as a seven-day moving average (the seven days up to and including the days shown in the table)

	Week 1	*Week 2*	*Week 3*	*Week 4*
Monday		130	124	119
Tuesday		129	123	117
Wednesday		128	123	117
Thursday		128	124	116
Friday		127	123	115
Saturday		127	116	117
Sunday	130	123	120	111

There are several things to note about Table 3.3:

- It contains 22 data points, not 28. This is because there are only 22 consecutive seven-day periods in 28 days, since we have no information about the sales before or after the period in question.
- A downward trend is now reasonably easy to discern, which was not readily apparent from looking at the original data – the daily fluctuations were disguising the information content in 'noise'. See Figure 3.4.
- Perhaps the trend indicates increased competition, or maybe it is nearing the end of the peak season for eating ice-cream. Without locating the month within the larger cycle (here, probably annual), we cannot interpret the results much further.

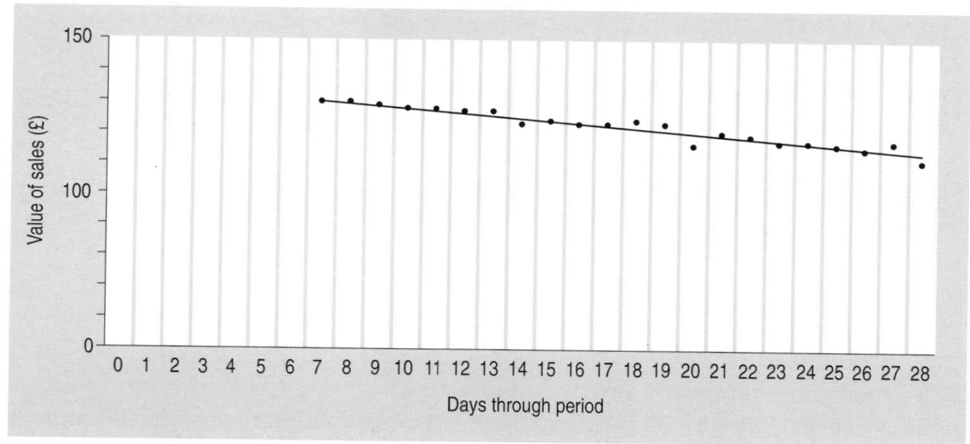

Figure 3.4 *Plot of daily sales with seven-day moving average*

The choice of seven days for the averaging period was quite deliberate. Since we know there is a significant variation in sales during the week, our seven-day period will always contain precisely one example of each of the days of the week. An average over, say, nine days would vary depending on whether there were one or two weekends in the period under consideration.

If our period of interest was the whole year, we might consider the use of, say, a four-week moving average. This would give us a new data point every week, made up of the average weekly sales over the previous four weeks. Plotting this seems to provide us with a more robust indicator of what is happening over the year (Figure 3.5).

Although we can now see the wood for the trees, our data still only describe the year in question. Did we have a good summer, and how typical was the pattern of this particular year? Mercifully, not everything is quite as seasonal as selling ice-cream.

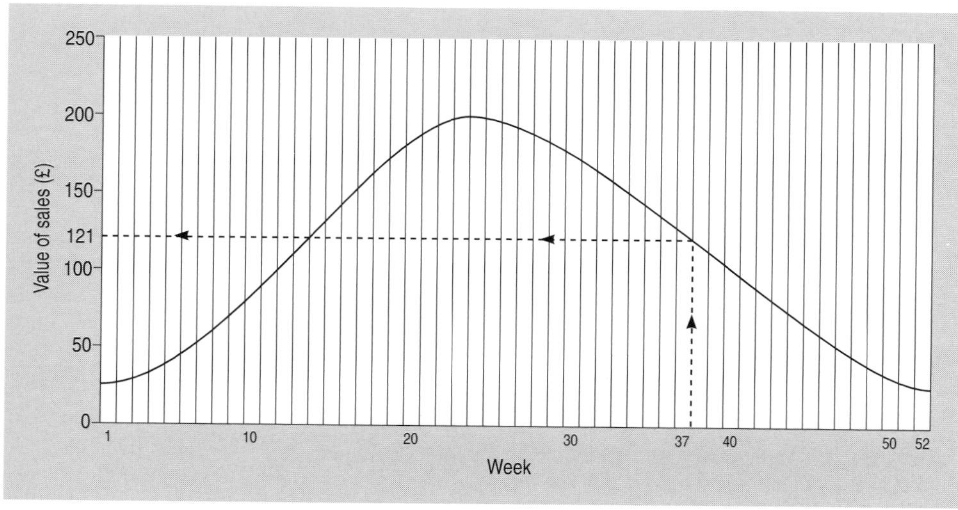

Figure 3.5 *Plot of four-week moving average sales over one year*

Index numbers

Index numbers are a very elementary concept. In essence they are no more than a simple ratio of a given quantity relative to a predetermined baseline. This baseline is usually chosen as 100 so that the result can be expressed as a percentage. The fact that index numbers are so straightforward has not prevented them from being the cause of at least as much confusion as any other statistical device.

'Widget' is used here generically and is not the thing found at the bottom of modern beer cans.

Suppose that you have started work on an assembly line. Your daily output of widgets is a measure of your productivity. On your first day, you are introduced to the department and required to attend a briefing with other new starters; you do not actually make any widgets. On day 2 you are sent to an experienced operative who provides some 'watch me' training. By lunch-time you have made your first widget, and that afternoon you hesitantly produce a further 38. Now that you know the ropes, your daily outputs for the remainder of the week are 88, 93 and 97. During the following week, you manage daily totals of, respectively, 100, 103, 104, 103 and 105. If we choose the Monday of this second week as the baseline (because by then you are regarded as 'up to speed', plus the fact that it simplifies the arithmetic), then the index of your performance on the second Friday, *relative to the preordained baseline*, is the ratio of 105 to 100, i.e. 1.05. (In practice, when referred to a base of 100, index numbers are usually denoted just by the number itself without actually calculating the ratio – in this case 105. We shall maintain this latter usage for the remainder of our discussion.)

An excellent example of the use of index numbers is provided by the Nationwide Building Society in its regularly published survey of house prices (Figure 3.6 and Table 3.4).

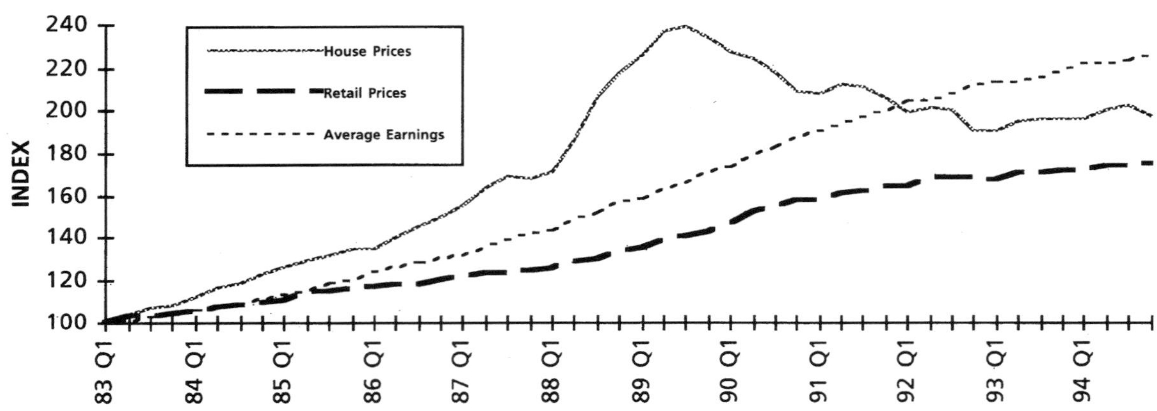

Figure 3.6 *Indices of house prices, retail prices and average earnings (Source: Nationwide, 1995, p. 3)*

You should note that the figures shown in Table 3.4 (and hence reflected in Figure 3.6) are all quoted relative to the same base: in this case the first quarter of 1983. If you want to determine the percentage change between any two dates, it is a simple matter of dividing the latter by the former, effectively *re-basing* the latter figure relative to the former. For example, the percentage change between Q1 1987 and Q1 1990 was, for All Houses, 226.5/155.4 = 1.4575, 45.75%.

The choice of baseline can dramatically affect the view given of the changes.

For example, using the 1983 Q1 house prices as the base shows the 1993 Q1 prices in a positive light as they are 190.6 or 90.6 per cent higher than 1983. However, if you had purchased a house in 1990 Q1, when the index was at 226.5 and house prices were booming, you would have lost a significant amount of value by 1993. If we re-based the data using 1990 Q1 prices as the base, 1993 Q1 would become $\frac{190.6}{226.5} \times 100 = 84.2$, which gives a very different picture of the buoyancy of the housing market.

Table 3.4 Nationwide house price indices and indices of retail prices and average earnings

Nationwide House Price Indices and Indices of Retail Prices and Average Earnings

United Kingdom (First Quarter 1983 =100)

Period	Mortgage Rate [1] %	Nationwide Mix Adjusted House Price Indices [2]				Retail Price Index	Average Earnings Index [3]	House Price / Earnings Ratio [4]
		All Houses	New Houses	Secondhand Houses				
				Modern	Older			
1982 Q1	13.5	91.9	94.8	90.4	91.4	95	92	3.19
1983 Q1	10.0	100.0	100.0	100.0	100.0	100	100	3.21
1984 Q1	10.25	112.8	112.5	112.7	113.7	105	106	3.42
1985 Q1	13.875	126.2	125.0	125.5	127.8	111	114	3.55
1986 Q1	12.75	135.5	134.3	134.0	138.4	116	124	3.52
1987 Q1	12.25	155.4	150.3	153.7	160.9	121	132	3.78
1988 Q1	10.3	171.4	164.5	169.5	175.6	125	144	3.84
1989 Q1	13.5	226.3	211.1	225.8	233.7	135	159	4.56
1990 Q1	15.4	226.5	205.1	224.2	239.7	145	174	4.18
Q2	15.4	224.2	201.5	222.2	238.5	152	180	4.01
Q3	15.4	217.6	198.7	218.1	230.9	154	183	3.82
Q4	14.5	208.8	191.8	211.8	220.2	157	187	3.58
1991 Q1	13.9	208.0	190.1	212.7	217.9	158	191	3.50
Q2	12.25	211.7	193.6	211.9	226.2	161	194	3.50
Q3	11.5	210.5	191.8	215.3	222.1	162	197	3.43
Q4	11.5	205.2	187.6	209.3	217.5	163	200	3.29
1992 Q1	10.99	199.6	187.0	204.6	209.4	164	204	3.13
Q2	10.7	200.9	184.9	204.2	212.8	168	205	3.13
Q3	9.95	199.8	187.4	203.0	211.8	168	208	3.08
Q4	8.55	190.6	183.3	193.1	200.1	168	212	2.89
1993 Q1	7.99	190.6	181.9	195.7	196.9	167	213	2.88
Q2	7.99	195.2	183.3	194.0	204.5	170	213	2.94
Q3	7.99	196.4	181.0	195.5	208.4	170	215	2.94
Q4	7.74	196.2	182.6	196.9	208.8	171	218	2.89
1994 Q1	7.74	195.5	189.2	194.6	209.4	171	222	2.83
Q2	7.74	199.9	186.0	198.6	212.6	174	222	2.89
Q3	8.14	202.0	191.5	201.4	216.5	174	223	2.91
Q4	8.14	197.3	190.9	194.8	211.0	175*	226*	2.81*

* Estimate

New properties are those not previously occupied. Modern properties are ones built in 1945 or later which are not new. Older properties are those built before 1945.

1 The mortgage rate shown is the gross rate charged to new borrowers at the end of the quarter. No allowance is made for large loan or other discounts.
2 The procedure used to calculate the Nationwide's mix-adjusted indices is applied individually to (a) *all* properties (b) the sample of new, modern and (c) to older properties bought by first time buyers and previous owner occupiers. It is possible for the percentage change for *all* properties to be greater or smaller than the percentage changes for the sub-sets shown in (b) and (c) above.
3 Average earnings relate to full time men, aged 21 years and over, in all occupations (excluding those whose pay was affected by absence) derived from the New Earnings Survey in April each year: the monthly index of average earnings is used for interpolation and extrapolation.
4 Ratio of the weighted price of all properties mortgaged to Nationwide to national average earnings.

The lesson you should learn from this exercise is that the choice of baseline is seldom arbitrary. It is much more likely to have been carefully selected. Your duty as a manager is not merely to be able to passively assimilate simple statistical information, but to actively interrogate it to discover the real significance (if any) that it portends.

3.5 Sampling

The introduction of sampling theory in courses such as this has traditionally been in relation to statistical process control; if I measure 10% of the output of my production line, and find that 5% of this sample is faulty, what can I predict about my overall quality? Such statistical process control techniques are currently unfashionable, in an environment where organizations are increasingly striving for 100% compliance with specification, i.e. zero defects. However, it is important that you should understand the basis of sampling.

Suppose you want to know something about a group, perhaps how your customers view your latest offering, but unfortunately (or fortunately?) there are too many of them for you to ask them all, and you have to make do with a sample. It seems reasonable to suppose that the sample will not behave *precisely* like the population from which it is drawn. The reasons for this inaccuracy take two distinct forms: *bias* and *sampling accuracy.*

Bias is ultimately due to inadequacies in the selection of the sample; *sampling error* arises from the limited size of the sample selected.

Sample selection

The most straightforward sampling technique is to take a random sample. Unfortunately, this does not mean you can just go and ask people 'at random'. Suppose you wanted to know about the shopping habits of supermarket customers. How realistic would it be to simply stand outside the exit from a supermarket and complete a questionnaire with every tenth person who came out? Well, if you managed to stand outside all day on every Wednesday in May, you could begin to build up a useful picture of people who used that particular supermarket on Wednesdays in May; the difficulty comes when you try to generalize your findings to a wider group.

If it were a High Street location, you might find that people who shopped at the out-of-town branches behaved differently. Wednesday shoppers would include a proportion of people doing their once-weekly shop, plus others who buy every day. Would the proportions be the same on Friday night or Saturday morning? And would findings in large cities be applicable to people living in rural areas?

In the 1936 US presidential campaign, the *Literary Digest* magazine did a survey of voting intentions. More than two million questionnaires were sent out, to a sample whose names and addresses had been 'randomly' drawn from lists of its subscribers, and from the telephone directory. The results from this huge sample were overwhelming in their endorsement of the Republican candidate. That the electorate at large voted for the Democrat, Franklin D. Roosevelt, merely suggests that there is more to the US electorate than magazine-reading telephone subscribers! Or, to be more precise, in 1936 the population consisting of telephone owners or *Literary Digest* subscribers did not represent well the whole electorate; it was badly skewed towards the more affluent, who in turn were more likely to vote Republican.

Self-selecting samples

How people respond, and indeed whether they respond at all, can defeat even the best chosen sample.

You may have heard of the infamous Kinsey Report. The intention was to investigate sexual behaviour in the USA, and the methodology (necessarily) relied heavily on volunteers and self-reported evidence. Retrospective studies have shown that not only were certain groupings heavily over-represented amongst Kinsey's subjects compared with the population at large but also those people agreeing to take part were in all probability significantly different from their less forthcoming brethren.

Many organizations conduct salary surveys of their members, including professional bodies and alumni associations. Whatever grouping we choose, we can rely on the fact that we will not elicit a 100% response. There will be people who are happy to divulge their salary, and those who are not. Probably those who believe that they are doing well will be significantly over-represented in the survey returns.

Even on a more parochial basis, we are all at some time or another guilty of generalizing from personal experience. How representative of the general populace are the people with whom you tend to interact? Most of us tend to associate with people with whom we have something in common. In our social circles we tend to cleave to those who hold similar views. Even at work we tend to meet people who by definition are also in employment. Never forget the psychiatrist who claims that everyone is neurotic nowadays; well, everybody *they* meet, anyway.

Sample size

Mercifully, the question of sample *size* is more of a science than an art, and we can begin to offer some guidance.

We will start with a simple scenario featuring a ridiculously small sample and see what we can learn about the representativeness of samples as their size increases. Let us suppose that 60% of the population start each day with a cup of tea, whilst 40% prefer coffee. (It will simplify matters if we assume that everybody drinks one or the other.) What are the possibilities if we ask a sample of just two people?

The alternatives are straightforward: we might get two coffees, two teas, coffee and tea, or tea and coffee (note the two different ways in which we can get 'one of each').

Based on our understanding of simple probability, we can construct Table 3.5.

There is a section on basic probability theory in Appendix 1.

Table 3.5 Coffee or tea drinkers

Number of tea-drinkers	*Percentage of sample*	*First response*	*Second response*	*Probability calculation*	*Probability of this result*
0	0	Coffee	Coffee	0.4 × 0.4	0.16
1	50	Coffee	Tea	0.4 × 0.6	0.48
		Tea	Coffee	0.6 × 0.4	
2	100	Tea	Tea	0.6 × 0.6	0.36

The column of particular interest is the last one. Given our extravagant choice of sample size, these last values give the probability that we will encounter the pattern of responses shown in column one. That is, we are least likely to get the answer 'no tea-drinkers' from our sample, and more likely to get the answer 'one' (or maybe 'two'). We could plot these expected results as a frequency distribution, as shown in Figure 3.7 (overleaf).

If we were to repeat the exercise using successively larger samples, by the same crude arithmetic process we would generate a series of sampling distributions as shown in Figure 3.8 (overleaf).

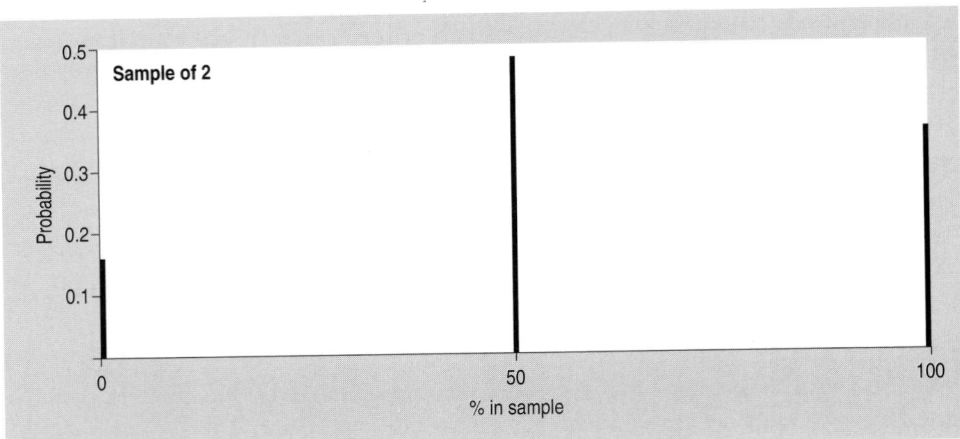

Figure 3.7 *Data from Table 3.5 plotted as a distribution curve*

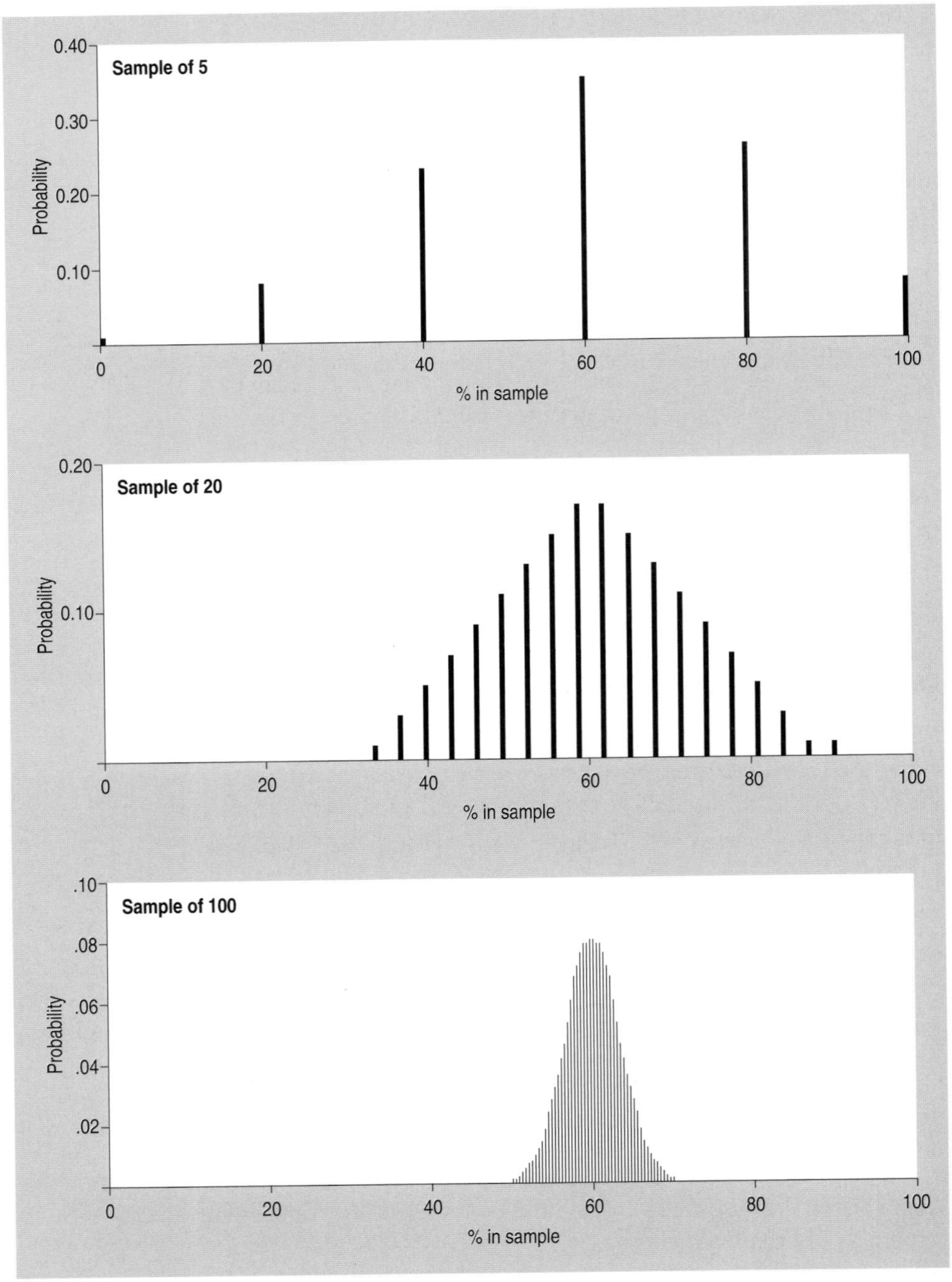

Sample of 5

Sample of 20

Sample of 100

Figure 3.8 *Distribution curves from samples of 5, 20 and 100 tea-drinkers*

As you can see, by the time we get to a sample size of 100, we have narrowed the range of expected results from our sample, which *is* likely to give us results clustered around the mean of the population at large, but any given sample of 100 could still lie anywhere in the range indicated.

As you should have noticed, the last curve in Figure 3.8 is beginning to look remarkably like a 'Normal' distribution and, for the purposes of this discussion, we can safely regard it as such. (Strictly speaking, the curve is slightly skewed, since there is more scope for values to exist above the mean than below it. Nevertheless, for larger samples, say greater than 50 or so, reflecting a population percentage between 10% and 90%, we can treat the curve as Normal.)

In our example, '10% population percentage' means a sample where 1 out of 10 drink tea, and 90% means a sample where 9 out of 10 are tea-drinkers.

From work earlier in this session, you should recall that a Normal distribution can be characterized in terms of two parameters, usually the mean and the standard deviation. When dealing with sampling distributions, the standard deviation is known as the 'standard error', and may be calculated as follows:

$$\text{Standard error} = \sqrt{\frac{\text{Population \%} \times (100 - \text{Population \%})}{\text{Sample size}}}$$

Thus, for a sample size of 100 and a population percentage of 40%, the standard error may be calculated as:

$$\sqrt{\frac{40 \times (100 - 40)}{100}} = \sqrt{24} \approx 4.9$$

You may remember from Figure 3.2 that approximately 95% of the values in a Normal probability distribution lie within ± 2 standard deviations of the mean. We may therefore conclude that 95% of our sample percentages will lie within ± 2 standard errors of the population percentage.

You should also note the unfortunate consequences of the $\frac{1}{\sqrt{\text{Sample size}}}$ part of the formula, whereby the sample size needs to quadruple before the standard error is halved. In managerial terms, this manifestation of the law of diminishing returns means that, since cost is usually related to sample size, reducing sampling error can become an expensive business.

3.6 Confidence testing

You may have noticed a practical problem with the formula above. In order to calculate the standard error of your sample, it seems necessary to have a knowledge of the population percentage, and yet it is precisely this population percentage that you are trying to uncover with your sampling!

In practice, for large samples the standard error may be approximated by the substitution of the sample percentage for the population percentage, to give an expression:

A sample size of over 30 would normally be regarded as large.

$$\text{Standard error} \approx \sqrt{\frac{\text{Sample \%} \times (100 - \text{Sample \%})}{\text{Sample size}}}$$

Given this, we can now estimate the population percentage (what we set out to do) with '95% confidence' as lying within ± 2 standard errors of our sample percentage as follows:

$$\text{Population \%} = \text{Sample \%} \pm 2 \times \sqrt{\frac{\text{Sample \%} \times (100 - \text{Sample \%})}{\text{Sample size}}}$$

See Box 3.2 for a worked example.

Box 3.2 Worked example – more 'widgets'

In a sample of 100 widgets taken from a large batch, 20% are found to be faulty and are rejected. What can we deduce about the larger batch from which they were drawn? If we are happy to make a statement about this larger batch 'with 95% confidence', then substituting in our formula gives the following:

$$\text{Population \%} \approx 20\% \pm 2 \times \sqrt{\frac{20 \times 80}{100}}$$

$$\approx 20 \pm 8\%$$

i.e. we can say with 95% certainty that the population sample contains between 12% and 28% of faulty widgets.

You should note that the '2' in the formula comes from the fact that 95% of values are included between the $\pm 2\sigma$ points as illustrated by Table 3.1 and Figure 3.2.

The other key managerial question is how to estimate the sample size necessary in order to achieve a certain sampling accuracy. Given the formula above, it is a relatively simple matter to derive an expression for required sample size in terms of a rough estimate of the population percentage:

$$\text{Sample size} = 4 \times \left(\frac{\text{Estimated percentage} \times (100 - \text{Estimated percentage})}{(\text{Required percentage error})^2}\right)$$

The value of 4 in the numerator gives a result that offers 95% confidence that the true population mean will lie between ± 2 standard errors of the sample mean. See Box 3.3 for a worked example.

Box 3.3 Worked example – 'widgets' revisited

Let us assume that we require a production process to generate 95% acceptable widgets, and that we want to be 95% confident that required error is only 1%, i.e. between 94% and 96% of all widgets are really acceptable.

Substituting our formula gives the following:

$$\text{Required sample size} = 4 \times \left(\frac{95 \times (100 - 95)}{1^2}\right) = 1900$$

As you can see, this does generate rather a large number. As was mentioned earlier, accuracy costs money! (Doubling the error required will reduce the sample needed by a factor of 4.)

Throughout this and previous examples, we are in no way advocating 5%, say, as an acceptable reject rate – it almost certainly is not. What you should gather is that prevention may be cheaper, and easier, than the cure.

QUESTION 3.2

(a) In a survey of 2000 businesses, 40% were discovered to be interested in distance-learning packages. Assuming that 95% confidence is needed in the result, what population percentage does this suggest?

(b) How big a sample size is needed to predict a population percentage of 75% ± 5% with 95% confidence?

3.7 Testing for significance

Much of the decision making in business is based on the detection of something significant and the subsequent action to make use of this significance. This is an area where subjectivity generally reigns supreme: that which is 'significant' is regarded purely as a matter of judgement, a commodity which many people claim to have been born with or acquired by dint of long experience in the particular field.

Nothing in statistics would ever claim to replace judgement; rather, it would claim to be able to inform and assist judgement. Luckily, there are some reasonably straightforward tests which can help us to establish significance (or otherwise).

The null hypothesis

Statisticians – indeed all people engaged in science-based research – look at the world rather differently from the average manager. The latter is usually looking for the unusual, the exception, whether for good or ill; this is sensible behaviour as it is often the unusual result or situation which requires managerial intervention. A person dealing with statistical data, on the other hand, will assume everything is normal ('normal', not necessarily 'Normal'!) until he or she is forced to reject this as overwhelmingly unlikely. In other words, the statistical analyst accepts the 'null hypothesis' that there is nothing unusual going on until made to change viewpoint by the pressure of extreme improbability coming from the evidence of the data.

When managers use statistical techniques, they, too, must take the view that everything is dull and normal, and require the data to prove that, in fact, something unlikely and exciting is probably happening. They must assume that their brilliant new delivery system is no better than its predecessor – until proven otherwise; that their hugely expensive advertising campaign adds nothing to sales – until the contrary is clearly demonstrated.

So, how does one decide whether one's actions have had an effect? The answer is: by constructing an appropriate 'null hypothesis', basically that there has been no perceivable effect, and then *testing* whether the collected data force one to reject the hypothesis as unreasonable. If it is no longer reasonable to hold that there has been no effect, then – and only then – may one conclude that there *has* been an effect. In statistical terms, that the event measured is *significant*.

The test we are about to use is called χ^2 (chi-squared) but, before looking at it, we need to note one more point. In the paragraphs above we have used words such as 'prove'. Statistics can never *prove* anything – at most, it can show that something is extremely unlikely to have occurred by chance alone, but this is not 'proof'. Unlikely events do occur – frequently. It is incredibly unlikely that any particular individual will win a State lottery, but *someone* wins the jackpot almost every time there is a draw. With these two ideas – assumption of 'no change', and the use of statistics to say this is *probably* untrue – we now look at a way of testing our hypothesis.

The Greek letter χ is pronounced 'ky' as in 'sky'.

The χ^2 (chi-squared) test

One of the classic problems of advertising is knowing whether it is successful or not. As someone once so succinctly put it: 'Half of my advertising budget is wasted. I just wish I knew which half!' Luckily, help is at hand.

Suppose we are promoting 'Sudso', the new miracle washing powder. It has been the subject of a concerted advertising campaign in the area served by one regional television station, but not in the similar area served by another. If we invest in some (very simple) market research, we might examine whether Sudso has made any headway against its main rival, 'Brand X', as a result of our campaign.

In an attempt to establish what has happened we employ a reputable market research firm to interview a representative sample of consumers. If you have followed the earlier arguments, you should be wondering whether the sample really was representative, but we have employed a respected firm and we shall assume for the sake of this discussion that it is. (Reputable market research firms take great pains to ensure the representativeness of their samples. Mistakes will inevitably be made, but not often, and not through any lack of diligence on their part.)

Results of the exercise

In Region A, which was subject to our advertising campaign, and Region B, which was not, canvassers approached a sample of respondents with the following results (Table 3.6). This presentation of the observed outcomes in rows and columns is known as a contingency table.

Table 3.6 A contingency table

	Region A	*Region B*
Prefer Sudso	81	72
Prefer Brand X	121	128
Don't know	35	29
Total	237	229

The basis of the χ^2 test is a comparison of the values actually obtained with the results that might normally have been expected. As described above, this involves the creation of a so-called *null hypothesis*, which in this case is the proposition that the advertising achieved nothing. Had this been the case, the *proportions* preferring Sudso in Region A would have been the same as in Region B.

We can calculate the *expected value* of those who prefer Sudso for Region A on this basis as the expected proportion (72/229) multiplied by the number of respondents in Region A (237) to give 74.52. Similar calculations reveal the complete table (Table 3.7).

Table 3.7 Expectations of preference

	Region A	E *(Expected from null hypothesis)*	*Region B*
Prefer Sudso	81	74.52	72
Prefer Brand X	121	132.47	128
Don't know	35	30.01	29
Total	237	(237)	229

If we compare the values actually obtained in Region A with those predicted by the null hypothesis, we can use the magnitude of the difference to determine the significance of the effect.

The first step is to calculate a value for the difference between observed and expected values. Do not worry about which is the larger and which the smaller; we are interested only in the magnitude of the difference. Once we have this value, we multiply it by itself and then divide it by the expected value.

The expression $\left[\frac{(\text{Observed value} - \text{Expected value})^2}{\text{Expected value}}\right]$ needs to be calculated for each of our observed results. In the case of those who prefer Sudso, for example, this will be $\left[\frac{(81 - 74.52)^2}{74.52}\right] = 0.56$

The full data are tabulated in Table 3.8.

Table 3.8 Comparison of observed (*O*) with expected (*E*)

	Region A Observed	E *(Expected from null hypothesis)*	$\frac{(O-E)^2}{E}$	*Region B Observed*
Prefer Sudso	81	74.52	0.56	72
Prefer Brand X	121	132.47	0.99	128
Don't know	35	30.01	0.83	29
Total	237	(237)	2.38	229

(You should note that, in this particular example, the value of $\frac{(O-E)^2}{E}$ for the results from Region B are actually zero. This is simply because Region B was itself chosen to represent our null hypothesis.)

Now the value of χ^2 is just the sum of the values of $\frac{(O-E)^2}{E}$ for all the cells.

Put in mathematical language:

$$\sum \frac{(\text{Observed value} - \text{Expected value})^2}{\text{Expected value}}$$

where Σ (Greek capital letter sigma) means the sum of the values.

In our particular case, this equals 2.38. So, now that we have obtained our value for χ^2, we need to look it up in a significance table such as Table 3.9.

Table 3.9 Critical values of χ^2 at various levels of probability

df	*.10*	*.05*	*.02*	*.01*	*.001*
1	2.71	3.84	5.41	6.64	10.83
2	4.60	5.99	7.82	9.21	13.82
3	6.25	7.82	9.84	11.34	16.27
4	7.78	9.49	11.67	13.28	18.46
5	9.24	11.07	13.39	15.09	20.52
6	10.64	12.59	15.03	16.81	22.46
7	12.02	14.07	16.62	18.48	24.32
8	13.36	15.51	18.17	20.09	16.12
10	14.68	16.92	19.68	21.67	27.88
11	17.28	19.68	22.62	24.72	31.26
12	18.55	21.03	24.05	26.22	32.91
13	19.81	22.36	25.47	27.69	34.53
14	21.06	23.68	26.87	29.14	36.12
15	22.31	25.00	28.26	30.58	37.70
16	23.54	26.30	29.63	32.00	39.29
17	24.77	27.59	31.00	33.41	40.75
18	25.99	28.87	32.35	34.80	42.31
19	27.20	30.14	33.69	36.19	43.82
20	28.41	31.41	35.02	37.57	45.32

For any particular *df*, the observed value of χ^2 is significant at a given level of significance if it is *equal to* or *larger than* the critical values shown in the table.

A glance at the significance table shows that, before we can check the significance of our value for χ^2, we need one further piece of information, the so-called degrees of freedom (*df*) of the situation with which we are dealing. Our original table of data showed three rows and two columns, i.e. three possible responses from each of the two regions. The number of degrees of freedom is calculated as (rows – 1) × (columns – 1) = (3 – 1) × (2 – 1) = 2.

If we check our value of χ^2 in the row for *df* = 2, we see that the 2.38 is less than *all* the critical values listed, which suggests that our results are *not significant*. This means that we cannot reject the null hypothesis since the differences we observed were quite possibly due entirely to chance.

The way to interpret the χ^2 table is, for any given degree of freedom, to regard the critical values as a series of hurdles of increasing height that our χ^2 has to clear to be significant at each of the levels indicated. In the case in point, if our χ^2 had been equal to 4.60, then there would have been .1 probability (10%) that this result could have arisen by chance. If it had reached 5.99, this represents only a .05 probability that it was merely a chance result, and so on across the table. A χ^2 of greater than 13.82 would have been significant at the .001 level, meaning that there was only one chance in a thousand that this would have arisen by chance.

So how then are we to interpret significance levels? Different circumstances demand different criteria. In the case of our market research, we may choose to follow the conventions of psychology and regard a 5% probability of the results arising by chance as tending to suggest a significant difference, and a 1% probability as being quite strongly supportive of the difference being significant. (You may see phrases such as $p < .05$; this means that the probability, p, of the quoted results arising by chance was less than 5%.)

A cautionary note

In case the numbers begin to appear too certain, we should offer a few words of caution:

- Because of the nature of the χ^2 test, it should not be used when any of the expected frequencies comes to less than 5. If this is the case, you should consider combining categories of response to bring the expected value to greater than 5.
- The degree of risk you are prepared to accept (that your results are merely due to chance) is a judgement you must make, and one that requires careful consideration of the circumstances. Effectiveness of washing powder advertising may be accepted at the $p < .05$ level; the results of trials on a new drug might require a higher degree of confidence.
- To return to the Sudso example, even if the results are accepted as significant, are you really sure that it was the advertising that was responsible for that difference? Have you eliminated the possibility that it was another factor that you have not considered, such as the pricing policy of a regional supermarket chain who were running a special offer at the time of your survey?

QUESTION 3.3

Assume that the results of our 'after' survey were actually:

Prefer Sudso	100
Prefer Brand X	105
Don't know	32

Does this suggest that the advertising campaign was successful and, if so, at what level?

3.8 How to interrogate a statistic

Statistics is a complicated business. In its more advanced and specialized forms, it requires significant training and a clear head. People who deal with statistics on a day-to-day basis usually take great care over the precision and accuracy of their work, and are generally very circumspect about drawing conclusions. They will often surround their results with the conditions, assumptions and circumstances that must be borne in mind when contemplating such results.

Sadly, today's culture is such that the 'headline figure' is often left to stand alone; any qualifications are at best relegated to a footnote, and often omitted altogether. The good news is that a complete mastery of statistics is not necessary in order to make intelligent use of the information that passes your way. What is needed is a healthy degree of scepticism, and the ability to ask some simple questions.

Who says so?

What is the source of the data? Not necessarily the original source, but specifically who is responsible for bringing it to your attention, and who made the decisions regarding the presentation design? Could they possibly have a vested interest in the results (or indeed your perception of them)?

Bias can be either conscious or subconscious. Have we got all the data, or just certain fragments? Why was that particular year chosen as the basis for comparison? What type of average are we dealing with, and who decided?

How do they know?

If you have travelled to the USA on a non-US passport you might recall the declaration that visitors are required to make before entry. The airlines give out little white cards which ask a series of questions along the lines of 'Are you entering the country with the intention of dealing in narcotics?' or 'Do you intend to attempt subversive action against the US Government?' You probably wondered what would happen if you answered yes to such questions, but you could guarantee that anyone with illicit intentions is unlikely to declare them up front. Nevertheless, we remain convinced that someone, somewhere, is compiling statistics based on our responses to the questions on those forms.

Business ethics is beginning to be a respectable subject for debate in business schools. Questionnaires are a traditional method of gathering data. What value should we place on a survey into insider trading (the practice of trading in stocks and shares on the basis of privileged information gained within the company concerned) that produced a 10% return of the questionnaire, and an analysis that revealed that 90% of those returned denied categorically that they had ever encountered the problem?

What is missing?

Human beings are actually rather good at working with limited information. We can often make sense of something given only a partial view of it. Sometimes, however, the conclusion that we jump to may be wrong. It must be said that there are people who play on this fact, provide limited information, and invite us to draw a conclusion that is not really there.

At the height of the Gulf War, it was allegedly costing £1,000,000 a day to maintain the British military presence in the Gulf. It was less easy to find out how much it would have cost anyway to keep the same forces in Germany/the North Atlantic/Aldershot. Only the *incremental* cost is really relevant.

The Boston Chamber of Commerce once chose its 'American Women of Achievement' and proudly proclaimed that the 16, who also appeared in *Who's Who*, could boast 60 academic degrees and 18 children between them. A little research revealed that two of the women concerned, Virginia Gildersleeve and Lillian Gilbreth, accounted for one-third of the degrees between them, while the latter had two-thirds of the children!

In the early 1990s, a then prominent political figure was apparently heard to be endorsing a clinic offering some unconventional cancer treatments. Much political capital was subsequently made when it was discovered that recovery rates were in fact significantly below the norms for the UK health service at large. What the newspaper concerned had conspicuously failed to communicate was that the clinic tended to admit only those patients who conventional medicine had said were beyond help.

What has changed?

You may often encounter two sets of circumstances, and be invited to make a comparison where the situations are not strictly comparable.

Official census returns for a Chinese Province once revealed a population of 105 million, whereas five years previously only 28 million had been reported. Was this evidence for some spectacular population growth? What is missing here is that something had changed. Far from being equivalent routine censuses (which might be conducted less often than every five years), it transpired that, whereas the earlier census had been conducted for reasons of tax and military service, the latter was for the purpose of famine relief.

In the late 1970s the 3M company promoted itself on the basis that there were more 3M photocopiers in the world than all other makes put together. If we also knew of Xerox's claim that 90% of the photocopies made in the world were made on *its* machines, we may begin to understand the shape of the market. (3M sold small copiers that made few copies, often to small businesses, whilst Xerox sold larger machines that produced many copies, often in a print-room environment.) Both claims were true, but neither piece of information conveyed the whole story.

Does it make sense?

The acid test is the test of reasonableness. If things are really as we are led to believe, what are the consequences? In some ways, this is similar to what the scientific method describes as *reduction ad absurdum.*

A UK Government statistic said that by the year 2015 there will be a 140% increase in road traffic. In addition to the 'Who says so?' and 'How do they know?' questions, you are really entitled to ask whether it really means a 140% increase, i.e. from 100% to 240% of today's figure. Ponder for a moment the implications for London's orbital motorway system, the M25. At the time of writing a fourth lane is being built, initially in the more heavily used stretches. If the above quoted statistic is taken at face value then, by 2015, a tenth lane may have to be on the drawing board. Will such a system really be acceptable, or will another oil crisis or ecological catastrophe mean the end of private vehicles, to be replaced with something fundamentally different? It is worth mentioning that serious concerns were being voiced at the start of the twentieth century that, *if things continue as they are*, the city of London would be overwhelmed by horse droppings as a result of the transport systems of the era. As has been mentioned several times in Session 2, extrapolation is a risky business and always has been.

Perhaps a final short extract from a work by Samuel Langhorne Clemens will help to illustrate dramatically the point being made:

> In the space of one hundred and seventy-six years the Lower Mississippi has shortened itself two hundred and forty-two miles. That is an average of a trifle over one mile and a third per year. Therefore, any calm person who is not blind or idiotic can see that in the Old Oölitic Silurian period, just a million years ago next November, the Lower Mississippi River was upward of one million three hundred thousand miles long, and stuck out over the Gulf of Mexico like a fishing-rod. And by the same token any person can see that seven hundred and forty-two years from now the Lower Mississippi will be only a mile and three-quarters long, and Cairo and New Orleans will have joined their streets together, and be plodding comfortably along under a single mayor and a mutual board of aldermen. There is something fascinating about science. One gets such wholesale returns of conjecture out of such a trifling investment of fact.
>
> (Mark Twain, 1874, *Life on the Mississippi*)

3.9 Summary

In this session you have been exposed to quite a wide variety of statistical ideas. Some were relatively straightforward, for example moving averages; others were quite complex, such as the subtlety of hypothesis testing. Unfortunately, they all share one attribute – they are, sometimes, perhaps often, misunderstood. You are not required to be a statistical expert, but you need to be aware of the uses and pitfalls associated with these types of analytical tool.

What we have tried to do in this session is to demonstrate certain truths about the presentation of information in general, and of statistics in particular.

- Far from speaking for themselves, facts are dumb; they require interpretation.
- People practised in this art of interpretation have many skills but, like us all, they are often prone to bias, whether it be conscious or unconscious.
- In order to make sense of the flood of data, information and statistics that washes over us in the modern world, we can no longer react passively to what we are told. We need actively to interrogate what we are presented with; a little knowledge, and the ability to ask some searching questions, can make a big difference.

The last word, as ever, belongs to Darrell Huff:

> … the crooks already know these tricks; honest men must learn them in self-defence.

Objectives

After studying this session you should be able to:

- For appropriate data, use Normal distribution analysis to estimate the likelihood of results being close to or far away from the average.
- Use moving averages to extract useful information about trends, cyclicity, etc. from 'noisy' time series data.
- Make sense of information provided in index form.
- Estimate population percentages, and calculate sample sizes for basic sampling investigations.
- Understand the principles underlying the construction of a null hypothesis and its testing by means of the χ^2 test.

DESIGNING OPERATIONS

SESSION 4

Contents

4.1 Introduction

Sessions 4 and 5 introduce some of the key concepts in operations management. Operations are activities which transform resources to produce goods and services. Operations managers are thus responsible for managing resources in order to satisfy the needs of the customers who make up their market.

This session tackles the important but often difficult and complex decisions involved in the design of operations. This often requires long time-scales so we look at some techniques for forecasting future demand, and some of the problems of using such forecasts. The importance of the interaction of people and technology in the operation process is identified as a key design issue, as is the relationship between product/service and process design.

Issues concerned with the design of operations contain some of the most important decisions for operations managers and indeed their whole organization. This is because such decisions are likely to involve major expenditure particularly of capital investment. The mistakes made can have extremely serious if not catastrophic effects in the organization. Major design decisions are taken only infrequently, reducing the opportunities for managers to learn from previous experience. Once made, these decisions are not easily or cheaply undone. Another significant consequence of design decisions is that they will set the limits to the operation's capacity to meet demand. In a rapidly changing world it is usually extremely difficult to predict the future with any certainty, but a future perspective is essential as design decisions usually take some time to implement.

Designers of operations are concerned with both what goods and services are to be produced and how they are to be produced. It is important that goods are designed with due consideration for how they are to be manufactured. In the case of services, issues of product and process are essentially inseparable. Choice of process type has a significant impact on both the volume and the variety of goods or services which can be produced by the operations process. Of particular concern is the choice of layout in terms of how materials or customers flow through the process. Decisions of process design will almost certainly involve considerations of how jobs of work are organized, what equipment should be used and the interaction of people and technology.

The aims of this session are:

- to familiarize you with the key issues involved in process design and the range of factors that need to be considered

- to provide an overview of the different types of operational process
- to introduce some of the main concepts and techniques used in process design.

4.2 Forecasting future demand

One of the principal objectives of operations management is to satisfy customers' needs. Before one can design an operating system it is vital to know what exactly is the purpose of the system. What goods and/or services is it to produce? What level of output is it to achieve? Herein then lies the main problem of design. What customer demand will there be for the output of the operations system?

There are a number of methods and techniques which have been developed to forecast the future. You may think that we have moved on a long way since the Romans used to examine chickens' entrails to predict the future, but the track record of many forecasters may leave you wondering.

Forecasting techniques

Approaches to forecasting can broadly be classified into three categories:

1 Extrapolation techniques
2 Causal techniques
3 Subjective techniques.

Extrapolation techniques

Also known as 'time series analysis', extrapolation techniques involve extending existing data (i.e. past data) into the future (see Figure 4.1). They are therefore based on the premise that future events can be based on past events. Analysis of a time series of, for example, sales is likely to reveal that the figures are composed of elements of trend, seasonality and random variations. The trend, either upwards or downwards, is the movement of the data over time. Seasonality is the pattern of movement of the figures throughout the year. Random variations follow no discernible pattern. Most extrapolation techniques are concerned with eliminating the random variation, and quantifying the seasonal variation, so that the underlying trend can be identified and extrapolated into the future (see Figure 4.2).

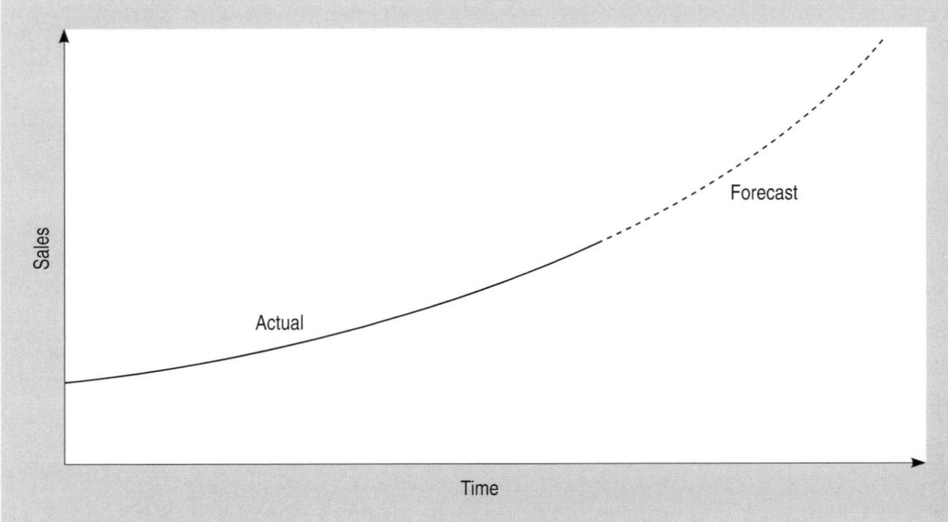

Figure 4.1 *Extrapolation: extending the past into the future*

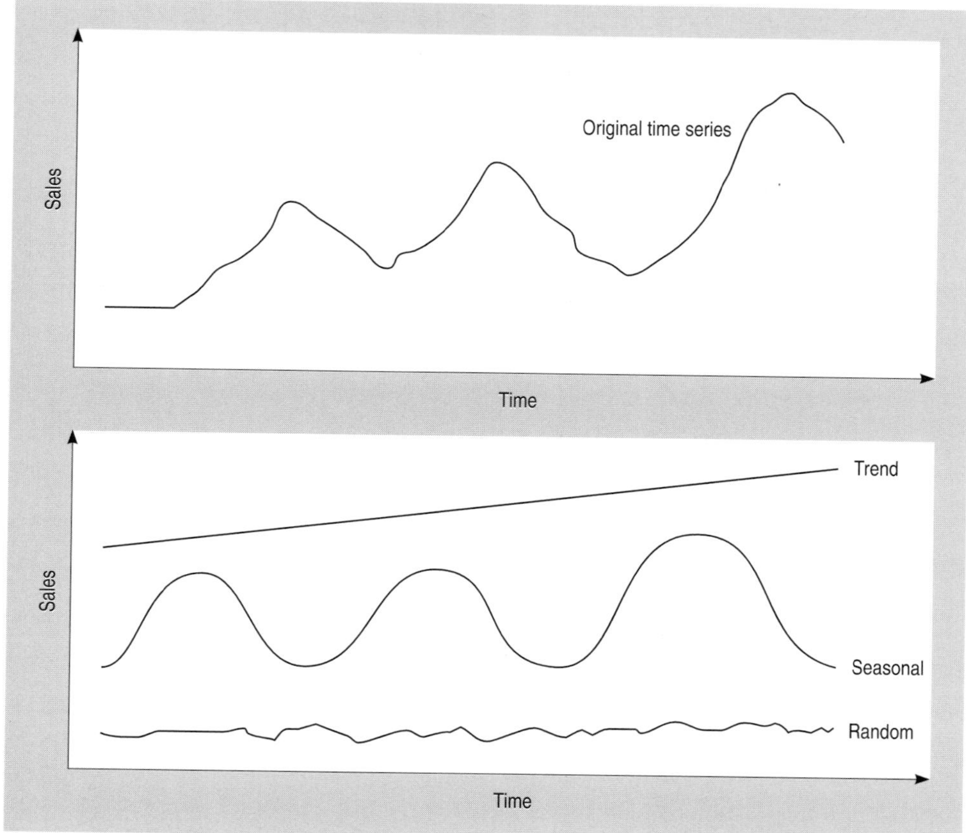

Figure 4.2 *Time series analysis*

The simplest extrapolation techniques are:

- *Moving averages* – the actual demand in the previous X periods is summed and divided by X to calculate the average demand for the last X period. These points are plotted progressively over time and then used to extrapolate into the future. Usually quarterly or annual figures are calculated.
- *Exponential smoothing* – using a simple formula, this method forecasts the next period's demand from the actual demand in the current period and the previous forecast demand for the current period. A smoothing constant is chosen for the formula which in effect weights the importance of previous information available to the forecaster. The earlier the information, the less importance is given to it.

Both these methods are cheap and easy to use. Other more complex and more costly techniques are available. The big problem with extrapolation is being able to determine whether the trend line will continue on its present path and when it will turn. This issue might be completely missed if extrapolation is treated only as a mathematical exercise, with potentially serious consequences.

Sales of many newly introduced products and services often follow – more or less closely – the so-called S-curve (see Figure 4.3 overleaf) particularly where new technology is substituting for old.

This should serve as a reminder to forecasters that no trend will go on forever, and that demand for any product or service will eventually peak. At a point part-way up the S-curve there is no way of knowing purely from sales data when that peak will be reached. Of course, what is required is understanding of the events which gave rise to the sales achieved. This would then help the

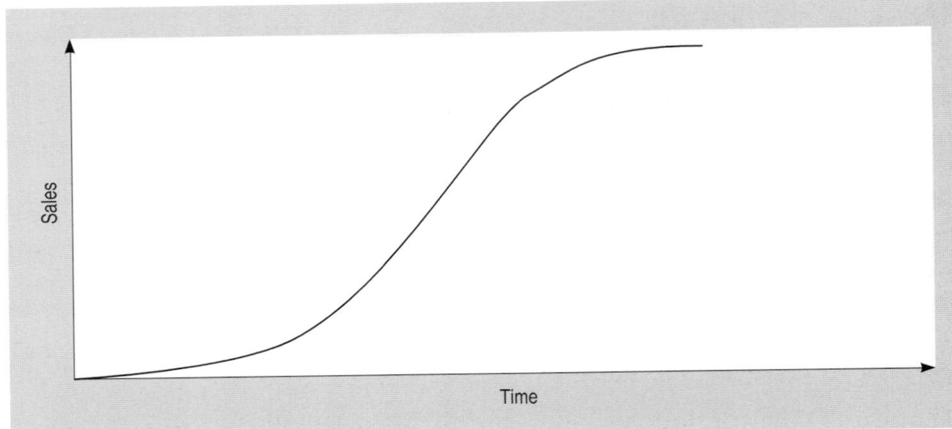

Figure 4.3 *The S-curve*

forecaster to predict when the trend line might bend. The method then ceases to be purely extrapolative and starts to become more causal.

Causal techniques

Causal techniques seek to identify cause-and-effect relationships between demand and other variables. For example, sales of ice-cream are likely to be related to summer temperature. Various mathematical techniques have been developed to make use of this concept. Linear regression is used where only one variable is thought to determine demand (such as summer temperature and ice-cream), whereas multiple regression uses more than one variable. Computers can be used to build models of such relationships. Econometrics uses this approach to model economic activity of particular sectors or entire national economies. The advantage claimed for causal techniques is that they should predict turning points in future demand, unlike extrapolation techniques. Their disadvantage is that they can be costly to use and may still not work.

Subjective techniques

Dissatisfaction with the results of the mathematical approaches described above led to the development of subjective techniques based on intuition and judgement. There are a number of such approaches.

The *Delphi technique* canvasses the opinion of a group of various experts by questioning them independently. Their initial forecasts are then circulated anonymously around the rest of the group. The experts can then, if they wish, review their forecasts. The process continues until a group consensus emerges.

Scenario planning seeks to construct a small number of potential future 'scenarios' based on different combinations of potential situations. The advantage claimed for this approach is that it forces managers to think about possible futures which may be quite different from the past.

Individual managerial judgement recognizes the value of the intuition of those closely involved in an industry. Managers' 'gut-feeling' or 'hunches' have been proved correct on many occasions and should not be lightly dismissed as 'unscientific'. The use of individual judgement, especially when based on sound experience and backed by good market information, can prove invaluable to forecasting the future. Market information can be obtained from the sales force, market research techniques or industry surveys.

Uses of forecasts

We have already highlighted some of the problems of the various forecasting techniques. Extrapolation merely projects the past into the future and this is only likely to be valid if the same conditions apply in the future as in the past. Causal techniques suppose that it is possible to know not only what factors determine demand but also their relationship. Developing appropriate models has proved to be expensive. In any case the accuracy of the method relies on a supposition that, whatever cause-and-effect relationships existed in the past, they will continue into the future. Subjective techniques rely on the skill, knowledge and expertise of often fallible human beings. No matter how well informed they are, people's view of the future is bound to be limited by their experience of the past.

This is a gloomy conclusion made worse by the empirically bad track record of some forecasters. The fact is that forecasts usually turn out to be wrong. The inaccuracy increases the further into the future the forecast goes, and the larger the unit of analysis of the forecast.

What then is to be done? What is likely to be the best method of forecasting? Should we bother with forecasting at all? Despite the difficulties, the best approach is probably one which combines a number of techniques. The informed use of appropriate mathematical techniques can help aid managerial thinking. This is, after all, the best outcome to hope for. In this sense any forecast is better than none and the process may be more useful than the product.

Perhaps unsurprisingly it is proving increasingly difficult to forecast demand in a fast-changing world in operating environments often described as turbulent. The main response to this from the people responsible for designing operations has been to design for flexibility wherever possible, which allows operations to respond to changing customer requirements. Slack (1989) distinguishes three types of flexibility:

- product/service flexibility – the ability to introduce new products/services
- mix flexibility – the ability to vary the volume or quantity of products/services
- delivery flexibility – the ability to vary the timing of delivery of products/services.

We will consider these issues in more detail below.

ACTIVITY 4.1

Investigate how forecasting future demand is carried out in your own organization. Which of the various approaches that we have described is used? Can you discover how accurate such forecasts have been in the past?

4.3 Generic process types

For manufacturing operations a number of distinct process types can be characterized.

Project – used for manufacturing discrete, often complex and highly customized products. Projects are usually large scale and, because of their physical scale, the work is usually done on a customer's site with all necessary resources (materials, people, equipment, etc.) being taken to the job. Examples would be large construction projects such as road or bridge building. Projects have a definable beginning and end, and often take long periods to complete.

Job – used to manufacture low volumes (even one-offs) of highly individual or customized products. Such products tend to be physically smaller than those manufactured by project operations and, being transportable, are made at the manufacturer's factory. Examples are small engineering firms, bespoke tailors or custom-made built-in furniture.

Batch – may have certain similarities with jobbing operations but will be used to manufacture larger volumes of similar or identical items. Whereas in jobbing operations the entire job, comprising various different stages, is often done by one operator, in batch operations each stage of the process tends to be done by different operators. At each stage the whole batch of items will be processed before being passed on to the next stage. If batch sizes are small the batch process may differ little from jobbing. As the batch becomes bigger, the batch process may start to resemble a line process (described below). Examples of batch processes include garment manufacture and metal casting.

Line – used in high volume repetitive manufacture of similar or identical items. A production line is set up, at each stage of which the same activity is performed on each item before it moves on to the next stage. Examples include motor car and domestic appliance manufacture.

Continuous processing – used in relatively inflexible processes where the products themselves are typically inseparable. The process will be designed to run for long periods, perhaps literally continuously for days or even weeks. Examples are chemical plants and electricity-generating plants.

The choice of process will have implications for both the variety of products and the volume of production which can be produced by the process (see Figure 4.4). Project operations offer almost limitless choice for the range of products which can be made. In fact, most projects are unique. However, the volume will be low; typically each project is for a single item. At the other extreme, a continuous processing operation will enable very high volumes to be achieved but the range of products will be very low. Some such processes may produce only one product (e.g. an oil refinery or a steel mill).

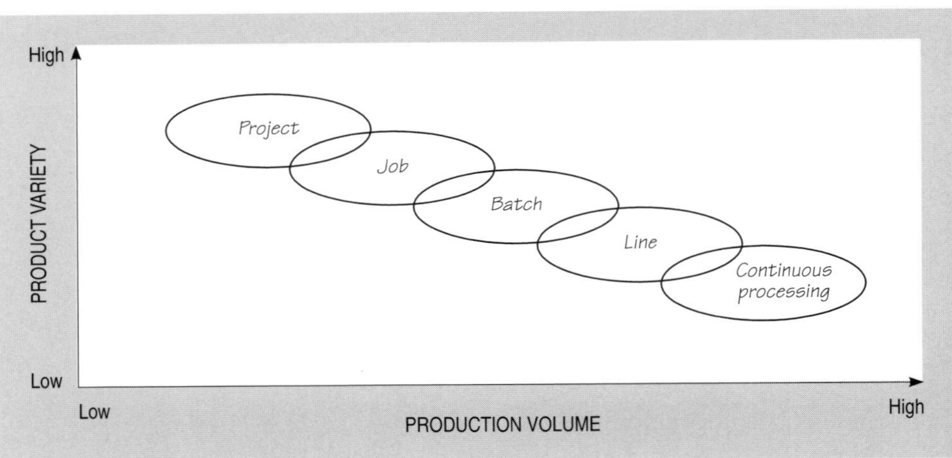

Figure 4.4 *Process types in manufacturing operations*

QUESTION 4.1

(a) In which of the generic process types would you place the following service processes?

A Table service in a restaurant

B Consultant outpatient clinics in a hospital

C A fast-food outlet

D Supervising rides in a theme park

E A management consultancy assignment

F Cheque-handling in the banking industry

(b) How helpful is the classification and hence what do you conclude about the applicability of these generic processes to service activities?

In considering service operations it is more useful to use a specifically service categorization, for example:

Professional services – these are characterized by their high degree of customer contact and customization. Customers may spend a lot of time in the process, which is highly adaptable to meet varying customer needs. Professional services emphasize the front office activities where staff have considerable discretion in service delivery decisions. Examples are management consultants and architects.

Mass services – these are at the opposite end of the scale to professional services. Mass services are characterized by limited customer contact. The service is likely to be tightly defined by the provider with little scope for customization. The emphasis is on back office operations leaving front office staff with little discretion in service delivery. Examples are supermarkets and airports.

Service shops – these are characterized by a combination of front and back office activities, intermediate between professional and mass services. Similarly, customer contact, customization and front office staff discretion will fall between two extremes. Examples include most high street retailers and restaurants.

This categorization has similar volume and variety implications to those for its manufacturing counterpart (see Figure 4.5).

Chase (1978) provides a service processes matrix using the two dimensions of degree of customer contact and degree of labour intensity (Figure 4.6 overleaf). Thus, professional services are labour intensive with a high degree of customer

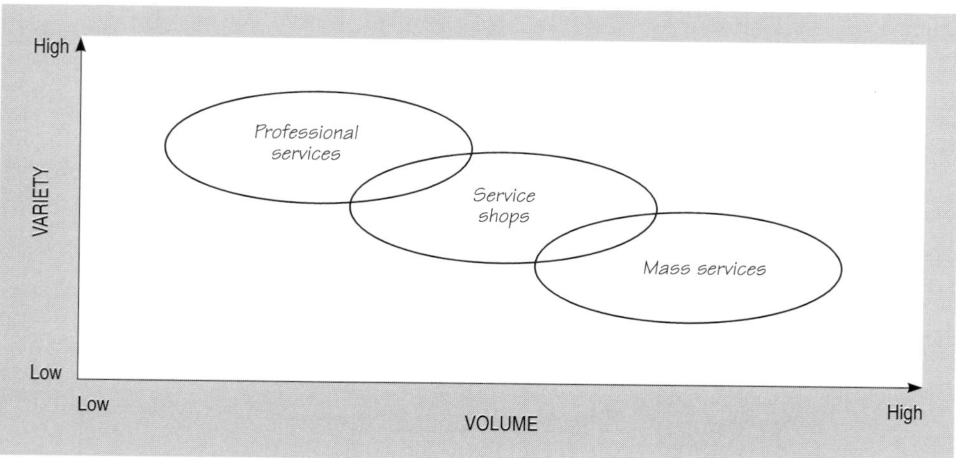

Figure 4.5 *Process types in service operations*

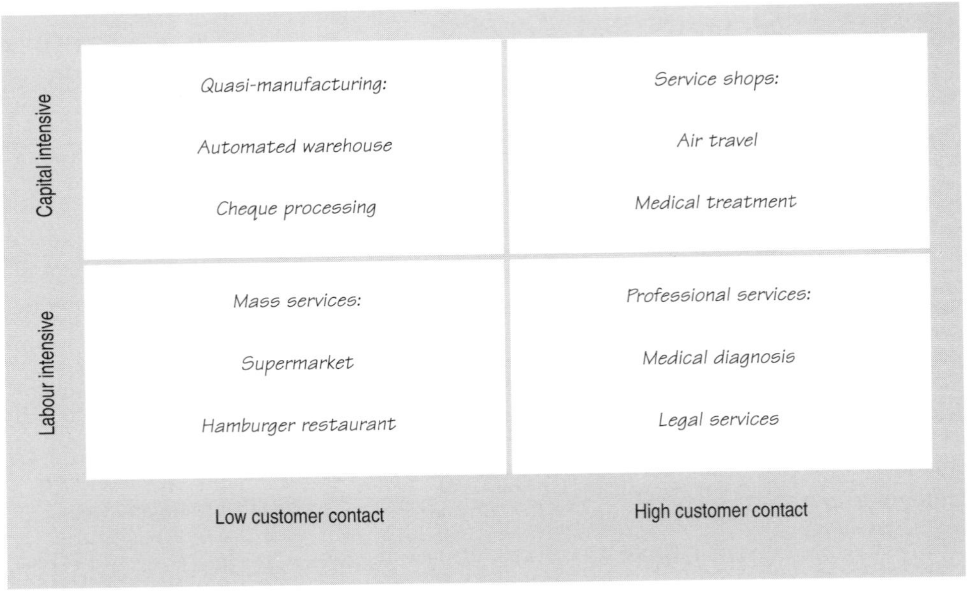

	Low customer contact	High customer contact
Capital intensive	*Quasi-manufacturing:* *Automated warehouse* *Cheque processing*	*Service shops:* *Air travel* *Medical treatment*
Labour intensive	*Mass services:* *Supermarket* *Hamburger restaurant*	*Professional services:* *Medical diagnosis* *Legal services*

Figure 4.6 *The service processes matrix*

contact, service shops have a high customer contact and are capital intensive, and mass services are labour intensive with low customer contact.

The term 'quasi-manufacturing' is introduced to describe services which have low customer contact and are capital intensive. These offer rigidly standardized services where back office operations predominate. Examples are automated warehouses and cheque-processing activities in a bank.

QUESTION 4.2

Think about how the different process types affect the volume, variety and flexibility of an operations system.

For each process type (for manufacturing and services operations), write down the implications for the production volume, the product/service variety and the flexibility of the operation.

Manufacturing:

	Production volume	*Product variety*	*Flexibility*
Project			
Jobbing			
Batch			
Line			
Continuous processing			

Services:

	Service volume	*Service variety*	*Flexibility*
Professional services			
Service shops			
Mass services			

Process choice is a fundamental decision in operations design. Which type of process is best will depend on the market characteristics that the goods and services being produced are designed to service. Hayes and Wheelwright (1984)

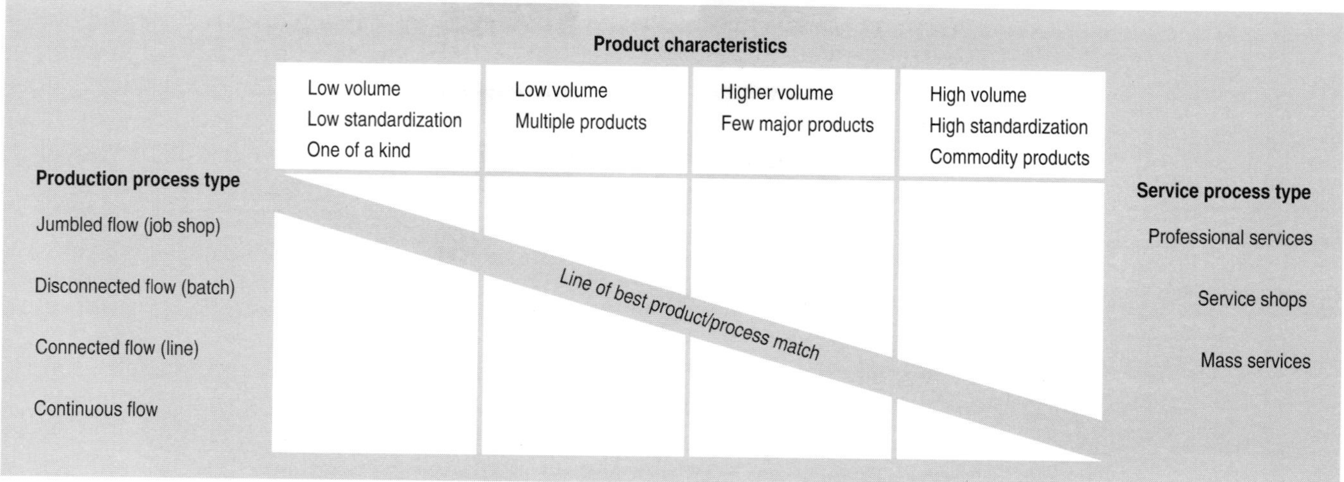

Figure 4.7 *Matching product and process types*

devised a matrix showing the match of product and process for an operating system (Figure 4.7). The lowest cost product/process combination will occur on the top-left to bottom-right diagonal.

Having determined the most appropriate process type the next stage in the process design task concerns issues of layout, job design and choice of technology. These are interrelated and will be discussed in turn.

ACTIVITY 4.2

(a) Where on Figure 4.7 would you place:

- (i) The product/process match of your organization's main activities?
- (ii) The product/process match of your department or area of work?

(b) What do the categories highlight, and what are the difficulties in applying them?

This activity is quite revealing in relation to The Open University whose operations combine characteristics of low standardization and a professional service (e.g. in course development, and in correspondence tuition) with high volume, highly standardized, mass services (e.g. The Open University's Social Science Foundation course alone has more registered students than Essex University). Perhaps, therefore, we should not be surprised that knitting together these completely different sorts of operational processes is not without its challenges!

4.4 Layout

After determining which process type is to be used, the design of the operations layout is the next most important process design decision. Layout decisions are concerned with the interaction of the equipment, people and materials involved in the transformation process. Choice of layout will determine both the physical location of the resources used to carry out the transformation (equipment, materials, staff, etc.) and the flow of the resources being transformed (materials, information or customers) by the operation process.

Inappropriate layout design can have a significant impact on the performance of the operation. Unnecessary movement of resources will reduce operating efficiency, adding costs whilst not adding value. Moving materials more times or over greater distances than necessary increases the risk of damage, thereby jeopardizing quality. Similarly, requiring customers to travel further than absolutely necessary in the transformation process is likely to reduce their perception of the quality of their experience. Choice of layout will also affect the operation's ability to respond to changes in customer demand, particularly in terms of volume and variety of product or service. Finally, if a layout has to be changed because of inadequate design, the subsequent disruption is likely to cause lost production and dissatisfied customers as well as incur considerable extra cost.

Once again, the main categories of layout derive originally from manufacturing. However, in this case they have more relevance to service operations. Indeed, the increasing scale and significance of service operations in advanced economies means that, in recent years, they have become a focus for operations analysis and design. The systematic re-examination of a wide range of service operations – from rubbish collection to hospital catering – has produced significant savings. For example, one hotel chain successfully redesigned its hotel rooms to minimize the time spent on cleaning operations (for instance, corners that gather dust and are hard to clean were eliminated from the bathroom and its fittings).

Layout types

There are essentially four different basic layout types:

- fixed position
- process
- product
- group (or cellular).

Although there can be exceptions, each of these types is most commonly used in one or at most two of the types of generic operations process discussed in Section 4.3 (see Figure 4.8).

Fixed position layout

In a fixed position layout there is no flow of material, customers or information through an operation. Rather, the resources required to carry out the transformation process are brought to the position where the operation is to be done, usually because it is physically impossible, inappropriate or inconvenient to move the resources which are to be transformed by the operation.

Most projects are characterized by a fixed layout (e.g. constructing a new office block or shipbuilding). Service examples would include on-site mainframe computer maintenance or staging a pop concert.

The main advantage of fixed position layouts is their great flexibility. Any resources required for any task in the operation can be brought to the position as and when required with minimum disruption for the product or customer.

The disadvantage is that unit costs can be high because of very low volumes. Also, scheduling activities can be very complex requiring tight control and accurate sequencing of the various activities. The physical constraints of the location only add to the complexity, for example restricting the quantity of material that can be stored.

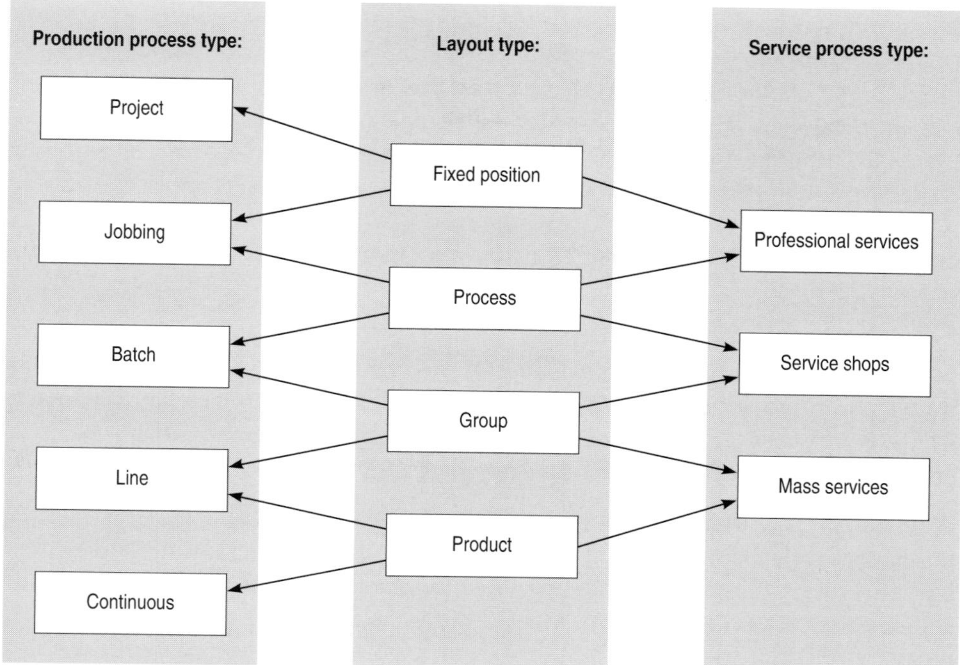

Figure 4.8 *Relationships between layout type and operations process types*

The discipline of project management has developed a number of techniques to aid the planning and control of activities in fixed layout processes. These are discussed in Section 5.4.

Process layout

In a process layout the resources required for a particular operation are brought together in separate areas. Each area is then dedicated to a particular specialist activity. The resources to be transformed (customers, materials or information) then move from one area to another depending on what activity is required. The sequencing of activities can be varied depending on exactly what product or service is required.

These different 'areas' may even be in different organizations.

A manufacturing example is an engineering factory with a machining shop, a drill shop, a welding shop, a paint shop, etc. The materials being processed to manufacture any one product can be sequenced to move from one shop to another in turn as required.

In the same way in a hospital, patients may be moved to specialist areas (operating theatre, radiography, intensive care, recovery ward, etc.) depending on their medical treatment. Also, in retail shops and supermarkets customers are largely free to move between specialist areas or departments to make their purchases.

In a process layout the bringing together of staff and equipment for specialization facilitates the development of expertise in particular operations functions which are frequently required to produce different goods and services. This allows the operations facility in total to respond with great flexibility to differing customer orders. The disadvantage of this arrangement is that flows of materials or customers can be complex, making control difficult. For materials, this can increase transportation costs and lead to the build-up of work-in-progress. For customers, this can lead to queuing and dissatisfaction.

The main task for the designer of a process layout is to minimize the distances that the material or customer is required to travel. This requires a detailed study of the frequency of movement between the various specialist areas in an actual or a simulated situation. The desirability (or otherwise) of different areas being close to one another is also assessed. From this information a preferred layout can be developed. This will inevitably be complex and several proprietary computer programs are available to aid these calculations. However, as with most operations management decisions, a number of trade-offs are involved which are often best resolved using managerial judgement based on a combination of quantitative and qualitative approaches.

Product layout

In a product layout the resources being transformed (customers, materials, information) move in a predetermined sequence from one area to the next. Each of these areas contains the necessary resources (staff, equipment, materials, etc.) to carry out only a very narrow range of activities.

A manufacturing example is a motor car assembly line where each work station on the line repeats the same activity for each car that passes (e.g. mounting the engine, bolting the wheels, inserting the windscreen, etc.). Similarly, in many self-service cafeterias each customer must pass each service point (soups, meats, vegetables, drinks, etc.) in turn to the cash desk. Although in this case the customer has the option of not using any particular service point.

Product layout is suitable for the production of large volumes of similar (possibly identical) goods and services. It ensures high utilization of specialist (and often expensive) equipment and hence ensures low unit costs. Also, the movement of materials or customers is minimized.

The disadvantages are its relative inflexibility and its vulnerability to disruption. A problem at any point in the line will cause delays at all points behind. Another price to pay for the efficient utilization of resources can be the repetitive and restrictive nature of the work at each work station. This can be a particular problem for operating staff who perform tasks where cycle times are very short. Staff boredom and frustration can lead to quality problems and worse.

The main task for designers of product layout is to ensure that each work station has a similar capacity so that a smooth flow can be achieved without any 'bottle-necks' (i.e. constraints at one particular point). This task is termed line-balancing and requires that the job of work at each work station be designed to take approximately the same time. This can be difficult if times vary because of the complexity or difficulty of a task. Where this is likely, designers often build in potential additional capacity (e.g. allowing a second operator to work at a work station or by having a parallel work station available). An example of the latter is where a second cash desk is opened at busy times in a self-service cafeteria.

Group (or cellular) layout

Again, the groups may actually be different small firms, each specializing in a range of operations.

Group layout is really an attempt to gain the advantages of variety and flexibility of a process layout and the advantages of smooth flow, high volume and low unit cost of a product layout.

A group layout is based on the concept of providing dedicated specialist areas containing all the necessary equipment, staff and other resources required to produce a range of similar goods or services.

In manufacturing this is often referred to as 'group technology'. 'Families' of products are identified on the basis of similar processing requirements. Each family is produced by a dedicated group of equipment and staff. Such groups are formed into 'cells', with individual cells often arranged in product layout for line processing. Cells often use U-shaped layouts to facilitate easy movement of staff between machines, potentially improving labour efficiency.

Service examples of group layout include the 'shop-within-a-shop' concept in retailing, which seeks to provide customers with a full range of goods for particular specialist requirements (e.g. all sports goods, clothing and equipment). In the same way a hospital maternity unit is a grouping of resources dedicated to providing a service to a clearly identified group of 'customers'.

The advantages of group layouts are high throughput and greater flexibility. Staff motivation is likely to be high as the arrangement offers the advantages of specialization without the disadvantages of a limited range of short cycle repetitive job tasks.

The disadvantages are the costs of setting up such an arrangement and the higher capital investment required for additional equipment. Equipment utilization may also be low.

The group layout designer has two levels of decisions to make. First, there are decisions about what group of products and services is to be designated for the cell to produce and what resources (equipment, staff, etc.) to place within the cell. This should principally be driven by strategic consideration of the markets which operations as a whole is seeking to serve. Secondly, there is the detailed consideration of the layout within the cell itself.

ACTIVITY 4.3

Which layout, or combination of layouts, best describes the arrangement of the activities for which you are responsible?

Which other type(s) of layout might be introduced, and with what advantages and disadvantages?

Established ways of doing things can exercise a tyranny over our thinking, and it is only when we consider a different pattern altogether that alternatives become apparent. In service industries it has been taken for granted for years that preparing, for example, a quotation involves documentation moving through a series of specialist checks and assessments – a process that is usually slow and unresponsive. Recently, variations of the cellular approach have been introduced, in which key staff each access the information and support they require to prepare particular types of proposal in one or two days, instead of several weeks.

4.5 Choice of technology and job design

There are very few operations which do not involve some kind of process equipment whether it be very basic or state of the art. It is not the purpose of this block, nor indeed of this course, to consider the detailed technology available in any particular industry. What we can do, however, is to consider the principles involved in making decisions about process technology irrespective of the precise context for its use.

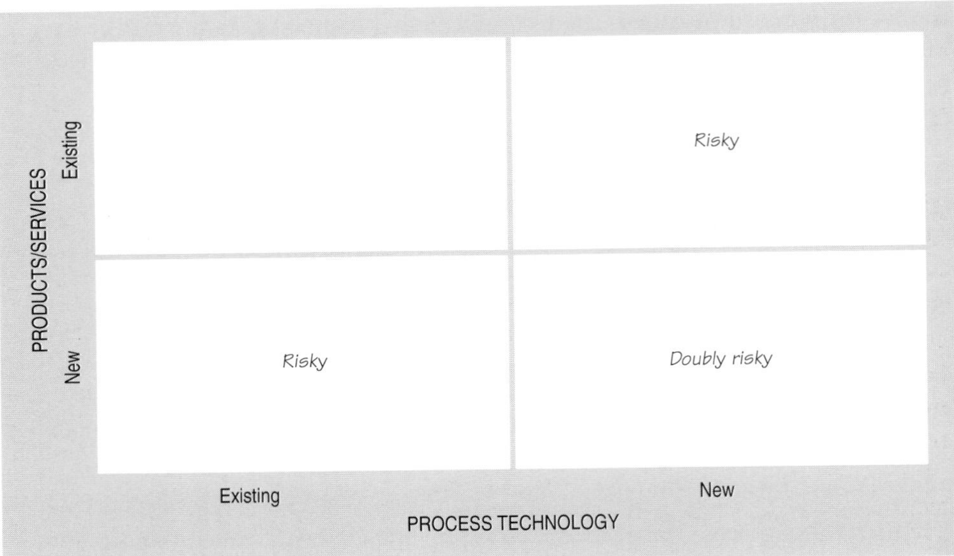

Figure 4.9 *The product/process matrix*

Clearly, operations processes should be designed to meet business objectives. Decisions concerning what process technology to use should thus be taken as part of an integrated operations strategy to meet those business objectives.

Risk is another important consideration: changing from the familiar to the unfamiliar carries a risk, as the product/process matrix (Figure 4.9) illustrates.

There is least risk in continuing to use known process technology to produce existing products/services. A change in one dimension carries obvious risk whether one is trying to change process technology or the product/service produced. Changing both of these dimensions simultaneously is, however, doubly risky.

General Motors, the American car giant, thought that advanced automation was the way to tackle the Japanese threat to its home markets in the mid-1980s. It invested $4 billion in its new high-tech Hamtramck factory which was designed to produce a new range of small cars to compete directly with Japanese imports.

> Hamtramck is a new factory with a new production system and a new product opened in 1985 with 260 robots for welding and painting cars, and 52 AGVs (automatic guided vehicles). There were also television cameras, computers and laser-based measuring systems to check quality.
>
> Hamtramck … an extraordinary gamble by GM with new technology spectacularly backfired. The production lines ground to a halt for hours while technicians tried to debug software. When they did work, the robots often began dismembering each other, smashing cars, spraying paint everywhere or even fitting the wrong equipment. AGVs installed to ferry parts around the factory, sometimes simply refused to move. What was meant to be a showcase plant turned into a nightmare.
>
> (*The Economist*, August 10, 1991, pp. 62–63)

Johnstone *et al.* (1993) advocate examining choices of process technology in three dimensions:

- the scale of the technology – its processing capacity
- the degree of automation – the extent to which it substitutes computer-controlled equipment and computer-executed algorithms for human activities and decisions

- the degree of integration – the extent to which individual pieces of technology are connected to one another to form an integral system.

The scale of technology

The design decision often comes down to whether to choose one large-scale piece of technology or two or more smaller pieces. The advantage of a single large capacity item or plant is that it benefits from economies of scale. If large volumes can be processed, low unit costs can be achieved. However, if demand for the output is less than anticipated, utilization rates will be low with consequently higher operating costs. This is obviously a risk if demand cannot be predicted with any certainty, particularly where growth is anticipated. This may lead to the organization having to increase marketing activity to find buyers to prevent this expensive capital investment from being idle. This is the very antithesis of being market-led. The other problem with very large pieces of technology is that they will almost certainly lack flexibility in terms of product/service mix. Also, any disruption or failure in their operation will obviously immediately take out a very large element of the organization's capacity. There is also the risk of the organization being stuck with a very large piece of obsolete equipment if technological advances are made. Finally, the adoption of a number of smaller pieces of technology may allow them to be sited nearer to different markets, not only reducing transport costs in the case of products, but also potentially generating more sales because of their closeness to the market. In short, the choice needs to be made with due regard for the basis on which the organization wants to serve its markets. This is a business rather than a technological decision.

The degree of automation

The extent to which people are required to operate technology can vary considerably. As yet there is no form of technology that never requires any attention from a human being although many can operate with very minimal human involvement.

The usual justification for automation is the cost reduction from labour savings. However, although this may reduce costs overall it is likely also to result in at least some increase in fixed costs. This inevitably means a higher break-even point for the operation with resultant pressure to achieve increased volumes. Automation is also likely to reduce the flexibility of the operation particularly to respond to demand from different products/services. There are particular issues for automation in service industries where the technology is operated by the customer. People usually prefer to be served by another human being, and even the most sophisticated machine can only as yet offer a limited range of standard product/service to customers. None the less, technology usually provides opportunities to make operations more reliable with resultant improved quality.

The degree of integration

Advances in technology, particularly in information technology, have increased the opportunities for linking previously separate pieces of technology to form integrated systems.

In manufacturing, the coupling of various machine tools with robots and other mechanical handling devices, to create so-called Flexible Manufacturing Systems (FMS), enables a complete range of components to be manufactured with little human involvement. This and further computer-based advances (e.g. CIM – Computer Integrated Manufacturing) can improve throughput times, lower work-in-progress inventories, achieve consistent quality, and increase machine utilization whilst still retaining considerable product mix flexibility. Like most capital investments it does, however, rely on relatively high volumes to achieve the required payback. The integrating technology is very expensive. The skills needed both to program such systems and maintain them are quite sophisticated. As with any interconnected system, a disruption or fault in any one area will bring the whole system to a halt.

In information-processing operations, linking computers in networks can reduce overall costs and allow users to share access to databases and exchange information with one another. As ever, such investments are costly and the disadvantage is the vulnerability of the whole system to breakdown, viruses or unauthorized use and interference (hacking).

In general, increasing any of these three dimensions (i.e. the processing capacity, the degree of automation, or the degree of integration) of the technology will tend to increase the volumes required for efficient production and at the same time reduce the variety of products/services which can be produced by the technology.

The choice of technology and job design

Another way of approaching the choice of technology is to consider which operations are best done by machines and which by people (or, more precisely, by people-with-equipment). Automation and integration reduce the number of people (directly) involved, but the fact that particular operations *can* be performed by machine does not necessarily mean it will be cost-effective for them to be done in that way. In general, robots, computers and machines offer repetitive precision and rapid calculation. People, on the other hand, offer diagnostic, problem-solving and learning abilities. Too often, though, process designers have viewed people negatively, as a source of unpredictability and error, to be marginalized and controlled as far as possible. The reasons for this go back a long way and continue to cast a shadow over process design.

At one level, the origins lie deep in the British Industrial Revolution. To ensure maximum efficiency in what were often quite simple tasks, factory owners adopted the principles of the division of labour. This allowed individual workers to become specialized in specific tasks by breaking down jobs into separate activities, each carried out by a different worker. These workers were able to become more proficient at a particular task, often utilizing specially devised tools. This approach also had the benefit from the factory owner's perspective of reducing the power of any individual worker.

The development of scientific management was essentially an extension of this approach. F.W. Taylor, followed by others, pioneered the approach that work could be done more efficiently by systematically improving the methods used for each job. The modern-day derivative of the scientific management approach is *work study*. This can be thought of as the systematic examination of work activities in order to seek improvements. *Method study* is that branch of work study which concentrates on finding the best way of doing a task. The other branch is *work measurement* which seeks to determine how long a particular job should take.

The combination of advancing production technologies and the philosophy of scientific management was hugely productive. But it institutionalized a separation not just between *planning* and *doing*, but also between consideration of the technical and the social, between the 'hard' aspects and the 'soft'. The best possible technical system was designed – and then people were selected, trained and required to fit it. As is well known, scientific management has been subject to much criticism.

QUESTION 4.3

From your study of job design in Book 2, Session 3, list the problems associated with the application of scientific management methods or techniques, adding any other criticisms of which you are aware.

Dissatisfaction with some of the results of scientific management meant some production engineers began to be influenced by the human relations movement in management and those theories of motivation which stressed the importance of people's desire to achieve job satisfaction and the social dimension to work.

It has to be said, however, that scientific management assumptions continued to dominate the field of industrial engineering and operations management. Whether this was because cost and control considerations really did demand such methods, or because those involved in designing production systems were predisposed towards such designs (and were ill-prepared to develop new approaches) is a moot point. In any event, the original debate between scientific and behavioural approaches to work organization has, in the last 10 years, been overtaken by the changing market requirements that production systems must meet. In particular, *flexibility* is now a key issue which renders traditionally designed, line-based working obsolete in many contexts. Hence the increased interest in teams, group working, cellular production, quality circles and empowerment.

Moreover, such considerations are particularly important in service organizations where customer contact is involved. It is actually undesirable to design such jobs in minute detail – they necessarily involve discretion. It is in the power of the employee to determine the level of customer satisfaction achieved. Whether the employee alienates the customer, potentially losing their business forever, or delights the customer, securing many future purchases, is not something over which a manager can exert direct control. There comes a point where managers have to cultivate and rely on the employee's commitment to the organization's goals and objectives, and even its values and beliefs.

In conclusion, therefore, it is important not to assume that technology is a given which must determine the jobs employees will do. The operation has to be designed as a socio-technical system and this involves devising a combination of machine facilities and human roles, to fit the goals and context.

4.6 Summary

This session has considered some of the most important decisions in operations management, namely design decisions. They are important not only because they are taken infrequently but also because they are likely to result in significant expenditure and will set the organization on a course that is not easily altered. In order to improve the quality of design decisions a future perspective is required. We examined several approaches to forecasting future customer demand. We concluded that, as the track record of forecasting and forecasters was very poor, a prudent designer might be wise to design for flexibility. We then discussed the design of the operations process. We identified a number of distinct process types: for manufacturing – project, jobbing, batch, line and continuous processing; and for services – professional, service shop and mass service. Both of these classifications exist on a continuum of increasing output volume and decreasing variety. We considered how layout design decisions were linked to choice of process type and identified four basic layout types; namely, fixed position, process, group and product layouts. Finally, we pointed out how the choice of technology introduces issues of job design. In the next session we will consider issues of how, once an operating system has been designed, its activities can be planned and controlled.

Objectives

After studying this session you should be able to:

- Distinguish between *extrapolative*, *causal* and *subjective* forecasts, recognizing the merits and limitations of each.
- Distinguish between the following types of manufacturing operations, and recognize the sorts of products for which each is suited: project, jobbing, batch, line and continuous process.
- Distinguish between the following forms of operations and recognize the contexts for which each is appropriate: professional, service shop and mass service.
- Recognize different layout types and use the categories of fixed position, process, group and product to consider alternative possibilities in a given situation.
- Analyse choices between different technological possibilities in terms of the scale of operations, the extent of automation, and the degree of integration, recognizing (in general terms) the potential costs, benefits and risks associated with the different choices.
- Contribute an awareness of job design issues to the choice and design of processes, layouts and technology.

PLANNING AND CONTROLLING OPERATIONS

SESSION 5

Contents

5.1 Introduction

An issue of central importance to all managers is how to plan and control activities to match supply and demand. Planning and controlling may involve long-term capacity investment decisions or short-term day-to-day activity scheduling.

The strategies and techniques available to managers are outlined and discussed in this session.

In many respects, planning and controlling are central to any operation and are likely to be one of, if not the, main concern of operations managers. Design decisions are taken only infrequently, and the main task for managers is to achieve their objectives with the resources at their disposal. Decisions about how to plan and control those resources will probably be taken regularly and frequently. It is a feature of operations management that such decisions will involve long as well as very short time-scales. Some planning and control decisions will be concerned with the next several months or even years, whilst some may relate to the next few hours or even minutes.

This session is written primarily for those who are *not* operational managers in manufacturing industry. Its aims are:

- To help you understand and work with operations managers and operations researchers by outlining the key issues, concepts and techniques associated with operations management.
- To encourage you to review the activities you are responsible for from an operations perspective.

5.2 Planning time-scales in operations management

It is perhaps a unique feature of the nature of operations management decisions that they are likely to encompass long as well as short time-scales. Thus planning decisions will range from long-term strategic capacity planning decisions about major investments in new facilities and equipment to very short-term real time decisions about the immediate deployment of resources. The full range of these time-scales is illustrated in Figure 5.1 for the several different levels of operations planning activities. These examples are

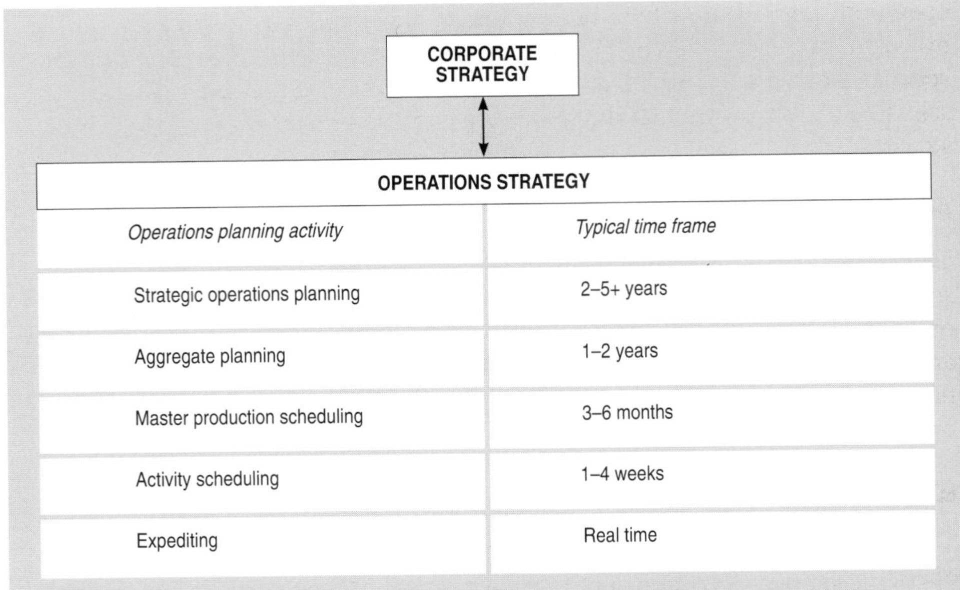

Figure 5.1 *Typical time-scales for different levels of operations planning*

illustrations only and different organizations in different industry sectors may have different planning practices. Time-scales may also need to be different depending on circumstances.

Strategic operations planning

This is concerned with long-term investment decisions for facilities or equipment which determine what capacity the organization will have. Such decisions are usually concerned with large-scale capital expenditure and so are likely to have to be approved at very high levels in the organization. They may involve setting up completely new facilities on new sites or involve replacements or additional equipment being installed at existing facilities. It can typically take many months or even years before such investments become available to operate. Thus investment decisions need to be taken on the basis of a long-term view of the future. This is usually provided using one or more of the forecasting approaches reviewed in Session 4.

Aggregate planning

This typically involves attempting to match the total operations capacity of the organization to forecast future demand for the next 12 months or so. It will usually do this on a month-by-month basis and on a facility-to-facility basis but is unlikely to go into product mix details at this stage. Its purpose is to determine whether there is sufficient capacity to meet forecast demand. If not, there may be actions that can be taken to provide additional capacity. Alternatively, there may be possibilities of taking action to manage demand. The other scenario is that there is insufficient demand for existing capacity. If actions cannot be taken to increase demand, then considerations will have to be given to reducing capacity.

We will discuss both the above two longer-term operations planning activities in more detail in Section 5.3.

Master production scheduling

This is a widely used term, obviously originating in manufacturing, but now used as the generic term to describe the activity of building up a detailed operations plan to show how sales orders and/or forecasts will be met by operations each week on a product-by-product basis. It must also take into account any existing order backlog. Its intention is to produce a realistic schedule and to ensure that the necessary parts and materials are available in stock, or are delivered as required. Materials control is discussed in Section 5.5.

Activity scheduling

This involves a further level of detail, desegregating the master production schedule to individual jobs for separate work units (work groups or individuals, or machines). It will also show when individual jobs are required to be started and finished and their route (if any) through different stages of the operations process. The result will be a detailed day-to-day schedule of activities for all the operations resources.

Expediting

This term usually refers to interventions in the day-to-day activities of the operation in order to reschedule activities in response to short-term requirements. There can be many reasons for this: perhaps a change in a customer's order, or a supply side problem (absent workers, faulty equipment, material shortage, etc.). These are the activities traditionally carried out at the supervisory level of management, but many organizations have been seeking to devolve this responsibility to individual operator level. This does, of course, raise questions of how it can be co-ordinated.

We will discuss these short-term planning and control activities, which we refer to as 'scheduling', in Section 5.4.

5.3 Planning and control of capacity and output

In general terms, the purpose of operations planning is to match the output of the process to an uncertain and fluctuating demand and to do so at the lowest possible cost. In practice, the goals of matching demand and minimizing costs will often diverge and, depending on their strategies in the market-place, organizations may quite reasonably give more weight to either demand or cost considerations. But, in any event, decisions about capacity and output have to take account of both these considerations. This is illustrated in Figure 5.2 (overleaf). In the short and medium term, operations managers have to decide the level of output, and whether an adjustment to capacity is required.

It is essential to realize, however, that Figure 5.2 simplifies the situation enormously. Why? Because it assumes one, integrated, operational process. In reality, of course, the process for any particular product or product line will often involve a network, or chain, of operations, some of which are also used in producing other goods or services, and each with somewhat different actual, or available, capacities. So it may not be the capacity of the system as a whole that matters as much as the capacity of particular *bottle-neck* processes, and how they may increase. And, even if it is a case of the capacity of a single, integrated process, the problems of achieving a balanced increase in output may simply shift to the constraints experienced by suppliers or distributors. In consequence, forming judgements about the feasibility of achieving particular levels of output, let alone the unit costs likely to be associated with them, may not be at all straightforward.

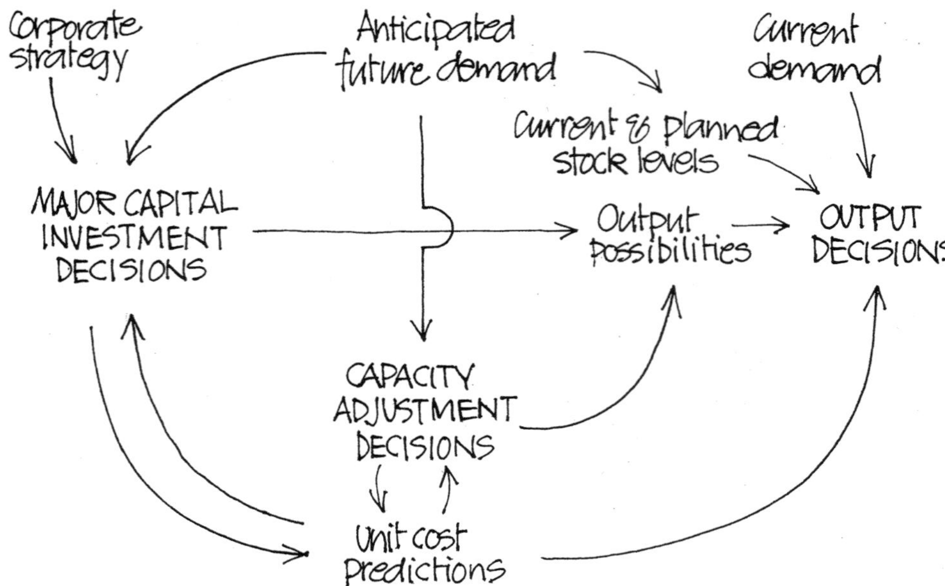

Figure 5.2 *The interrelationship of factors affecting capacity and output decisions*

That said, the underlying principles are the same in simple cases as in complex ones. So the discussion will continue to assume a single integrated unit. After considering briefly how output costs tend to behave as volume changes, the main options in adjusting capacity and then output are discussed. Finally, the possibilities for acting on customer demand in order to improve the match with capacity and output are described.

Understanding unit costs

Once a particular operation has been designed and installed it is tempting to think that the lowest average unit costs can be achieved by operating at its maximum possible rate. This is because its fixed costs can be spread over the greatest output, whilst variable costs will remain constant.

In reality the unit costs curve will often start to rise again as output reaches its maximum. There are a number of reasons for this:

- Fixed costs may not all be incurred at the point where the operation starts up. There may be step increases at higher levels.
- Variable costs may not be constant. For example, working outside normal hours (by overtime, at night or weekends) may incur higher labour rates.
- Operating efficiency may fall at higher output rates. For example, people's productivity may fall if they work longer hours, and equipment may break down if it is run for extended periods which do not allow for adequate maintenance. This is illustrated in Figure 5.3.

In reality, of course, the relationships between volume and unit costs are usually far more complex, involving step functions, time conditions or other constraints – and considerable uncertainty. Nevertheless, some estimate of unit costs will usually be important in making decisions on output levels and the investments to increase capacity.

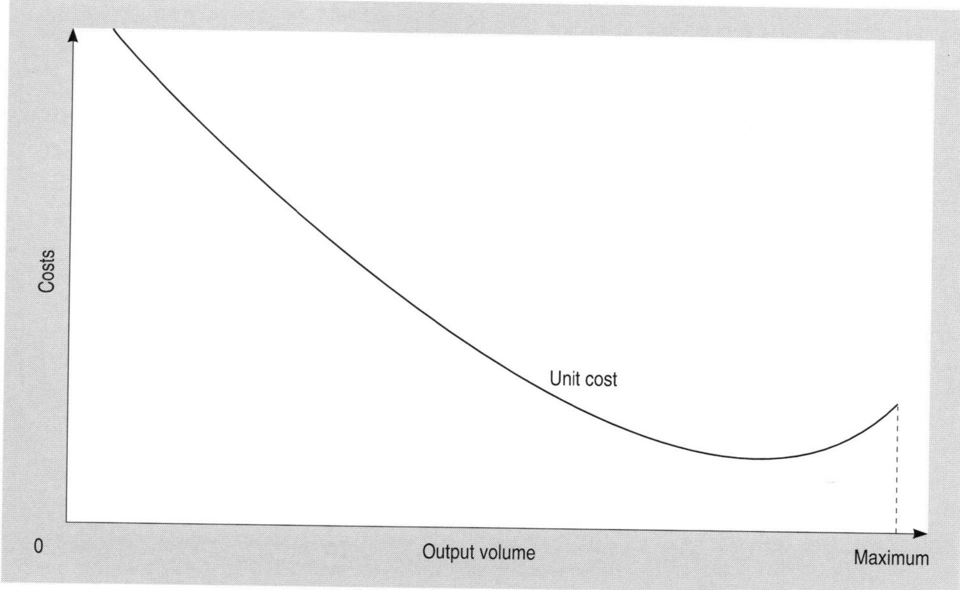

Figure 5.3 *The relationship of unit costs and output volume as capacity limits are approached*

Capacity strategies and decisions

In broad terms there are two approaches to the timing of capital investment decisions:

1. Capacity Leads Demand – i.e. provide sufficient capacity so that forecast demand can be met. This leads to the advantage of always being able to satisfy customer demand and so maximize revenue. The problem is that utilization rates may be low and so unit costs high. It also carries the risk of over-capacity if forecast demand does not materialize.
2. Capacity Lags Demand – i.e. only invest when demand will meet or exceed capacity. This will ensure consistently high utilization and predictably low unit costs. However, it carries the risk of dissatisfied customers and missed revenue opportunities whenever demand exceeds capacity.

The choice will depend on a range of factors, and in particular the company's competitive strategy in the market in question, e.g. is it competing on price – or on quality and availability?

Given a particular level of investment in facilities and equipment, operations planners have two basic strategies that they can follow in response to changes in demand:

- chase demand
- level capacity and output.

It may also be possible to follow a strategy which to some extent combines these two approaches.

Chase demand

In this strategy the operation changes its output in response to changes in customer demand. This requires it to be able to flex its capacity as required. For most operations this means adjustments to staffing arrangements. For many service operations this may be the only way they can implement this strategy. For producers of goods, it may be possible to meet increases in demand from inventory. Finished or part-finished goods may be held in stock to cope with such eventualities. Irrespective of stockholding decisions, followers of a chase demand strategy need supply arrangements which can cope with fluctuations in demand. All these approaches have an associated cost to them, not least that the operation (and its suppliers if necessary) will need to have capacity which for at least some periods of time will be underused. A chase demand strategy is therefore unlikely to be one of least operating costs. It may, nevertheless, offer opportunities for revenue and/or profit maximization.

Level capacity and output

In this strategy the operation is run at a fixed rate of output irrespective of customer demand. If the level can be optimized, operating costs can be minimized. In a service situation, however, this means that, when demand exceeds supply, customers will be forced to wait. Some may not be prepared to do this and their business (and sales revenue) will be lost. In a manufacturing situation, the output level could be ordered so that *over time* supply will still match demand. In this case finished goods will be stored in times of low demand, and used to meet forecast future increases in demand. This is particularly appropriate where demand is predictably seasonal. (See Figure 5.4.)

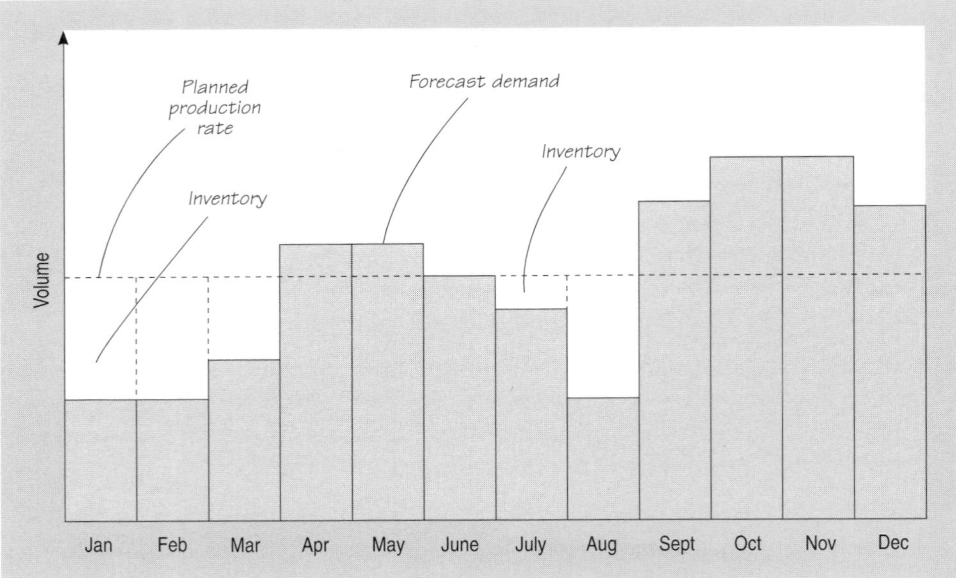

Figure 5.4 *Level production plan designed to meet total annual demand*

A mixed strategy would involve planning to increase capacity at different times to meet anticipated changes in demand. For a manufacturer, the costs of external production could be offset against the inventory-carrying costs that a level plan involves.

Adjusting capacity and output

Operations managers can flex their operations capacity and output in the following ways:

1 *Hire and fire staff* – as well as the attendant costs this practice also carries implications as far as employee relations, productivity and staff morale are concerned. In many European countries, despite current attempts to 'liberalize' labour markets, it may not be an option to reduce staff quickly, because of local laws or practices. It may, however, be possible to make use of other measures such as hiring freezes, early retirement, natural wastage,

but these are not generally short-term measures. Even with the relatively high levels of unemployment in Europe, there may not be suitably qualified people available to recruit as required. Training will take time and may be costly.

2 *Overtime/short-time working* – overtime working is used to a lesser or greater extent in many industries in many countries. There may, however, be legal or contractual limits on its use. As well as the extra costs involved (overtime usually involves premium payments to staff), levels of productivity of workers are likely to fall if overtime is long or used frequently. Short-time working is the practice of employing workers for less than the full normal working week. It may not be permitted in some countries and in any case will have implications for staff morale.

3 *Part-time staff* – the employment of part-time staff is a subject of considerable controversy in the UK at the moment. It is increasingly used particularly in service industries which are more likely to follow a chase demand strategy. Such organizations see it as an ideal way of being able to plan to respond flexibly to changing customer demand. There have been recent examples of retailers (e.g. Burton's) laying off full-time staff and hiring part-time staff. The practice is viewed by some people as exploitative and it is likely to be subject to increased legislation in many countries. Despite the flexibility advantages, there may be problems in recruiting and retaining suitable part-time staff, particularly if skill levels are required to be high.

4 *Temporary staff* – again this practice seems to be on the increase. Temporary staff are employed by the organization as and when required. Contractual periods of such employment may be for quite short periods of time (days or weeks) or for much longer periods of time (up to two years). Sometimes such staff are provided by agencies who provide a contact point for such workers. Again, such practices offer scope for flexibility but the commitment to the organization of such employees may be questionable.

5 *Stockholding* – holding stock acts as a buffer to protect the production activities of the organization from fluctuations in demand. It can also be used to protect operations from fluctuations in supply. Stock can take the form of raw materials, work-in-progress, or finished goods. Remember that holding stock costs money. Such costs include cost of capital, cost of storage space, obsolescence and deterioration. Stockholding costs can account for up to 30% of stock value, so it is not surprising that most organizations seek ways of reducing their stocks.

6 *Subcontracting* – at times of peak demand operations may seek to use the productive capacity of other operations, usually from outside their own organization. Manufacturers may buy in part-completed goods or sub-assemblies, which they might otherwise produce themselves. They may even subcontract the entire job, even to a potential competitor. Service operations can also use subcontract arrangements. Many transport companies use independent owner–drivers when their own fleet is fully utilized. Airlines may transfer passengers to their competitors if they are fully booked. Such approaches again offer much scope for flexibility. However, it may be wise to consider whether such subcontractors will always have the capacity as and when required, and whether their performance will be of the required standard. There are also many other implications if one is using a potential competitor to do the work, not least whether your customer will become your subcontractor's customer more permanently.

7 *Customer participation* – in service operations it may be possible to increase the level of participation of the customer. This approach is often used in catering operations with, for example, self-service salad bars at busy times. This is also effectively what is happening when banks provide ATMs (automatic teller machines) inside their branches as well as human cashiers.

Demand management

Managing demand is sometimes thought of as only the concern of the marketing function. Whilst this may have some truth in manufacturing operations, in services the operations come directly into contact with the customer. There are a number of actions which operations managers can use to manage demand. Some of them need to be considered jointly between operations and marketing, and may be applicable in both service and manufacturing situations.

1 *Pricing* – the pricing weapon can always be used to affect demand. Differential pricing is commonly used to reduce peak demand or to stimulate demand in off-peak periods. Off-peak travel fares and out-of-season holidays are just two such examples.

2 *Promotions* – advertising and other promotional activities can be used to stimulate demand in periods of low demand.

3 *Reservations* – reserving future capacity in advance can be effective for both the operation and the customer. This is particularly the case if the reservation allows the customer to receive the goods or the service at the time it is required. This is commonly used in many service situations (e.g. restaurants, hairdressers). For manufactured products, certainty of delivery time may be more important to the customer than speed of delivery.

4 *Waiting* – although unavoidable if demand exceeds capacity, this is often an unsatisfactory approach. In a competitive situation customers may well not be prepared to wait and the sale may be lost. Sometimes customers may be prepared to wait, especially if they can be promised a time when their needs can be met by reserving future capacity as discussed above. Once a customer is waiting, particularly if it is a physical wait in a queue, research and experience have shown the importance of managing the queue. Davis and Heineke (1994) showed that customers' satisfaction with the actual performance depends on their perception of waiting. This can be affected by such factors as whether the wait is perceived to be fair, comfortable, explained, occupied, anxious or whether the opposite happens in each case. Queue management thus calls for attention to both the physical aspects of the delivery system and the psychological state of the waiting customer. We will discuss these issues in more detail in Section 5.4.

5 *Complementary products/services* – the intention here is to use the excess capacity at off-peak times to produce goods/services for which there is no demand at that time. For example, a lawn mower manufacturer might produce snow-clearing equipment in the winter, or a fast food restaurant might offer breakfasts. Another aspect of this approach can be provided by service organizations as part of the queuing process discussed above. For example, to make the wait more pleasant (and to increase revenue) restaurants keep waiting customers in an adjacent bar.

ACTIVITY 5.1

(a) Write notes to answer the questions below.

	For the main output of your organization	*For your department, or the area for which you are responsible*
On what basis are investment decisions about underlying operational capacity made?		
In what ways are capacity and output adjusted to meet demand?		
In what ways is demand influenced or controlled?		

(b) What alternatives or improvements does this discussion suggest?

Most organizations use a combination of different methods and it should be possible to find instances of most of them. Even if you think you have nothing to do with operations management, you will probably find the ideas in this section can be readily related to, for example, the ways in which decisions are made about increases in secretarial provision, or the ways in which you or your staff handle surges of work that threaten to overload you.

5.4 What (or who) is next?

Operations management involves taking the longer term, aggregate operations plans of the organization and developing them in increasing detail, matching the capacity of the constituent operational processes to customer demand over progressively shorter time periods. The ultimate outcome is a daily schedule, indicating how available resources will be allocated across different activity centres within the operations area as a whole. It will determine what is to be done, when, by whom and with what equipment.

In service operations a different but related problem arises: it is people who are being 'processed' and often there will be little or no control over the timing of arrivals, and perhaps also considerable variation in the time required by customers who are receiving the service. The factors give rise to the familiar, but none the less difficult and important, problems associated with queues and queuing.

Activity scheduling

The first step in work scheduling is to develop a Master Production Schedule (MPS) from the aggregate operations plan. This needs to detail the weekly production of individual goods/services. The aggregate plan does not consider individual product lines but the master schedules need customer orders and sales forecasts by product line. Armed with this information and knowledge of the operations capacity, the scheduler attempts to match available supply with demand, using available resources as efficiently as possible to meet customer demand. This is usually a trial-and-error process through so-called 'rough cut' capacity planning. Several computer models are available to help schedulers, but they can be expensive as they may have to be tailored to individual operations. Through a number of iterations the scheduler produces an MPS, typically for the next 12 weeks or so. Frequently the production of the MPS highlights dilemmas requiring decisions on whether to increase short-term capacity or whether to permit demand to remain unmet, requiring customers to wait for their orders.

The role of activity scheduling is to develop the MPS into sufficient detail so that operations managers can assign work on a daily basis to the people and equipment in their control. There are a number of factors which must be considered in producing such schedules.

Routeing

In operations which are not line or continuous processes, any particular job (it is usually material or information which is being processed, but it may be a customer) will have its own unique route through the various stages (work centres) in the process. It is essential to know this route in order to determine the requirements to be placed on each work centre in a given period of time.

Loading

This involves determining what work is to be assigned to or 'loaded' on to each work centre. Knowing how long each job should take, it is possible to calculate when each job will be completed at each work centre. If capacity is exceeded, resultant waiting times can be calculated.

There are two approaches to loading:

1 *Forward loading* – this starts at the present time and loads jobs forward in time utilizing the available capacity. Thus, within existing capacity constraints, this will enable jobs to be finished at the earliest possible time. If this is not acceptable (because of customer requirements) decisions will be needed about whether additional resources can be provided.

2 *Backwards loading* – this starts with the due date for each job and works back, assigning the required processing time to the jobs at each work centre, ignoring capacity constraints. This will highlight any overloads forcing the scheduler to take action, e.g. reallocating work between work centres or providing extra resources.

Sequencing

This is concerned with decisions on how to prioritize the exact order of work at each work centre. The objective is to achieve agreed completion times for each job, whilst minimizing costs. When there are many jobs and many work centres this is an exceptionally complex task, and one unlikely to lend itself to an optimum solution in a realistic time-scale. To help provide a practical solution to the task, and bearing in mind that schedulers may do this every week or even every day, a number of sequencing (or dispatch) rules have been developed. These are rules of thumb, which are applied in any given situation to provide an answer to the question 'What should be done next?' Some alternatives are:

1 *Shortest processing time* – always do the next job available which has the shortest processing time at the work centre concerned. This is aimed at achieving a high rate of work flow and machine utilization.

2 *Minimum slack time* – 'slack time' is the time remaining until the due date, less the remaining processing time. This is aimed at always achieving the due date.

3 *First come, first served* – based on the 'fairness' approach to processing queues. If it is customers who are being processed rather than materials or information, this may be the only realistic rule to use.

4 *Minimum planned start time* – using planned start times from existing schedules, always process the job with the minimum planned start time first.

5 *Minimum due date* – always process the job with the earliest due date first.

There are other dispatch rules. Which one an organization uses depends on what criteria are considered most important. Some rules are more likely to achieve higher resource utilization, some lower costs, some greater on-time job completion rates, etc.

ACTIVITY 5.2

All managers face sequencing decisions every day when they tackle their in-trays and E-mail messages. Which of the decision rules listed above do you use most in dealing with the demands on your own time?

What other decision rules do you, or should you, use more?

Many of us are 'deadline junkies', using the 'minimum due date' rule. The decision rules you use may also depend on your energy level – for example, by the end of the day the 'shortest processing time' rule may allow you to clear away several simple items.

Basis of resource allocation

Scheduling involves the often complex allocation of resources to jobs. In most situations it is useful to draw up a schedule for the jobs and for the resources being allocated to the jobs. Useful types of schedule are:

1 *Job order schedule* – this shows the sequence of job start and finish times and their constituent processes. Bar charts (Gantt charts) are often used to display this information.

2 *Human resource schedule* – this shows what work each person will be doing during that day or week.

3 *Equipment schedule* – this shows how the capacity of each piece of processing equipment will be assigned during the planning period.

4 *Material schedule* – this shows what materials will be required. We will discuss materials control in more detail in Section 5.5.

Resource constraints

There will inevitably be constraints on the use of resources which schedulers will need to take into account. These will include:

1 *Equipment* – some machines may have different processing capabilities to others depending on the task. There may be requirements for their maintenance. They may require certain times for change-over and set-up between different tasks.

2 *People* – as well as planned holidays and other absences, people may not be available for other reasons (e.g. training). However desirable, it is rare indeed for all workers to be so multi-skilled that they are totally interchangeable.

3 *Materials* – there may be long lead times or other problems for certain materials.

You will appreciate from the above discussion that activity scheduling is one of the most challenging tasks in operations management.

Sam Goldwyn was a founder of MGM (Metro-Goldwyn-Mayer), the US film production company.

Indeed, there may come a point where it is simply too complicated, and the costs of trying to maintain a coherent schedule that minimizes production time (for customers) and maximizes the efficiency of resource use within the different work centres, become excessive (Sam Goldwyn's famous remark about 'sparing no expense to cut costs' comes to mind). In other words, any gains in production speed and efficiency are more than offset by the overhead costs of employing squads of production controllers and progress chasers, or investing in sophisticated information systems and the staff to operate them and keep them up-to-date. Hence, although organizations rightly try to minimize stocks of work-in-progress, idle time, machine down-time, and so on, it is worth being aware that there comes a point when such efforts become self-defeating. Some degree of 'slack' in the system is beneficial because it prevents even minor problems from sending shock waves through the whole system.

The insoluble complexity of scheduling large numbers of jobs effectively and efficiently through large facilities containing many different work centres also helps to explain why group (or cellular) production systems have become more common. Because they often involve higher levels of equipment provision and more skilled staff ('slack' elements in the sense that some equipment and skills may not be heavily utilized) one might expect them to be less cost-effective. But, by breaking the operation down into manageable self-contained tasks capable of much faster response times, other costs are massively reduced – in particular, a large, expensive production planning and control function is no longer necessary.

QUESTION 5.1

Which of the four schedules (job order, human resource, equipment and material) is likely to be affected by the following?

- The sickness of a skilled employee
- A rush order from an important customer
- A machine breakdown
- A material stock-out (perhaps arising from a delivery failure)

(Note: one obvious answer is wrong!)

Queuing

In many service situations involving customer processing, there is no choice but to allow customers to arrive when they wish and serve them on a first come, first served basis. It is a common misconception to believe that if the average processing rate is greater than average demand then capacity will be adequate. This is not necessarily true. Let us examine a common queuing situation, with one server, and assume that:

- All customers will wait to be served irrespective of length of queue.
- Arrivals are independent of one another but on average the arrival rate does not change over time.

- Arrivals can be described by a Poisson probability distribution (see Figure 5.5) and come from a (statistically) very large (statistical) population.

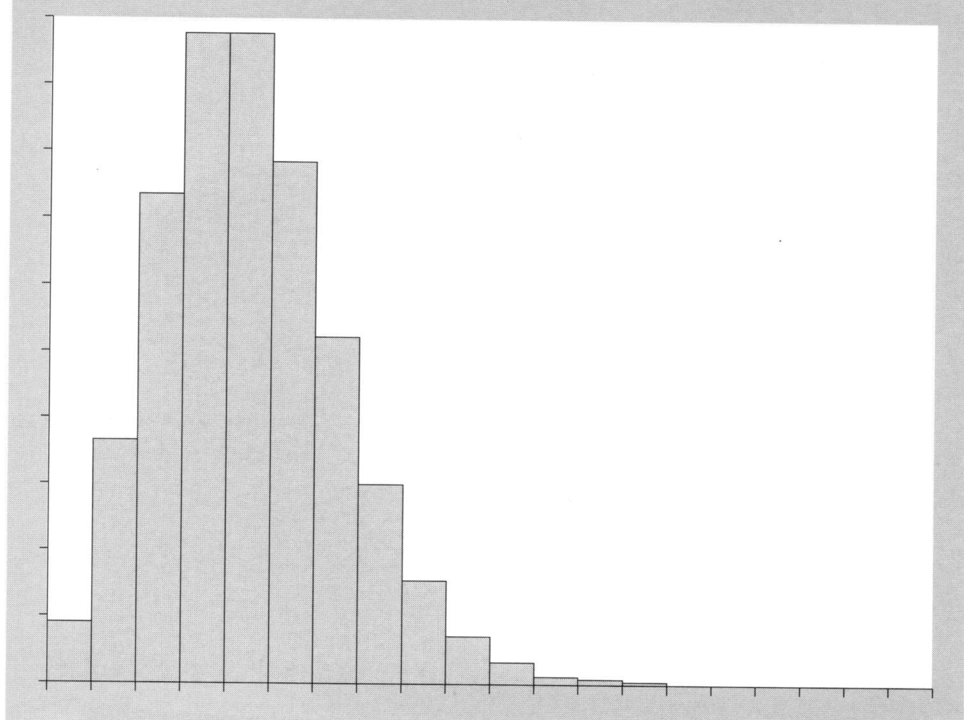

Figure 5.5 *The Poisson probability distribution*

- Service times vary from customer to customer, are independent of one another, but their average rate is known.
- Service times vary according to the negative exponential probability distribution (see Figure 5.6 opposite).
- Average service rate is faster than average arrival rate.

If all these assumptions hold true (and commonly they do) statistical theory shows that if:

a = Average number of customers arriving per hour and

c = Average number of customers arriving per hour that the server is capable of handling

then

$$\text{Average queue length} = \frac{a}{(c - a)}$$

and

$$\text{Average customer waiting time} = \frac{a}{c(c - a)} \text{ hours}$$

Suppose $a = 9$ and $c = 10$ (i.e. capacity is 11.1% more than demand)

The average wait = 0.9 hours, i.e. 54 minutes!

This strikes most people as surprising.

Plotting the average wait against the average arrival rate (Figure 5.7) shows that, even when there is 25% 'over-capacity', waiting times will still probably be unacceptable at 18 minutes on average.

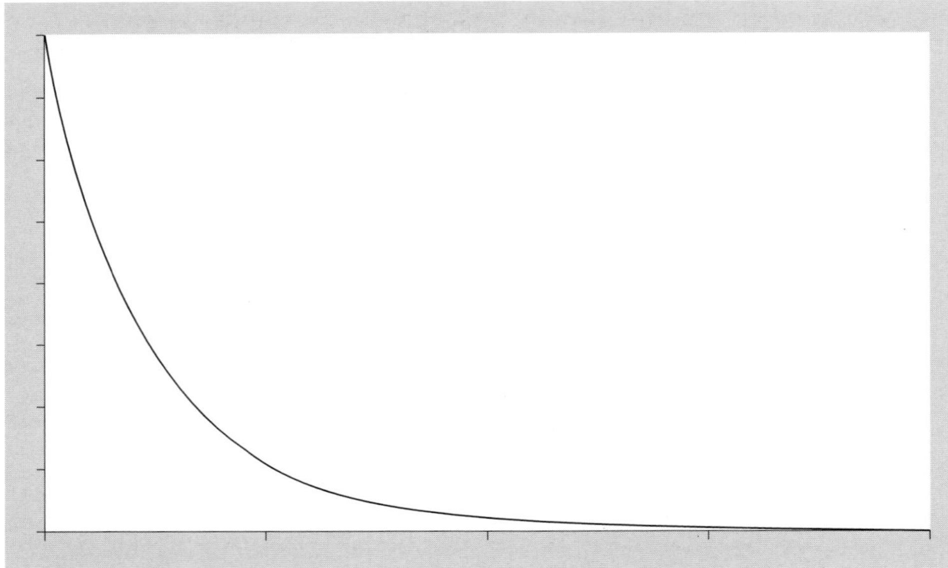

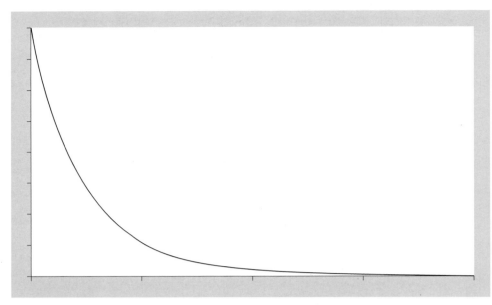

Figure 5.6 *The negative exponential probability distribution*

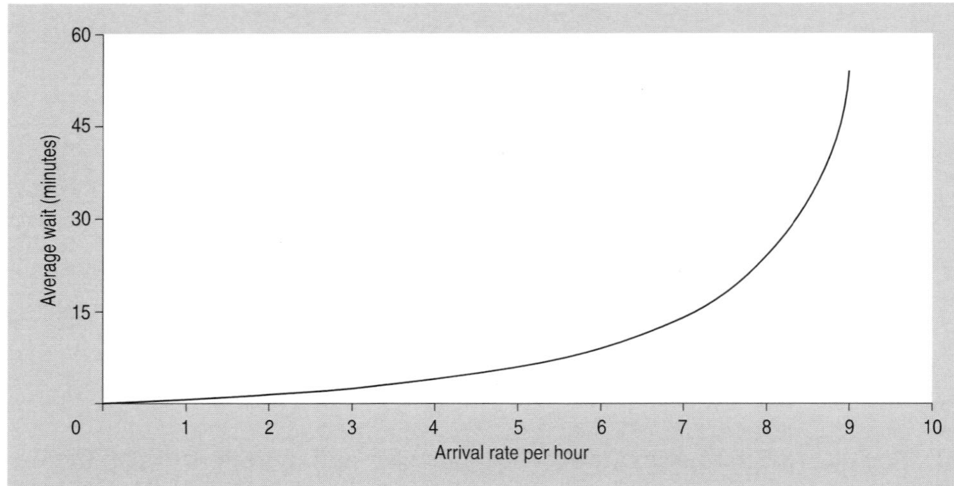

Figure 5.7 *Average waiting time for a simple queue (average service rate = 10 per hour)*

In practice, for a given capacity utilization, queues may be even greater if:

- demand is more variable than independent arrivals (e.g. people arrive in groups)
- demand varies over the day (peak times)
- service times vary more than exponential (a wide range of tasks)
- service capacity varies over time (e.g. at meal breaks).

In practice, this can mean that, even with average utilization as low as 50% of nominal capacity, queues may be unacceptably long, leading to angry customers and some who may choose not to wait and whose business may be lost forever.

Figure 5.8 (opposite) illustrates four commonly used queuing systems. Operations researchers have developed mathematical models to describe their performances which are much more complex than the above simple example. Unusual queuing situations can be modelled using the technique of simulation. Both these approaches are beyond the scope of the Finance Block.

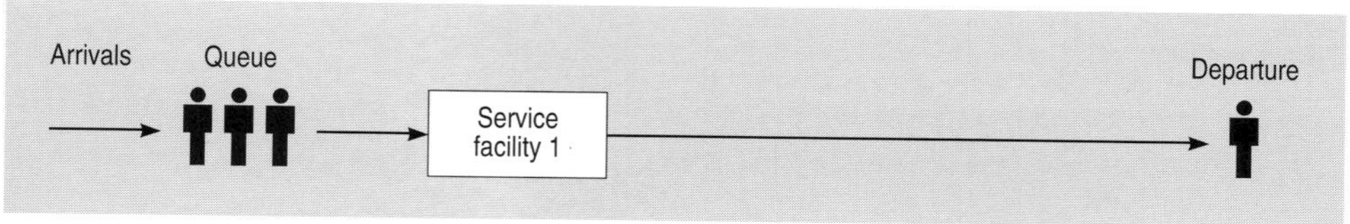

(i) Single channel, single phase

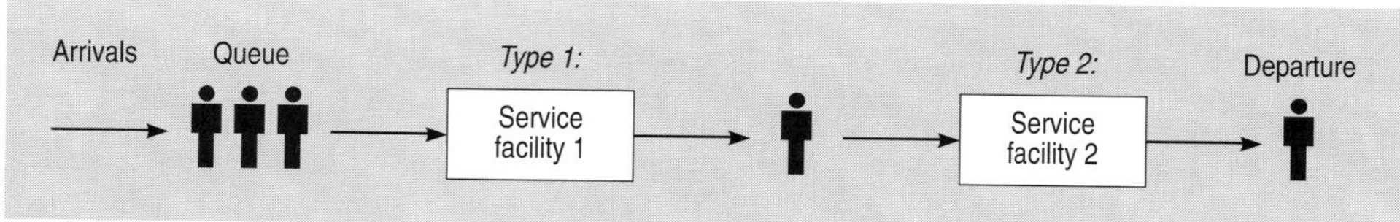

(ii) Single channel, multiple phase

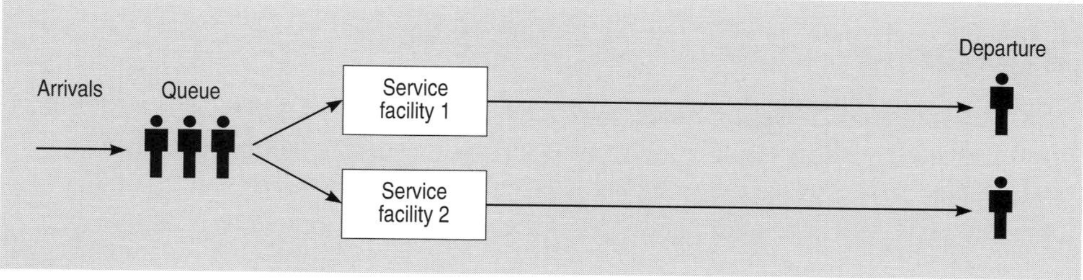

(iii) Multiple channel, single phase

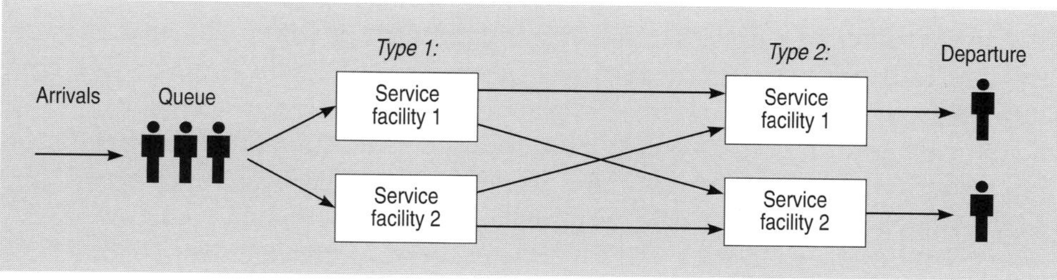

(iv) Multiple channel, multiple phase

Figure 5.8 *Some common queuing configurations*

The mathematics of queuing can apply equally well to queues of material or information awaiting processing. However, in all the mathematics, operations managers should never lose sight of the fact that customers are human beings with psychological needs. Maister (1985) identifies eight factors which influence customers' perceptions of their queuing experience:

1 Unoccupied time feels longer than occupied time.
2 Pre-process time feels longer than in-process waits.
3 Anxiety makes waits feel longer.
4 Uncertain waits are longer than certain waits.
5 Unexplained waits are longer than explained waits.
6 Unfair waits are longer than equitable ones.
7 The more valuable the service, the longer people will wait.
8 Solo waiting feels longer than group waiting.

Service operations managers are increasingly using these factors in managing their queues where queuing is unavoidable.

ACTIVITY 5.3

Where in your organization, or part of the organization, do queues occur? How might the psychology of waiting have been used to good effect?

The Disney organization are acknowledged experts in 'the art of queuing'. Next time you visit a theme park notice the subtle ways in which you are induced to accept the queues. Indeed, a certain amount of waiting is necessary to build up anticipation and excitement for the forthcoming ride.

An understanding of the psychology of waiting is now more in evidence: for example, theme parks indicate waiting times at different points in the queues for popular rides; large post offices install video displays (of advertising) alongside queues; mirrors fixed to lift doors take people's minds off their wait (and on to themselves!).

Expediting

No matter how well the planning and scheduling is done, there will inevitably be reasons why short-term intervention will be required. There may be an unexpected material shortage because of problems with a supplier; a key operator may suffer a sudden illness; a piece of equipment may break down; an important customer may request the more speedy completion of a particular order. The intervention required to deal with such unforeseen eventualities is generally referred to as 'expediting'. With the complexities of scheduling and the uncertainties of a dynamic external environment, it would be naïve in the extreme to believe that such interventions can be completely eliminated or that they necessarily point to a failure in planning. Expediting is a vital and necessary part of day-to-day shop-floor management. Thus it is essential that the authority to take these 'real-time' decisions is placed were it belongs, at shop-floor level. Whether this can be devolved to individual operators or whether there is a need for some supervisory level of management is not a debate that we can hold here. However, if such decisions cannot be taken at the time and in the place required, then, at best, there will be costly delays and, at worst, inappropriate decisions will be taken, with potentially even more costly consequences. Although expediting is unavoidable, its level must be closely monitored. Not all jobs can be rush jobs, and merely responding to 'who shouts loudest' is not the basis of a sound operations strategy. It is therefore a vital part of the operations manager's role to investigate recurring scheduling problems and take steps to eliminate them.

5.5 Materials control

It is rare indeed for an organization not to use materials in any of its operations. The control of materials is often particularly important in manufacturing industries. Many service industries also require significant amounts of materials in their operations, even if the operations process is principally concerned with processing customers or information. One of the main decisions for all users of material is 'What level of stock should we hold?' We will consider this question in this section by differentiating between different types of stock and discussing why stock should be held at all. We will then review some different approaches to materials control including MRP (materials requirements planning) and JIT (just in time).

Why hold stock?

First we will consider the different types of stock. In an operation primarily concerned with processing materials we can distinguish between the following:

- raw materials – materials which have been received from a supplier and are awaiting processing
- work-in-progress (WIP) – materials which have undergone at least one stage of processing and are awaiting the next stage
- finished goods – products which have been fully processed and are awaiting sale to a customer.

Most operations, whether service or manufacturing, are also likely to require items which are used in the operation process but which do not themselves form part of the output of the process. These include spares and other maintenance items for equipment, work clothing, consumables, tools, etc. and are often referred to as MRO items – Maintenance, Repairs and Operating.

The reasons for holding stock vary according to the type of stock:

Raw materials

- As a buffer against uncertainty of supply, which may disrupt operations.
- To buy in large enough quantities to secure quantity discounts or avoid small order surcharges.
- To buy when prices are low or before a known or anticipated price rise.
- As an insurance against anticipated shortages.
- As a buffer against unpredictable demand in operations.

Work-in-progress

To decouple the different stages in the operations and so:

- Facilitate flexibility in scheduling different operations.
- Improve utilization rates of the various operations by facilitating longer production runs and fewer change-overs.

Finished goods

- Make goods available to customers off-the-shelf.
- As a buffer against variability or uncertainty, in supply or operations.
- As a buffer against fluctuations in demand.
- To build up stock to service anticipated increased sales because of seasonality or marketing activity.

MRO

- As a buffer against uncertain demand for items whose non-availability carries a high risk of disruption to operations.
- As a buffer against uncertain supply.
- In anticipation of extra demand due to planned maintenance.

In discussing material stocks it is important to distinguish between independent and dependent demand.

- *Independent demand* – this is where the demand for an item occurs separately from that for any other item. Typically, demand for finished goods is influenced primarily from the market. Many MRO items will exhibit a random pattern of demand. Approaches to stock control for independent demand items centre on forecasting likely demand and maintaining a suitable level of stock to ensure customers can be supplied on demand. The emphasis is on replenishing the stock as it runs down to ensure that it never runs out.

- *Dependent demand* – this is where demand for an item is linked to that for another item. So, for example, knowing how many motor cars are to be manufactured, a car assembly plant will know how many engines, wheels, seats, etc. it will need for those cars. Thus the approach for dependent demand items is to calculate their requirement and ensure their availability in time for their use.

Independent demand inventory

Here we will examine the ways in which stock of independent demand items can be controlled in order to ensure that levels of stocks do not reach zero. The main requirements of such stock control systems are to determine when to order and how much to order from suppliers. There are basically two approaches to this, although hybrids are also possible.

Reorder level system

In this system, stock levels are monitored continuously. When they fall to a predetermined level, the reorder level, an order is placed with the supplier for a predetermined quantity, the reorder quantity. The reorder quantity is determined from the usual usage rate for that stock item and lead time quoted by the supplier. The intention is that the replacement stock should arrive just before stocks run out. To safeguard against any uncertainties in demand or any unreliability in supply, it is usual to plan to keep a certain level of safety stock. Figure 5.9 illustrates this system.

For the reorder level system:

Safety stock = Demand rate × Average lead time.

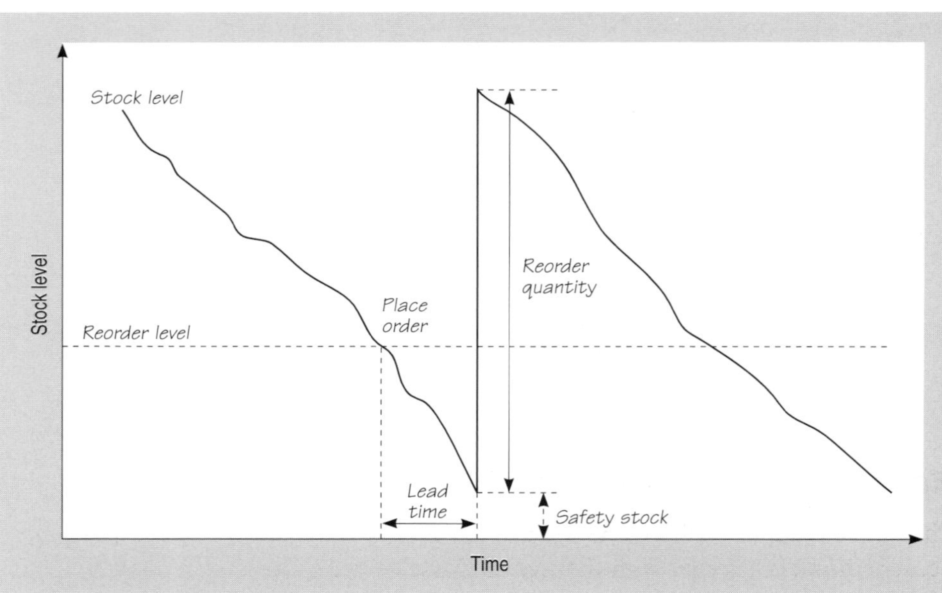

Figure 5.9 *Reorder level system of stock control*

Continuous review system

In this case, the stock level is checked at regular review times (e.g. once a week, or every month). An order is then placed with the supplier for a quantity calculated as the difference between a predetermined maximum (or ceiling) level and the current stock level. Thus the order quantity will vary each time an order is placed. Figure 5.10 illustrates this system. The ceiling level is set to cover demand until the next review time plus the delivery lead time.

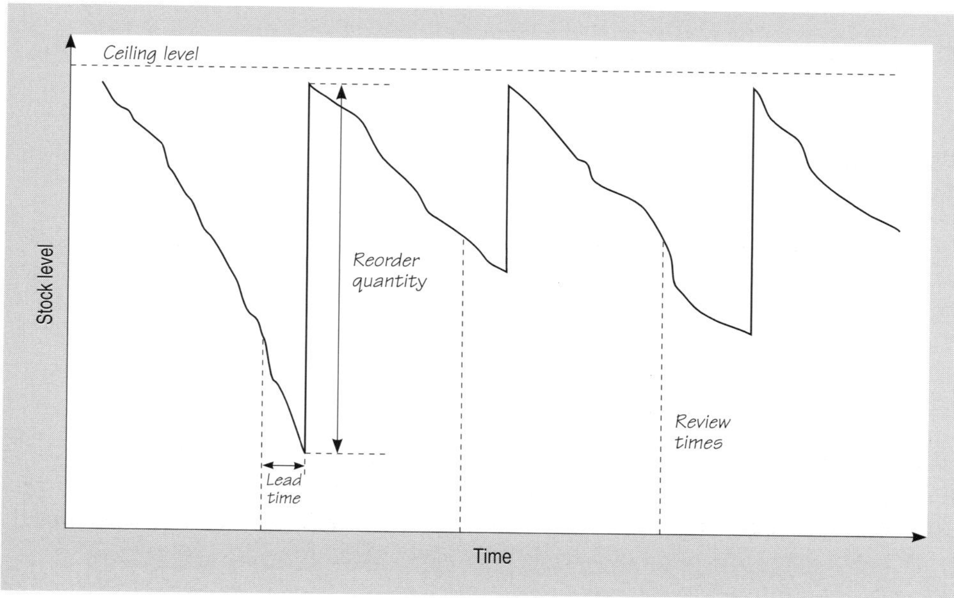

Figure 5.10 *Continuous review system of stock control*

For the continuous review system:

Safety stock = Demand rate × (Review time + Average lead time)

Comparison of the two stock control systems

The relative advantages of the reorder level system are:

- smaller safety stocks are required for the same level of service
- order quantities will be the same or similar
- it is easier to take advantage of quantity discounts for suppliers.

For the continuous review system:

- it is easier to plan work load for staff
- orders for different items can be dealt with together, making the buying process more convenient and facilitating supplier discounts based on order value.

Economic order quantity (EOQ)

This is a formula which can be used to calculate what the order quantity should be. It is commonly used with the reorder level system:

$$\text{EOQ} = \sqrt{\frac{2AS}{RV}}$$

where A is the cost of placing an order, S is the annual demand (in units) for the item, R is the stockholding cost (expressed as %), V is the cost (purchase price) of the item. The EOQ formula is based on a number of assumptions:

1. The rate of demand is known and is constant. It also assumes the past pattern of demand will hold good into the future.
2. The lead time is constant and known.
3. The unit cost (purchase price) is constant.
4. No stock-outs are allowed.
5. Material is ordered and arrives in one batch (i.e. there are no part deliveries).
6. The item is not dependent on any other product.

QUESTION 5.2

Look closely at the EOQ formula and the assumption on which it is based. Identify at least four problems that might arise either in calculating EOQ or concerning the assumptions on which it is based.

Despite its limitations EOQ is still a widely used formula and is frequently found in software used in computer stock control systems. As long as one is aware of the basis on which it is derived, the formula can be used to reduce the costs of ordering and holding stocks.

The EOQ formula can also be used to calculate the optimum size of batch (or lot) to be manufactured. In this case:

The Economic Batch Size, EBS $= \sqrt{\dfrac{2AS}{RV}}$

where A is the set-up cost for the process and the other symbols are the same as in the EOQ formula.

As well as the other shortcomings of the EOQ formula discussed above, using it to calculate a production batch size has an additional problem. It takes the set-up cost, A, as a given. The JIT approach to manufacturing, by contrast, considers this as a factor to be reduced and has led to dramatic improvements in set-up times and costs.

ABC inventory management

The 80:20 or Pareto rule is a tool of analysis which can be usefully applied to inventory management. An analysis of the annual usage value (i.e. quantity used × unit cost) allows inventory to be classified into three broad categories:

- Class A – the small proportion (typically 10%) of items which account for the majority of costs (say 70%)
- Class B – a middle group of, say, the next 20% of items which account for approximately the next 20% of costs
- Class C – the large number of items (say 70%) with little value (say 10% of costs).

A typical plot of usage value against numbers of stock items is shown in Figure 5.11. These figures are only a rule-of-thumb, but using this general principle will enable the classification to be applied in practice.

Categorizing stock in this way enables tight control of the high value Class A items, an intermediate level of control of Class B, whilst Class C would have the lowest level of control.

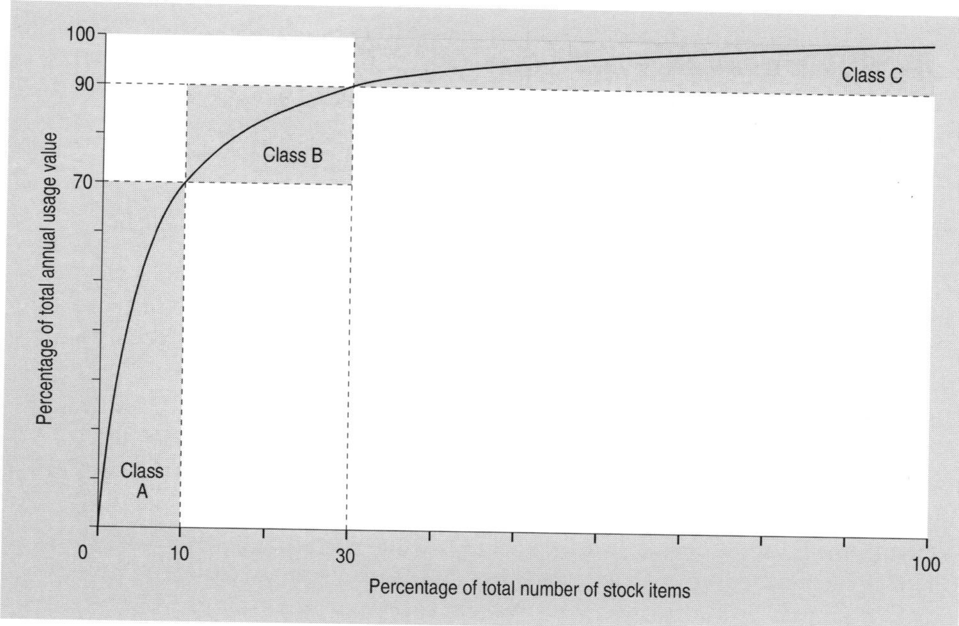

Figure 5.11 *ABC analysis of stock*

Dependent demand inventory and MRP

Dependent demand items have demand which can be calculated from independent demand items. They are typically the components and raw materials used to manufacture a product.

MRP (Materials Requirement Planning) systems can be used to calculate what dependent demand items will be required, and when they will be required, in the manufacturing process. MRP is driven from the Master Production Schedule (MPS) for a future period. The MPS will have been devised from known and forecast customer orders. To calculate what items are required, MRP needs detailed knowledge of every item that is required to manufacture a particular product. To provide this a Bill of Materials, listing exact details of all materials for each item, is drawn up. It is important to appreciate that what is required is *detail*, down to literally the last nut and bolt. The other input to the MRP system is the detail of the inventory status in the organization. This means current details of stock on hand and material on order including quoted lead times.

The MRP system then calculates what orders will need to be placed with suppliers and when, in order to meet the requirements of the MPS. In most practical situations, the system has extremely lengthy calculations to perform based on large quantities of data. Thus an MRP system is computer-based. Figure 5.12 illustrates the basic concept.

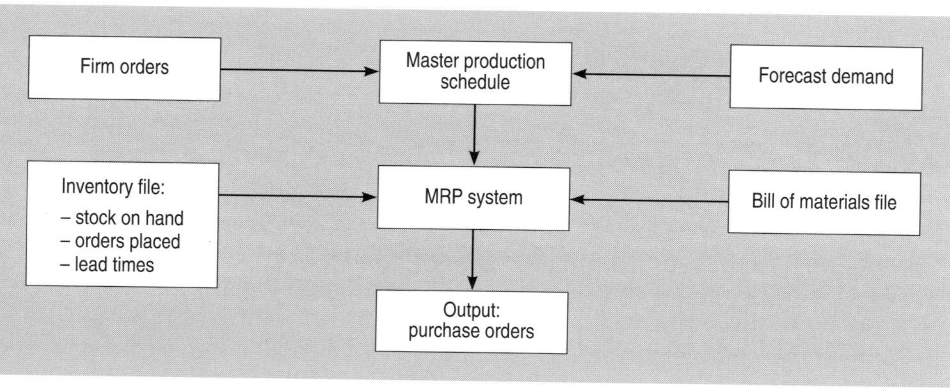

Figure 5.12 *Basic MRP system*

Although the principle of MRP seems quite simple, remember that it operates under dynamic conditions. Any change in any of the inputs will need to be taken into account. Thus the system needs regular and constant updating if it is to produce the benefits that MRP appears to offer. Like any computer system, the output from an MRP system is only as good as its input.

Benefits of MRP

The traditional order point system (reorder level, continuous review) discussed above performs quite well in independent demand situations because it is based on the assumption that historical demand patterns will continue into the future, and that demand will be reasonably constant over time. This may not be the case for dependent demand. Indeed, by its very nature dependent demand may be 'lumpy', that is a large batch may be required at a particular time but otherwise demand may be zero (i.e. an all-or-nothing situation). The order point system will either have to carry very large stocks of items for long periods when they are not required or may risk stock-out when the items are required. MRP is future focused: requirements for all materials are calculated on the basis of known or forecast demand. Whereas order point systems typically use EOQ calculations to determine order quantities (remember that they are based on historical data), MRP calculates order quantities on the basis of known demand. Thus order point systems should work best for finished goods and MRO stocks, and MRP best for some materials and WIP.

The basic approach to the co-ordination and control of operations that has been discussed (and taken for granted) so far is the traditional Western one. It is sometimes called the 'supply-push' approach. Its aim is to maximize the performance of each sub-system and thereby that of the whole system. It is achieved by controlling the activities of each sub-system process from a central control point (see Figure 5.13). This has traditionally been seen as the role of management, supported if necessary by production planners, controllers, schedulers, stock controllers, etc. As we have seen, increasingly sophisticated computer software has become available to aid management in this task (e.g. MRP 2, which is described below).

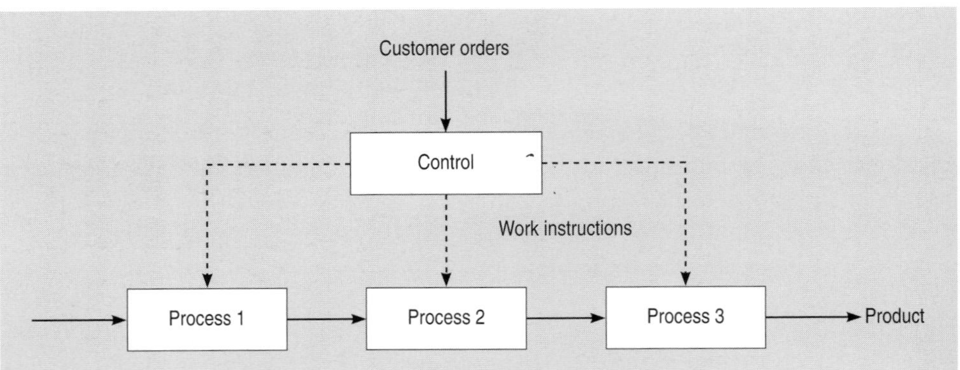

Figure 5.13 *Supply-push control*

Problems with MRP

In practice, MRP systems have often failed to deliver the lower inventory levels they promise. Problems seem to arise from the implementation rather than the theory of MRP. As we mentioned above, the MRP system needs to operate with accurate up-to-date information if it is to produce meaningful results. Implementation problems seem to centre around the MRP computer system not being advised of changes. There are so many possibilities for change: changes in design, changes in customer order quantities or timing, times not being met, part instead of full order deliveries, etc. If the situation is very dynamic, action to expedite overdue or priority orders may lead to the 'informal' system taking over from the formal MRP system. This situation can be particularly prevalent when installing MRP amongst staff who harbour reservations or even resentment about a computer-based system superseding 'their' system. Thus suspicion of the fallibility of MRP becomes self-fulfilling as people fail to operate the systems properly.

Manufacturing resources planning (MRP 2)

A further development of MRP is termed Manufacturing Resources Planning, usually known as MRP 2 (or MRP II). This is a computer-based system which is used to plan and control all manufacturing resources including materials, equipment, staff, and ultimately cash. In some systems MRP II is used to plan and control all business activities including sales and finance. As with MRP, there have been fairly mixed reports of MRP II's success in practice.

None the less, its basis is still a central controller issuing work instructions to all the separate processes within the system. It is the role of each sub-system to produce its output and make it available for the upstream process as instructed by the central controller. The sub-systems do not communicate directly with the next process but merely obey the instructions from the controller. In other words, they 'push' their output at the next process regardless of whether it is required. This obviously relies on the controller being provided with regular updated information so that instructions can be amended to account for changes in customer order, the progress of the work, breakdowns, material problems, etc. This can obviously become a highly complex task. It is perhaps then not surprising that so many problems continue to be reported by practitioners of this approach despite the availability of ever-increasing computer power. Problems arise if there is a disruption in any one process. If this disruption is not spotted and acted upon quickly enough, output from the downstream processes will continue and result in work-in-progress accumulating. There may in fact be an unwillingness to stop activities at these processes as their performance will be seen to deteriorate. Reward systems may even exacerbate this. If such disruption occurs regularly, upstream stations will want to build up stocks of input materials just in case of future disruption. Again their desire will be to optimize their performance. It is asking much of the controller to co-ordinate these activities to achieve optimal total system performance.

An alternative approach to supply-push, originating in Japan, has gained many Western adherents in recent years. This is demand-pull which is the basis of the 'Kanban' system of control and of the just-in-time (JIT) approach. The demand-pull approach aims to optimize the performance of the whole system irrespective of the performance of any one sub-system. The basis of this approach is that each process produces only what is required by the next upstream process in the next time period. Their instructions for this come directly from that process. If the work is not progressing as planned, the upstream processes will adjust their instructions to their supplying process to suit. In this way work-in-progress stocks are not allowed to build up. If a disruption occurs in any one process, it is quite acceptable for upstream processes to stop producing until the problem is resolved. Indeed, it is a central tenet of this approach that it is everyone's responsibility to remedy a problem anywhere in the system so that the performance of the whole system can be improved (see Figure 5.14).

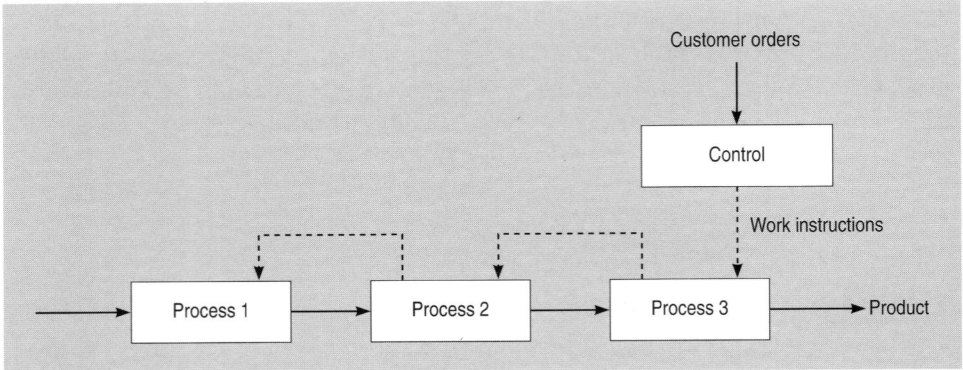

Figure 5.14 Demand-pull control

The demand-pull approach relies on close co-operation not only within the system but also with suppliers to the system. They need to be close-coupled to meet the requirements for their outputs. The role of the controller is considerably reduced in this approach, which does not require the use of computer power.

An alternative approach: 'demand-pull' and just in time (JIT)

JIT has become increasingly popular in Western manufacturing companies as they seek to emulate the success of the Japanese motor car manufacturers (particularly Toyota) who originated it.

JIT inventory control is based on a view that, far from being thought of as assets as accountants classify them, inventories are in fact undesirable and should therefore be driven from the manufacturing system. Thus the objective of JIT is zero inventories. As this is in fact impossible, we can view JIT as part of a wider philosophy of always seeking improvement. The approach of JIT to inventory control is to produce only exactly what is required 'just in time' for its use. JIT is based on the 'demand-pull' approach to operation control described above. In this, demand for material in one operation is signalled to the preceding operation. Thus one requirement for JIT is that operations are organized in a series of discrete activities. The method used to control the demand for, and supply of, material from one operation to another is, as mentioned before, referred to as 'Kanban' (Japanese for a card). This was the original Toyota method, by which instructions were sent from one operation to the next on such a card. Only those items listed on the card would be produced by the preceding operation, and in exactly the quantities listed on the card. The usual approach is to issue these instructions on a daily basis for delivery the next day. The objective is to synchronize production at each operation on a day-to-day basis. Clearly, there needs to be a reasonable degree of stability in the scheduling. This is usually achieved by fixing production schedules for a period of one to three months in advance. Assuming that each operation is required to produce more than one product type on any one day (and, given the need to produce small lot sizes, this is likely), there will probably be a need for change-overs on machines. Thus, JIT requires set-up times to be reduced to an absolute minimum. Similarly, the systems cannot tolerate breakdown or quality defects. Thus a decision to adopt JIT has far-reaching implications considerably removed from mere inventory concerns. It requires changes in working practices which may necessitate changes in equipment, physical layout, skill levels, reward systems, etc.

An interesting aspect of Japanese society made it easier, in a 'business culture' sense, for them to see how JIT could be made to work. The streets in Japanese cities and towns are very narrow, so deliveries have to be made by small trucks and vans. Hence the Japanese were used to the idea of small, frequent deliveries and could adapt more readily to the rigours of Kanban.

As well as having significant implications internally, JIT will also impact on the relationship with suppliers. In a JIT system they become an integral part of the production process, in effect an extension of the factory which happens to be off-site. Suppliers are required to deliver in small quantities, exactly as required, usually several times a day. For this to work:

- there must be very few suppliers (maybe a single supplier for each component or item of raw material)
- suppliers need to be close geographically
- the relationship with the supplier needs to be very close, implying a long-term relationship, built on trust.

ACTIVITY 5.4

Looking from a supplier's point of view, what would they want from the purchaser to encourage them to provide the level of service and quality demanded by JIT?

Apart from a higher price (which in any case may not be achievable in a competitive market) the supplier would probably look for: a long-term commitment to enable them to invest in the necessary systems (and perhaps equipment) for the contract; simple order systems with minimal paperwork; a guarantee of regular prompt payment against weekly, or more likely monthly, invoices.

Clearly, a move to JIT implies a significant change in relationships with suppliers and indeed all purchasing practices. The principal features of JIT are compared with more traditional practices in Table 5.1.

Table 5.1 Comparison of purchasing for JIT and more traditional purchasing practices

	JIT	*Traditional practice*
Purchase lot size	Small and frequent	Large
Supplier selection	Single source	Multiple sources
	Long-term contract	Short-term contract
	Local	
Inspection	Rely on supplier	Buyer is responsible
Negotiation	To achieve quality and reliability at a 'fair' price	To achieve best price (and delivery)
Transport	Determined by purchaser	Left to supplier
Product specification	In terms of performance	Rigid design specification
Paperwork	Minimal	Vast amounts
Packaging	Small, standard, well marked containers	Left to supplier
Basis of relationship	Co-operation	Adversarial

Note that JIT is not necessarily a computer-based system, although many practitioners do now use computer-based systems. JIT is principally aimed at driving out raw materials and WIP inventories. It can only be used to reduce finished goods stock if there is some certainty of demand from customers. Where this does not exist then finished goods stock will need to be held to protect the manufacturing system against fluctuations in market demand.

JIT is not an easy option or a 'quick fix'. Like most Japanese manufacturing approaches, its most successful exponents have been practising it for many years, in some cases decades. In those cases significant improvements have been reported not only in reducing inventories but also in many other aspects of operations.

5.6 Summary

This session has covered a great deal of ground. The aim has not been to turn you into an operations manager but to introduce you to the issues, language and techniques of operations management. To this end we highlighted the fact that operations managers are typically working to several different time-scales more or less simultaneously – from immediate 'real time' decision-making through to planning a year or more ahead. We outlined the different approaches to the problem of matching uncertain demand to capacity and output, and noted the strategic issues that such decisions may raise. The problems of scheduling work to minimize both costs and delivery times were then considered, and the corresponding challenge for service industries – queuing. Finally, the issues associated with determining appropriate stock levels and order dates were considered. This led into a brief discussion of JIT delivery and the rather different 'demand-pull' approach to production integration that it embodies.

Objectives

After studying this session you should be able to:

- Explain briefly in your own words the options for relating capacity and output to demand, and the main costs and benefits associated with them.
- Recognize in your own organization and work the different ways in which output is (and might be) adjusted to meet fluctuations in demand, and in which demand may be controlled to match output.
- Explain briefly in your own words the main issues associated with activity scheduling and use the following terms appropriately: MPS, routeing, loading, sequencing, slack.
- Recognize instances of queuing problems and explain briefly the contribution of both operations research models and psychological studies in understanding and addressing them.
- Use the following terms appropriately in discussions of stock levels: raw materials, work-in-progress, finished goods, MRO, independent demand, dependent demand, reorder level, ceiling level, EOQ, ABC inventory management, MRP system, JIT.

PROJECT MANAGEMENT

Contents

6.1 Introduction

We introduced the concept of projects as one of the generic types of operations in the discussion of process design in Session 4.

The most significant feature of a project is that it is unique, an unrepeatable one-off. Some organizations work almost entirely on a project basis: construction companies, management consultants, computer programmers producing bespoke software, etc. These types of organization employ specialist full-time project managers. You may consider that such people work in very different circumstances than most operations managers and it is true that project management involves distinctive skills and attitudes. However, from time to time all managers are responsible for projects of some kind – reorganizing an office or a workshop, moving to a new location, organizing a new product launch – and project management techniques can prove valuable. Indeed, in increasingly turbulent times, fewer management jobs at any level concern only the continuation of established operations. Project management is an increasingly important part of most managers' work.

Hence tnis session has two aims:

- To enable you to work more easily with specialist project managers by explaining the challenges they face and some of the techniques available to them.
- To familiarize you with basic project management ideas and tools that you can use to enhance the project elements in your own work.

6.2 Distinctive features of project management

A project manager is someone who is given overall responsibility for achieving the objectives of the project. These are likely to include:

- completing the project by an agreed time
- keeping cost within an agreed budget
- ensuring that the work complies with acceptable or specified quality standards

- keeping disruption to their client, their suppliers and the environment to a minimum.

Sometimes these objectives will conflict and, as is often the case in operations management, an acceptable trade-off will be required.

The task of project management can present operations managers with challenges which may be different from those they normally encounter in their work. These include:

- The difficulty of estimating the cost and time of the individual activities which make up the project. Because the project is unique, judgements have to be made based on limited knowledge and experience. This increases the likelihood that they will be wrong.

This reaches its limit with event managers, many of whom have no organization as such. They are freelance, and use networks of contacts in a wide range of businesses. Most of their time is spent on the telephone.

- A project usually involves the management of a team of people who may well not have worked together before. They are likely to be from different functional areas and have very different backgrounds. They may work for different organizations – partners or subcontractors. The project manager must ensure that they can quickly establish appropriate working relationships.
- Often members of the team work on the project only on a part-time basis. They still have their regular responsibilities. This is likely to result in them having problems in managing and monitoring their time.
- Because it is difficult to draw up exact specifications and requirements for all aspects of a project beforehand, it is not unusual for clients to require changes during the course of the project. These inevitably have cost and time implications and can cause friction between client and supplier.
- It is difficult to set appropriate performance targets for staff for project activities because of the unique nature of the tasks. This can make it difficult for the project manager to monitor staff performance.
- For project managers and their teams the initial phase of project planning and design may be relatively relaxed, but it is commonplace for the pace and pressure of work to build up steadily. Time speeds up as the deadline approaches.

The project management task can be thought of in terms of planning, scheduling and co-ordination and control.

Planning

The starting point of any project should be to agree with the client what the required output from the project is. This will enable project goals and objectives to be set, and time and resource requirements to be established. The major tasks within the project can be identified and a budget agreed. The project team can then be organized and key staff appointed.

Scheduling

This is concerned with drawing up a detailed work breakdown, task by task. Each task will need to have appropriate resources (people, equipment, materials, etc.) assigned to it, together with time and cost budgets. Activities will need to be sequenced in the appropriate order with required start and finish times established. It is likely that activities will need to be rescheduled (maybe several times) as the project progresses.

Co-ordination and control

In order to maintain control, all project activities will need to be monitored in terms of time, cost and quality against the project plan.

No matter how careful the planning, the uncertainty inherent in complex one-off projects means that things will not work out as intended – quite apart from client-requested changes to the specification or other matters outside the project team's control. Difficulties that threaten, more or less seriously, the schedule, cost or standard of the product, service or event are bound to arise, and it is silly to say they all could and should have been anticipated. A project manager's rationality, like everyone else's, is *bounded*. So a major part of project management involves problem-solving by modifying plans, shifting resources, and devising new ways of doing things. More specifically, since the overall task will have been broken down, in the planning phase, into its constituent parts, to be undertaken by different individuals or sub-groups, a major role of the project manager is in co-ordinating the progress of the parts. Each time one part of the project wants to do things differently the implications for other parts of the project have to be considered and negotiated.

The following sections consider various planning and scheduling tools as they are the common basis for managing projects of all sorts, and they also provide the basis for much of the co-ordination and control.

6.3 Key events charts

Key events charts are a very simple technique. Their main use is to specify the overall framework so that other people may prepare their detailed plans to fit in with the key events.

Let us consider an example. A new factory is nearing completion and will be opened by a celebrity. A small team is planning the opening ceremony in close consultation with the Managing Director and the celebrity's Public Relations Officer. The key events plan has been drawn up as in Box 6.1.

The plan is *not* a comprehensive list of everything that must happen to achieve a successful opening ceremony. Its purpose is to highlight the dates on which *key* events are planned to occur and by which the activities which contribute to those events must be complete. This will enable the individuals responsible for the different aspects of the event (for example, publicity, catering, handover of the building, etc.) to gear their own plans to the dates of the key events and to identify any possible problems in meeting those dates.

The key events plan in Box 6.1 can be easily amended or added to in the light of changing requirements. For example, you can add an extra column to indicate who is responsible for ensuring that each event occurs as scheduled and those people could then produce more detailed schedules of their own. In this way it can provide a starting point for planning much more complex projects.

Box 6.2 shows a standard production schedule used in planning and controlling the preparation of a monthly magazine. By filling in the dates and other details on this form the staff are setting the framework for a particular issue. Although some of the activities stretch over several weeks, the schedule puts dates on the key events in preparing the magazine, in particular the three crucial deadlines printed in bold type.

Box 6.1 A key events plan for the opening of a new factory

Version 2 – 22 June 199X

Prepared by: AW McG.

Circulation: RHD, UK, BO'L, DVG, PSO

Date	*Key event*	*Other events*
2nd July	Hold planned meeting	Receive project status reports
		Issue detailed plans for each department
6th July	Send outline plan of ceremony to celebrity	Distribute internally
		Receive departmental updates
		Building, plant and equipment status report
16th July	Celebrity's Public Relations Officer visits	Receive draft of publicity material
		Agree press arrangements
		Confirm catering plans
		Agree guest list
24th July	Receive comments from Public Relations Officer	Distribute comments
		Order publicity material
		Confirm press arrangements
		Check whole project status
27th July	Handover of building	Check completion of equipping
		Test-run equipment
30th July	Planning meeting	Review handover of building
		Receive final lists of problems from departments
2nd August	Rehearsal	
6th August	Final planning meeting	Review publicity material
		Review status of all problems
13th August	Opening day	

Box 6.2 Magazine production schedule

Issue number and date:		Editor:
Subject:		Second editor:
Weeks to go	**Action**	**Date**
16	Initial thinking on magazine	
15	First magazine proposal to editorial meeting	
14	Refined magazine proposal received: commissioning starts	
13	Commissioning finished. Work starts on:	
12	… editorial research …	
11	… facts spread …	
10	… visuals and photo research …	
9	**DEADLINE FOR CONTRIBUTORS**	
8	Work on articles, recommissioning if necessary	
7	Finalize copy on disk …	
6	Finalize … photos … visuals … facts, etc.	
5	**ALL SCRIPTS, VISUALS, OUTSIDE SECTIONS INTO STUDIO** (except letters and advertisements)	
	Design and typesetting begin …	
4	… production continues …	
3	Letters and advertisements to studio	
2	Corrections	
1	**MAGAZINE TO PRINTERS**	
	Distribution date	

ACTIVITY 6.1

Reflect on your use of schedules and charts.

When do you use them and why?

If you do not use schedules and charts much, or at all, which of the following reasons apply?

They are not often needed in my type of work, which is fairly routine.	❑
I have never thought of using them.	❑
I did not know how to go about preparing them.	❑
I am usually too busy.	❑
I do not want to admit that things are not going to be done in time.	❑
Other people prepare the schedules.	❑
I am afraid no one else would keep to the schedules.	❑

I am the sort of person who thinks ahead anyway. ❑

I do enough in my personal organizer. ❑

What further use of schedules and charts might you make in:

(a) The work of your organization/department/team?

(b) Your own individual work?

(c) Your studies on this course? (For example, have you used the Course Planner – essentially a key events chart – supplied in the Course File?)

6.4 Gantt charts

The Gantt chart, named after its creator, is one of the most commonly used techniques for planning the sequence of activities and for showing how long each activity will take. Figure 6.1 is an example. Activities are drawn as bars positioned along a time-scale – which is why they are also known as *bar charts*. The length of each bar represents the expected duration of the particular activity. A Gantt chart is easy to draw and it presents the plan in a visual form which is readily understood.

The Gantt chart can be used at every level in the planning process from initial outline planning down to planning individual tasks. It is useful for planning complex undertakings as well as simple ones. But, as schemes become bigger, any single bar on the master chart might have to be broken down and represented by another more detailed bar chart which, in turn, might need to be further broken down. Thus Gantt charts for projects, or ongoing work, which

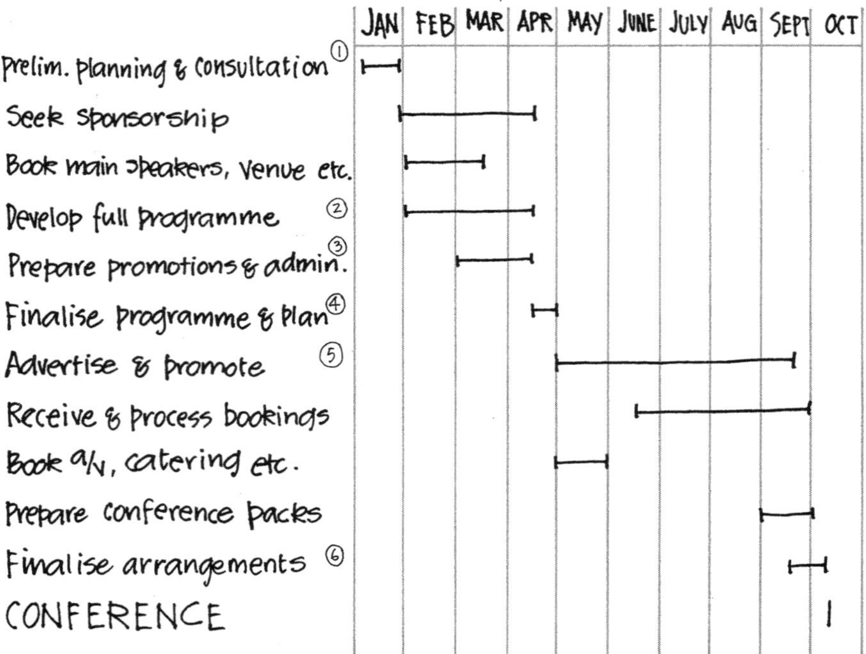

Figure 6.1 *Gantt chart of main tasks in preparing a conference*

involve many activities can be extremely complex. In some cases the interrelationships between activities and events may still be unclear and this is where the use of *networks* becomes worth while – of which more presently.

QUESTION 6.1

If you are not already familiar with them, the following exercise will ensure that you can draw and interpret Gantt charts.

Refer back to the production schedule in Box 6.2 and, using the blank Gantt chart in Figure 6.2, plan the production of three consecutive issues of the magazine (to avoid complications, assume four-week months and no Christmas). Start by listing the activities (we have done the first three for you) and then draw in their bars.

Then, write brief answers to the following questions:

- What difference in the pattern of work can you see between those people working in the studio and those working on the editorial content?
- If external contributors for a particular issue produce poor work, or work that is late, what difficulties is this likely to cause?
- What steps would you guess the publishers take to protect their schedules from such disturbances (apart from trying to choose reliable contributors)?

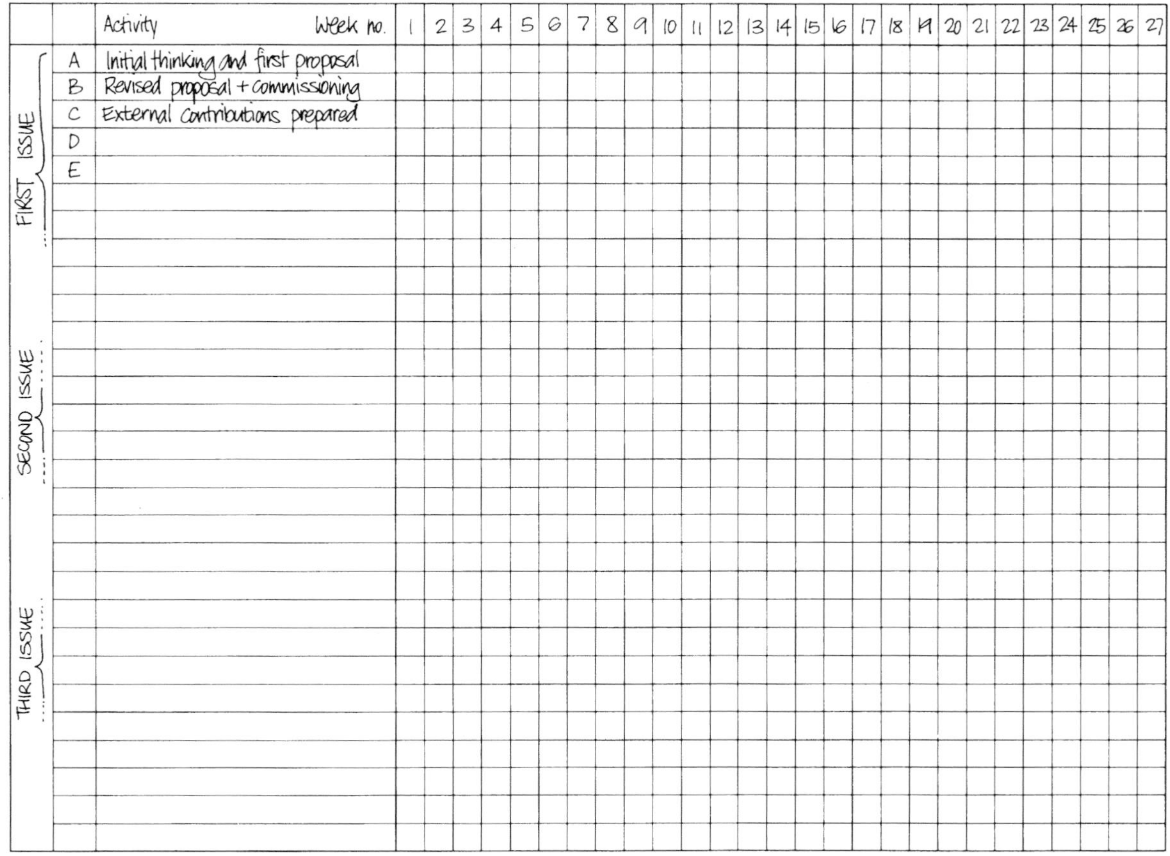

Figure 6.2 *Blank Gantt chart*

6.5 Networks

You may have come across PERT – an acronym for Program Evaluation and Review Technique – an early US implementation of network ideas for managing large military projects.

Many managers will not need to use network diagrams (or *critical path analysis*) in order to plan the completion of projects in minimum time and within resource constraints. But anyone undertaking a large, complex project to a strict deadline will find this technique practically essential, and those who frequently have to schedule moderately complicated events and projects will also find it helpful. In addition, everyone involved in scheduling activities should be aware of what is meant by the term 'critical path'. This section does no more than outline the construction and use of network diagrams. If you decide you want to learn more, you are encouraged to try out PC software for project planning – in your own time.

This was an actual problem facing one of the authors at the time of writing this book.

A simple planning network is shown in Figure 6.3 where the objective is to complete 12 interrelated activities in the shortest possible time. A simple case is sufficient to explain the underlying ideas and does so more easily. The network was constructed from the information in Table 6.1 (overleaf) using Microsoft 'Project' PC software.

Study Figure 6.3 and Table 6.1 for a few minutes so that you start to see how the network was constructed and what it all means. Here are some key points in understanding it.

- The network is made up of arrows and nodes.
- Each activity is represented by a node.
- There is a START node and a FINISH node.
- The arrows identify the immediately preceding activities. For example, Activity C is immediately preceded by Activities B and G as shown by the two arrows from nodes B and G that are directed at C.

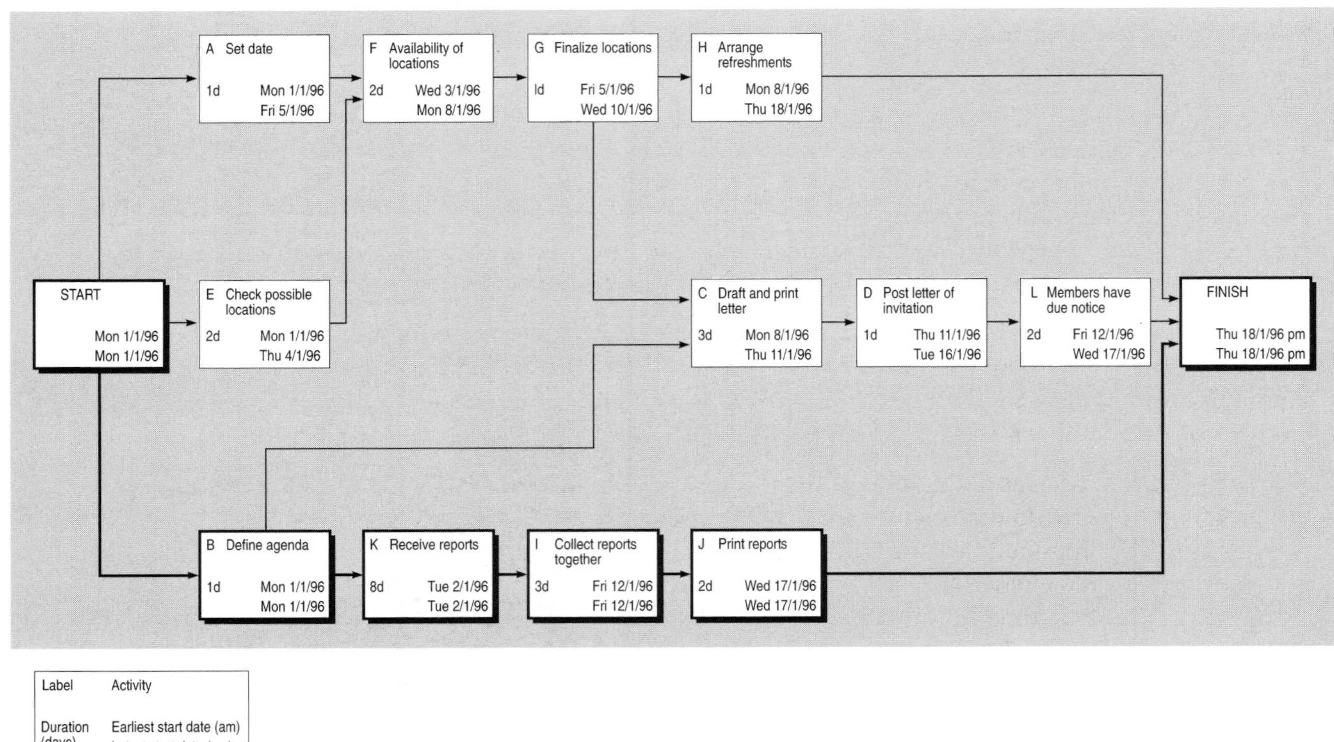

Figure 6.3 *Network diagram of activities in preparation for a meeting (activity on node)*

Table 6.1 Activities in preparing for a meeting, showing their duration and the immediately preceding activities. A start can be made first thing on Monday 1 January 1996

Activity label	*Description of activity*	*Duration (days)*	*Immediately preceding activities*
A	Set date	1	–
B	Define agenda	1	–
C	Draft and print letter	3	B, G
D	Post letter of invitation	1	C
E	Check possible locations	2	–
F	Availability of locations	2	A, E
G	Finalize locations	1	F
H	Arrange refreshments	1	G
I	Collect reports together	3	K
J	Print reports	2	I
K	Receive reports	8	B
L	Members have due notice	2	D

- Each node specifies the nature of the activity, the duration in days (d is an abbreviation for day), and two dates – the earliest start time and latest start time for the activity (9.00 am on the given dates).
- However, the FINISH node shows the date of the final day's work (i.e. the work is completed last thing on Thursday 18/1/96).
- The earliest start times (ESTs) are calculated by working forwards from the START to the FINISH nodes. So, for example, the EST for Activity D on Thursday 11/1/96 is calculated from the EST for the immediately preceding Activity C on Monday 8/1/96 plus the duration of Activity C which is three working days.

  Where an activity, such as F, involves the completion of two or more immediately preceding activities (A and E), the EST is always the highest such figure – which is only to say that an activity cannot start until all the activities on which it depends have been completed. Activity F cannot start on Tuesday 2/1/96 when A has been completed, because E is not yet complete.
- The latest start times (LSTs) are calculated by working backwards from the FINISH to the START nodes. So the LST for Activity F on Monday 8/1/96 is calculated from the LST for Activity G on Wednesday 10/1/96 less the duration of Activity F which is two working days.

  Where an activity, such as G, has two or more following activities (C and H), its LST will be the lowest such figure – which is only to say that an activity must start in time to ensure that none of the immediately following activities are delayed beyond their LSTs. Activity G cannot be delayed to Wednesday 17/1/96 in time for the latest start for Activity H, because Activity C must start on Thursday 11/1/96 at the latest.

Table 6.2 has been compiled from just some of the ESTs and LSTs shown in Figure 6.3. There are four activities where the ESTs and the LSTs are the same – so there is no choice when these may be started if the project is to be completed in the minimum time of 14 working days – i.e. at the end of Thursday 18/1/96. That is, Activities B, I, J and K have zero 'float' and are thus described as *critical activities.* The remaining activities have LSTs that lie after their ESTs and so they have some float. These activities can start at any time within this interval without holding up the entire project and they are described as *non-critical.*

The critical activities form a *critical path* from START to FINISH in Figure 6.3 (which is all to do with getting reports in and printed). Your eye is drawn to the critical activities which have a 'shadow' box and the bold arrows that form the critical path. Each of these critical activities must be started as soon as the preceding activities are completed. But if there is a delay, or if any critical activity takes longer than planned, it will hold up the entire project. In contrast, non-critical activities need not be started immediately. So, for example, Activity G may be started on Friday 5/1/96 but Figure 6.3 shows that it would not be necessary to start it until Wednesday 10/1/96, because it has a 'float' of three working days.

QUESTION 6.2

Complete the missing entries (for Activities F, G and H) in Table 6.2.

By now, we suspect, you will either be confused or revelling in the elegant logic – or perhaps feeling a mixture of both reactions. Network analysis is *not* obviously straightforward at first sight. However, it is an exceptionally powerful tool for highlighting those activities whose delay will delay the whole project – whether they are on the original critical path, or whether they simply become 'critical' as a result of delays beyond the LST of earlier activities. The availability of user-friendly PC software was transformed the utility of the technique from the domain of the specialist to the tool bag of the general manager.

In a simple case, such as planning a meeting, the ideas of 'float' and 'critical path' can be shown very clearly on a Gantt chart. The activities on the Gantt chart in Figure 6.4 have been sorted in order of their earliest start times.

Table 6.2 Some earliest and latest start times and floats

Activity	*Earliest start time*	*Latest start time*	*Float = Latest – Earliest start times*
A	Monday 1/1/96	Friday 5/1/96	4 working days
B	Monday 1/1/96	Monday 1/1/96	0*
C	Monday 8/1/96	Thursday 11/1/96	3
D	Thursday 11/1/96	Tuesday 16/1/96	3
E	Monday 1/1/96	Thursday 4/1/96	3
F		Monday 8/1/96	
G	Friday 5/1/96		
H			
I	Friday 12/1/96	Friday 12/1/96	0*
J	Wednesday 17/1/96	Wednesday 17/1/96	0*
K	Tuesday 2/1/96	Tuesday 2/1/96	0*
L	Friday 12/1/96	Wednesday 17/1/96	3

*Indicates a critical activity.

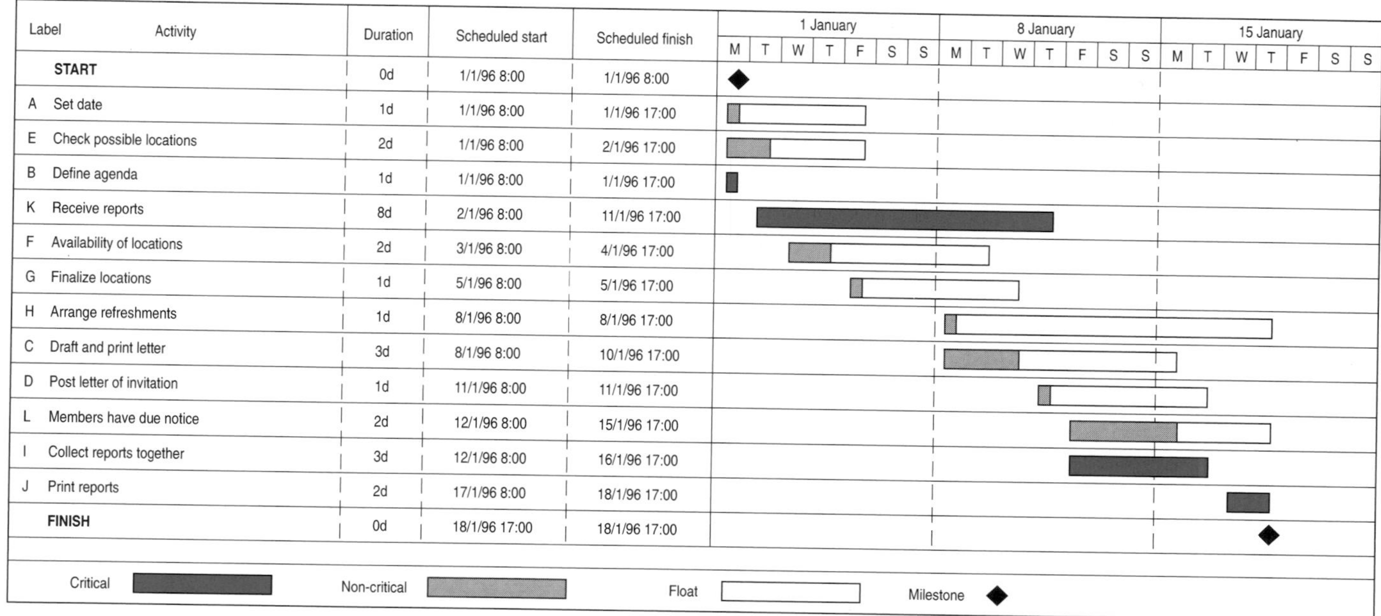

Label	Activity	Duration	Scheduled start	Scheduled finish
	START	0d	1/1/96 8:00	1/1/96 8:00
A	Set date	1d	1/1/96 8:00	1/1/96 17:00
E	Check possible locations	2d	1/1/96 8:00	2/1/96 17:00
B	Define agenda	1d	1/1/96 8:00	1/1/96 17:00
K	Receive reports	8d	2/1/96 8:00	11/1/96 17:00
F	Availability of locations	2d	3/1/96 8:00	4/1/96 17:00
G	Finalize locations	1d	5/1/96 8:00	5/1/96 17:00
H	Arrange refreshments	1d	8/1/96 8:00	8/1/96 17:00
C	Draft and print letter	3d	8/1/96 8:00	10/1/96 17:00
D	Post letter of invitation	1d	11/1/96 8:00	11/1/96 17:00
L	Members have due notice	2d	12/1/96 8:00	15/1/96 17:00
I	Collect reports together	3d	12/1/96 8:00	16/1/96 17:00
J	Print reports	2d	17/1/96 8:00	18/1/96 17:00
	FINISH	0d	18/1/96 17:00	18/1/96 17:00

Figure 6.4 *Gantt chart showing 'float' and the 'critical path'*

When we introduced Gantt charts we said the bar represented the duration of the activity; but here the bar is used in a more sophisticated manner to indicate the EST, the earliest finish time, the latest finish time, and the float of non-critical activities. For example, there is obviously considerable freedom in making arrangements for refreshments!

6.6 Conclusions

The three techniques described in this session provide a framework within which you can present and communicate the details of a plan (or draft plan). Secondly, they provide one means of checking progress against plans. Lastly, they focus attention on the following issues:

- Identifying the key events and deadlines.
- Disentangling the different activities and estimating how long each will take.
- Examining the relationship between activities, in terms of both *dependency* and *work load.*
- Working out which activities have priority (because they are, or may soon be, 'critical') and which ones still have time in hand (float).

Float was defined as the difference between the earliest and latest start times – but this is clearly the same thing as the difference between the earliest and latest finish times.

Gantt charts are widely used in management. The basic idea can be refined or elaborated to suit different purposes.

These are the important ideas on which the planning techniques are based and which make them valuable. The finer points of the techniques are much less important by comparison – indeed, if you were to glance through old management textbooks you would come across several slightly different versions of each one (such as activity on arrow networks). So it is a matter of choosing a technique that is adequate for your purposes, one that you are comfortable with, and developing or adapting it to the particular planning issues that you face.

The days when all these techniques had to be laboriously done by hand have gone for ever. The better PC software for project planning is user-friendly and offers very many facilities which a manager facing a complex project will find very helpful. Many managers without specialist knowledge find that their project planning software tools are absolutely invaluable.

After a while, moreover, the resulting document will need modifying or updating. This is another good reason why these techniques are ideally suited to PCs.

QUESTION 6.3

Construct a network for an office automation project which involves the 10 activities identified in Table 6.3. Then, assuming a start in Week 1 of the calendar overleaf, identify the critical activities and the earliest that the project could be completed. Which activity has the largest float? Draw up a Gantt chart showing the activities commencing at their earliest start times.

Table 6.3 Activities in an office automation project showing their duration and the immediately preceding activities

Activity label	*Description of activity*	*Duration (weeks)*	*Immediately preceding activities*
A	Construct a shortlist of suitable systems	4	–
B	Appraise selected systems	8	A
C	Make a final choice of systems	3	B
D	Order and obtain selected systems	12	C
E	Develop new systems and procedures	24	C, H
F	Train staff in new procedures	8	D, E
G	Phase in the new procedures	4	F, I, J
H	Recruit systems analysts	6	–
I	Document the new procedures	12	E
J	Arrange maintenance contracts	5	C

ACTIVITY 6.2

Which of the ideas or techniques in this session are likely to be relevant to your work?

What projects can you anticipate in the next few months that would provide occasions to use the techniques in earnest?

Calendar for use in Question 6.3

Week number	1	2	3	4	5	6	7	8
Week commencing	1/1/96	8/1/96	15/1/96	22/1/96	29/1/96	5/2/96	12/2/96	19/2/96
Week number	9	10	11	12	13	14	15	16
Week commencing	26/2/96	4/3/96	11/3/96	18/3/96	25/3/96	1/4/96	8/4/96	15/4/96
Week number	17	18	19	20	21	22	23	24
Week commencing	22/4/96	29/4/96	6/5/96	13/5/96	20/5/96	27/5/96	3/6/96	10/6/96
Week number	25	26	27	28	29	30	31	32
Week commencing	17/6/96	24/6/96	1/7/96	8/7/96	15/7/96	22/7/96	29/7/96	5/8/96
Week number	33	34	35	36	37	38	39	40
Week commencing	12/8/96	19/8/96	26/8/96	2/9/96	9/9/96	16/9/96	23/9/96	30/9/96
Week number	41	42	43	44	45	46	47	48
Week commencing	7/10/96	14/10/96	21/10/96	28/10/96	4/11/96	11/11/96	18/11/96	25/11/96
Week number	49	50	51	52	53	54	55	56
Week commencing	2/12/96	9/12/96	16/12/96	23/12/96	30/12/96	6/1/97	13/1/97	20/1/97

Objectives

After studying this session you should be able to:

- Appreciate and anticipate the distinctive demands of project management.
- Use key events charts and Gantt charts to plan and schedule projects for which you are responsible.
- Recognize occasions when project planning software is likely to help in planning a project.
- Interpret network diagrams and use the terms 'critical path' and 'float' appropriately.

QUESTION 3.1

(a) One-half (50%) of the widgets have weights above the mean; corresponding to $\sigma = 0$.

(b) 2.28%. Expressed in terms of the mean and standard deviation, 550 g is equal to the mean plus two standard deviations. Looking at Table 3.1, column B (the area in one tail), for $\sigma = 2.0$ there will be 2.28% of the values in that tail, i.e. 2.28% of the sample of weights greater than 550 g.

(c) 84.13%. The key point here is that 525 g represents 1σ above the mean. Since we want to know how many values lie below 525 g, we look up the area outside one tail (column C in Table 3.1) for a value of $\sigma = 1.0$.

(d) 31.08%. The values of 490 and 510 are 10 g either side of the mean. Since σ is 25 g, 10 g is 0.4σ i.e. $\left(\frac{10}{25}\right)$ and we are looking for how many values lie between the values of $\sigma = \pm 0.4$ (column E in Table 3.1).

(e) 1.64%. This is a little more difficult, but essentially uses the same principles as (d). The limiting values are 440 g and 560 g. In terms of means and standard deviations, these can be described as 500±60, i.e. the mean $\pm 2.4\ \sigma$. We are looking for how many widgets fall outside this range ('in two tails'), so we look up $\sigma = 2.4$ in column D (in 2 tails).

QUESTION 3.2

(a) By application of the formula:

$$\text{Estimate of population percentage} = \text{Sample }\% \pm 2 \times \sqrt{\frac{\text{Sample }\% \times (100 - \text{Sample }\%)}{\text{Sample size}}}$$

$$= 40\% \pm 2 \times \sqrt{\frac{40 \times 60}{2000}}$$

$$= 40\% \pm 2.2\%.$$

(b) By application of the formula:

$$\text{Sample size} = 4 \times \left(\frac{\text{Estimated percentage} \times (100 - \text{Estimated percentage})}{(\text{Required percentage error})}\right)$$

$$= 4 \times \left(\frac{75 \times 25}{5^2}\right) = \frac{7500}{25}$$

$$= 300.$$

QUESTION 3.3

Our new contingency table (after Table 3.6) will look as follows:

	After advertising campaign	*Before advertising campaign*
Prefer Sudso	100	72
Prefer Brand X	105	128
Don't know	32	29
Total	237	229

If we now set up our null hypothesis that the advertising had no effect, we need to create a table of expected values for the 'after' survey (i.e. by using the 'before' proportions on the 237 respondents to the 'after' survey). Thus:

	After advertising campaign	*Expected from null hypothesis*	*Before advertising campaign*
Prefer Sudso	100	74.52	72
Prefer Brand X	105	132.47	128
Don't know	32	30.01	29
Total	237	(237)	229

We now need to create a column to provide the values of

$\frac{(O-E)^2}{E}$ to produce the following table:

	After (O)	*Expected from null hypothesis* (E)	$\frac{O - E^2}{E}$	*Before*
Prefer Sudso	100	74.52	8.71	72
Prefer Brand X	105	132.47	5.7	128
Don't know	32	30.01	0.13	29
Total	237	(237)	**14.54**	229

As before, our problem has two degrees of freedom (remember (rows – 1) × (columns – 1) from the original contingency table).

Looking across the $df = 2$ row of Table 3.9, we can see that our value of $\chi^2 = 14.54$ exceeds even the value for $p = 0.001$. Thus, we can safely say that there was only one chance in a thousand that this change in washing powder preferences was due to chance.

If we are confident that 'other factors' were adequately controlled, we may begin to congratulate ourselves on the effectiveness of our advertising.

QUESTION 4.1

(a) A Perhaps this has some similarities with batch production?

B A sort of job operation?

C This has some clear parallels with line production in so far as evolving products move along predetermined routes.

D Customers usually move through in batches.

E Clearly, this is project management.

F This will involve a line process.

(b) Although there are some parallels, we did not find the classification, overall, particularly helpful. Arguably, the generic process types do not really fit service activities.

QUESTION 4.2

Manufacturing:

	Production volume	*Product variety*	*Flexibility*
Project	Very low	High	High
Job	Low	High	High
Batch	Medium	Medium	Medium
Line	High	Low	Low
Continuous processing	Very high	Very low	Very low

Services:

	Service volume	*Service variety*	*Flexibility*
Professional services	Low	High	High
Service shops	Medium	Medium	Medium
Mass services	High	Low	Low

QUESTION 4.3

(a) It produces monotonous jobs for people, condemning them to boredom and frustration at work. This leads to negative effects such as increases in absenteeism and staff turnover, poor quality work or even deliberate sabotage.

(b) The lack of employee control means that the jobs often result in stress and stress-related illness.

(c) It is more concerned with increasing the quantity than the quality of output.

(d) Short cycle repetitive jobs carry the risk of physical injury through the overuse of a narrow range of body movements. This is termed repetitive strain injury (RSI).

(e) Job specialization makes it difficult for workers to do other tasks. This reduces flexibility making it difficult for the operation to respond to changes in customer demand.

(f) Job specialization leads to demarcation problems and can introduce technical inefficiencies – the so-called 'line balancing problem' – as some jobs on the line are underused while others are overloaded. It can also lead to problems at one point in the production process, causing a complete stoppage of all other areas which rely on the output of that area.

(g) It concentrates knowledge, information, power and control in the hands of management. This can lead to poor employee relations and an authoritarian management style to which workers may well react in a very negative or destructive way. This reaction appears to confirm the assumption that it is only management who can achieve improvement and workers should be marginalized within the process.

QUESTION 5.1

Any of these events is almost certain to affect *all four* schedules. Hence, matching the problems listed to the schedule on which it would have its most obvious and direct impact (i.e. employee sickness affects the human resource schedule, and so on) misses the point.

QUESTION 5.2

There are many problems and shortcomings with the EOQ formula. The main ones are as follows.

In reality it is very difficult (if not impossible) to calculate a meaningful figure for A, the cost of placing and processing an individual order. At best any figure is likely to be an average over all purchasing activities.

Whilst it is possible to calculate S, the annual demand for the item on previous year's figures, how likely is it that they will prove to hold good for next year? Also will that demand be constant over the year? If it fluctuates significantly then EOQ calculations are likely to lead to either overstocking or stock-outs.

The cost of holding stock, R, is difficult to calculate in practice. It is likely to be made up of:

- the cost of capital which may vary over time as interest rates change
- insurance costs – (do these depend on the type of stock being held?)
- storage costs – these depend on building costs and any special facilities that the items may require (e.g. heat, cold, humidity)
- obsolescence – this will vary especially if fashion or technology are involved
- deterioration and damage – again this depends on the items
- pilferage or other losses.

The cost of the items, V, may vary over time (because of inflation or other macro-economic conditions) and may also be subject to quantity discounts or small order surcharges.

Lead times may vary for many reasons including the performance of suppliers or their suppliers.

Part deliveries may be unavoidable, or even desirable, in some cases.

Many items are purchased alongside others, and therefore the non-dependency assumption is often not valid.

QUESTION 6.1

Our Gantt chart is shown in Diagram A (overleaf).

Your chart may well be slightly different, but also quite correct. The difference between the two areas of work is that the editorial team have to be working on several issues simultaneously, whereas in the studio the issues go through one after the other. If external contributors let the staff down, the danger is that it would seriously affect work on one or both of the next two issues as well as jeopardize the issue in question. The staff might be too busy 'catching' to do the research for the next issue, and the preliminary thinking for the next but one issue. We guess that the publishers deal with this as follows:

(a) They try to keep a small stock of draft articles in reserve, to fill any gaps.

(b) The schedule contains some 'slack' so that they can cope with 'normal' problems and, if all goes smoothly, they can work ahead or on articles for the stock.

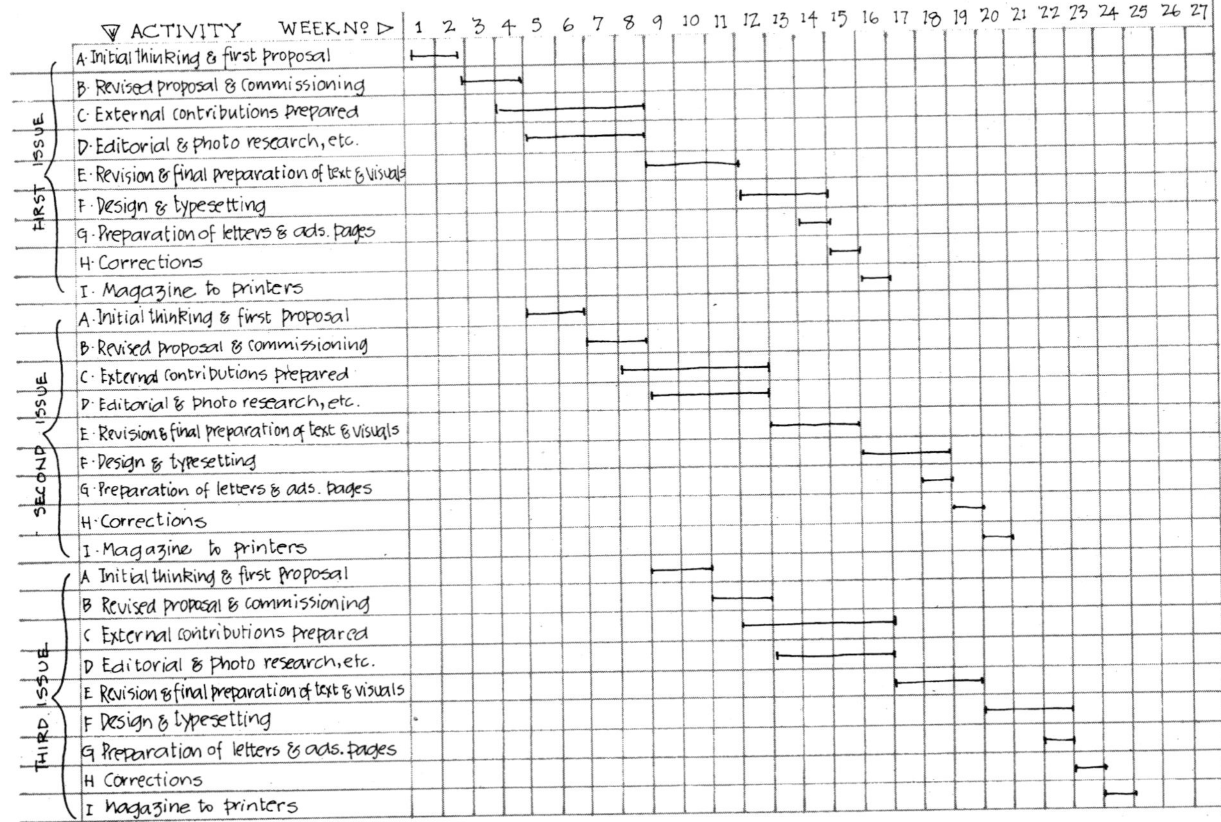

Diagram A *Completed Gantt chart*

QUESTION 6.2

Activity	*Earliest start time*	*Latest start time*	*Float*
F	Wednesday 3/1/96		3
G		Wednesday 10/1/96	3
H	Monday 8/1/96	Thursday 18/1/96	8

Note that only 8 of the 10 days between the EST and LST on Activity H are *working* days.

QUESTION 6.3

Our network diagram and Gantt chart are shown in Diagrams B and C.

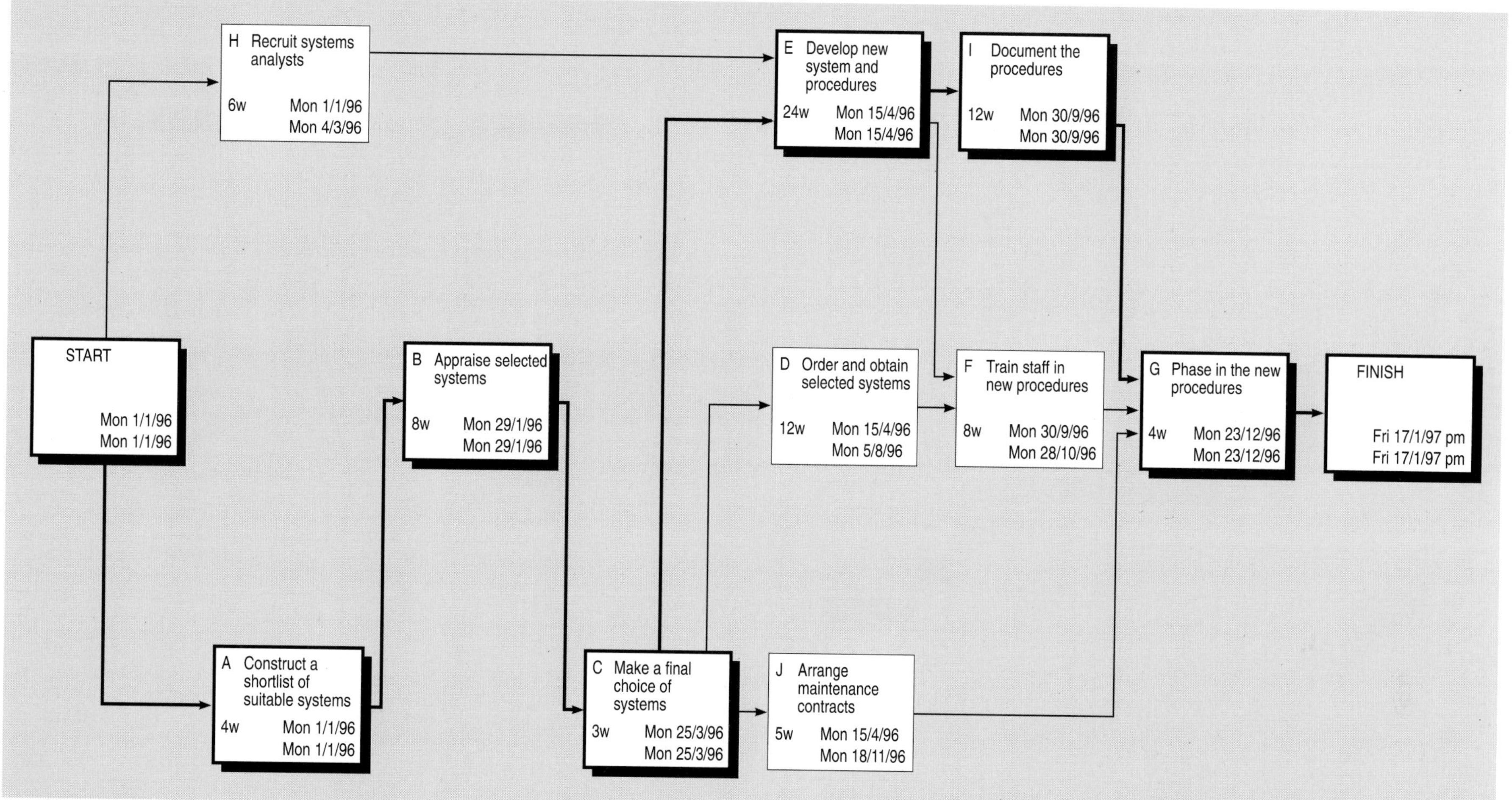

Label	Activity
Duration (weeks)	Earliest start date (am) Latest start date (am)

Diagram B *Completed network diagram*

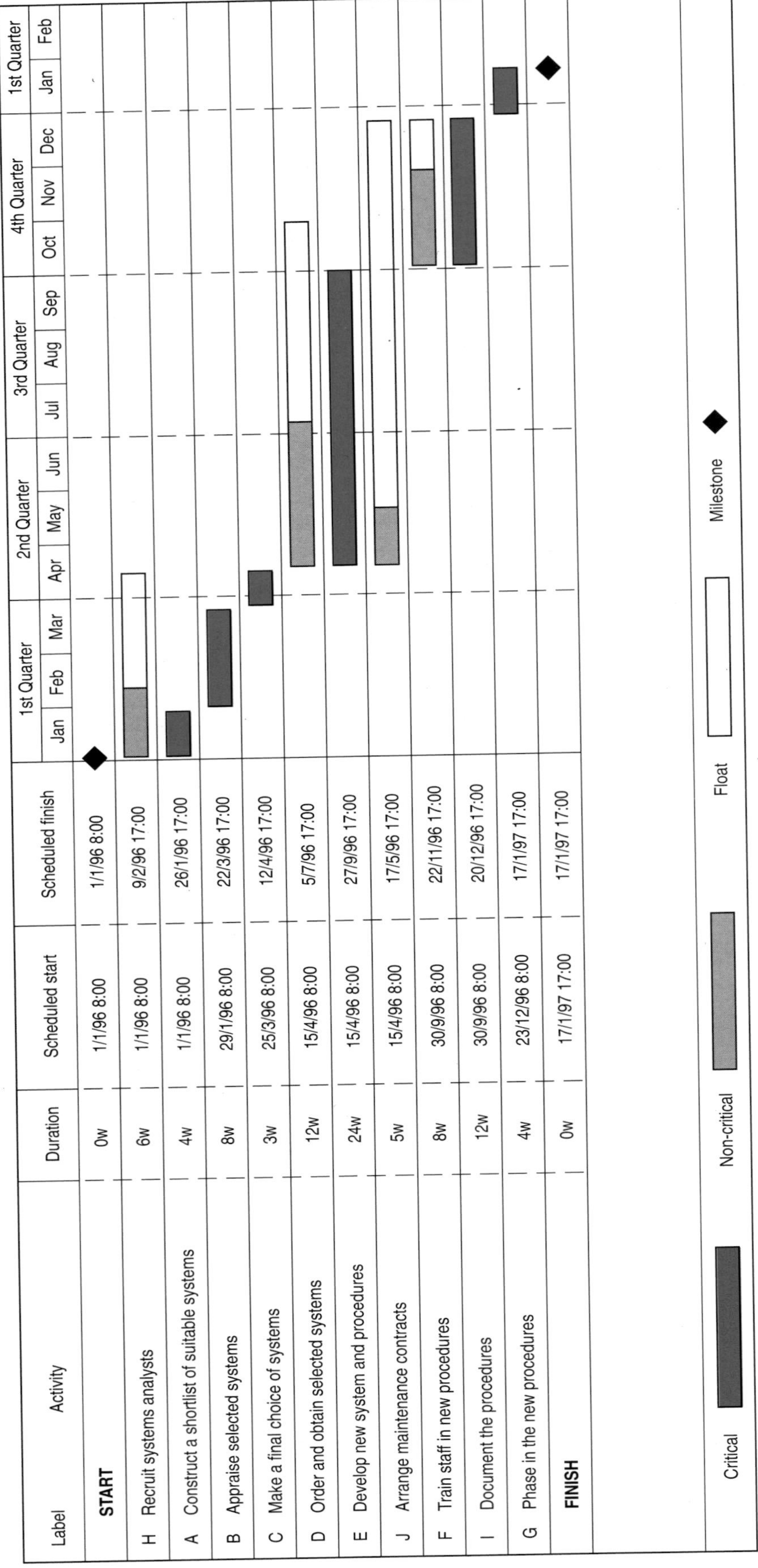

Label	Activity	Duration	Scheduled start	Scheduled finish
	START	0w	1/1/96 8:00	1/1/96 8:00
H	Recruit systems analysts	6w	1/1/96 8:00	9/2/96 17:00
A	Construct a shortlist of suitable systems	4w	1/1/96 8:00	26/1/96 17:00
B	Appraise selected systems	8w	29/1/96 8:00	22/3/96 17:00
C	Make a final choice of systems	3w	25/3/96 8:00	12/4/96 17:00
D	Order and obtain selected systems	12w	15/4/96 8:00	5/7/96 17:00
E	Develop new system and procedures	24w	15/4/96 8:00	27/9/96 17:00
J	Arrange maintenance contracts	5w	15/4/96 8:00	17/5/96 17:00
F	Train staff in new procedures	8w	30/9/96 8:00	22/11/96 17:00
I	Document the procedures	12w	30/9/96 8:00	20/12/96 17:00
G	Phase in the new procedures	4w	23/12/96 8:00	17/1/97 17:00
	FINISH	0w	17/1/97 17:00	17/1/97 17:00

***Diagram C** Completed Gantt chart*

REFERENCES

Chambers, A.D. (1981) *Computer Auditing*, Pitman, London.

Chase, R. (1978) 'Where does the customer fit in Service Operations?', *Harvard Business Review*, No. 56 (November–December), pp. 137–142.

Clark, K. and Fujimoto, T. (1989) 'Reducing the time to market: the case of the world auto industry', in Henry, J. and Walker, D. (eds) (1991) *Managing Innovation*, Sage/ The Open University, London.

Davis, M.M. and Heineke, J. (1994) 'Understanding the roles of the customer and the operation for better queue management', *International Journal of Operations in Production Management*, Vol. 14, No. 5, pp. 21–34.

Department of Health (1991) *The Health of the Nation*, HMSO, London.

Eurostat (1991) *Environment*.

Hackman, J.R. and Oldham, G. (1975) 'A new strategy for job enrichment', *California Management Review*, Vol. 17, Summer, pp. 57–71.

Hayes, R.H. and Wheelwright, S.C. (1984) *Restoring Our Competitive Edge Through Manufacturing*, John Wiley, New York, p. 209.

Huff, D. (1965) *How to Take a Chance*, Pelican, London.

Huff, D. (1991) *How to Lie with Statistics*, Penguin, London.

Johnstone, R. *et al.* (1993) *Cases in Operations Management*, Pitman, London.

Kendall, M. and Stuart, A. (1979) *Advanced Theory of Statistics* (4th edn), Vol. 2, Charles Griffin.

Maister, D. (1985) 'The psychology of waiting lines', in Cjerical, J.A. *et al.* (eds) *The Service Encounter*, Lexington Books, Massachusetts.

National Radiological Protection Board (no date) *Statement on Radon in Homes*, HMSO, London.

Nationwide (1995) *House Prices in 1994*, Nationwide Building Society, Swindon.

Schroeden, R.G. (1993) *Operations Management* (4th edn), McGraw-Hill, New York, p. 58.

Slack, N. (1989) 'Focus on flexibility', in Wild, R. (ed.) *International Handbook of Production/Operation Management*, Cassell, London.

ACKNOWLEDGEMENTS

Grateful acknowledgement is made to the following sources for permission to reproduce material in this book.

Figures

Figures 2.1 and 2.3: Department of Health (1991) *The Health of the Nation*, © Crown Copyright. Reproduced with the permission of the Controller of Her Majesty's Stationery Office; *Figure 2.6*: Central Statistical Office (1994), *Social Trends*, Vol. 24, © Crown Copyright. Reproduced with the permission of the Controller of Her Majesty's Stationery Office; *Figures 2.13, 2.14, 2.15, 2.16 and 2.17*: NHS Training Directorate/Open University (1992), B795 *Managing Health Service Information*, Part I, *Presenting and Analysing Data*, © Crown Copyright. Reproduced with the permission of the Controller of Her Majesty's Stationery Office; *Figure 3.6*: Courtesy of Nationwide Building Society.

Tables

Table 2.1: From *Leisure Futures*, courtesy of The Henley Centre for Forecasting; *Table 3.4*: Courtesy of Nationwide Building Society.

Cover

Images Colour Library.

DEALING WITH NUMBERS, INDICES AND PROBABILITIES

APPENDIX **1**

Contents

A1.1 Numbers

Number representation

What does the number 13,762 really mean? It consists of six symbols, that is, five digits and a comma. We know that any number of this type can be written using the digits 0, 1, 2, 3, 4, 5, 6, 7, 8 and 9, together with one or more commas, which separate the digits into groups of three. This use of commas is just a device that makes it easier to grasp the magnitude of a number. For example, if we write 3,268,147 it is easier to see that this number is more than three million than if we write 3268147.

We get a better idea of what 13,762 might mean if we read the number to ourselves; 'thirteen thousand seven hundred and sixty two'. The position of the 13 tells us how many thousands contribute to the number, the position of the 7 how many hundreds, the position of the 6 how many tens and the position of the 2 how many units.

We can put this into a simple table:

	Thousands	*Hundreds*	*Tens*	*Units*
13,762	13	7	6	2

This table can be extended to the left to cope with larger numbers, for example:

	Hundred thousands	*Ten thousands*	*Thousands*	*Hundreds*	*Tens*	*Units*
754,132	7	5	4	1	3	2

Moving from right to left across the columns of these tables is equivalent to multiplying by 10 and moving from left to right is equivalent to dividing by 10. This, together with the fact that we need 10 different symbols (0, 1, 2, 3, 4, 5, 6, 7, 8 and 9) to represent the different possibilities for the entries in a column, is why we often speak of numbers written to the *base 10*, or written in the *decimal notation*.

If we look again at the columns of these tables above we see that we can keep moving to the left, which is equivalent to multiplying the place value by 10, or moving to the right, which is equivalent to dividing the place value by 10. Just as the original table can be extended to the left, it can be extended to the right, for example:

Hundreds	*Tens*	*Units*	*Tenths*	*Hundredths*	*Thousandths*

Using a comma to separate groups of three digits and a full stop for the decimal point is the method used in the UK, USA, English-speaking Canada, much of the Far East, etc., but it is not the only system. For example, Spain and Germany use full stops to separate groups of three digits and a comma for the decimal point. France uses a comma for the decimal point, but just leaves a space to separate 000s.

We need one further symbol for the decimal point in order to distinguish the transition point between the units and tenths when, as is usually the case, the columns are not explicitly labelled. We now have all the ingredients of the standard decimal notation for numbers such as 127.35, where the full stop represents the decimal point. This can be represented using the table of columns as follows.

	Hundreds	*Tens*	*Units*	*Tenths*	*Hundredths*
127.35	1	2	7	3	5

This approach to representing numbers, using columns, makes it easy to see what happens with bases other than 10. For example, if we write numbers in the binary system, to the base 2, then we need two symbols to represent the digits. The symbols 0 and 1 are usually used, and we have to remember that moving across the columns from right to left is equivalent to multiplying by 2 and moving from left to right is equivalent to dividing by 2.

	Sixteens	*Eights*	*Fours*	*Twos*	*Units*	*Halves*	*Quarters*
11011.11	1	1	0	1	1	1	1

Do not be too concerned about this binary method. It is included mainly for interest as it is what your computer uses, since it only requires 'on' and 'off' – very easy for electronics.

The table helps us translate this number to the base 2 into a number to the base 10. The entry in a column tells us how much of the number represented by that column to include as part of the total number. So, using the binary number above, we can write:

$$11011.11 = 1 \text{ times } 16 + 1 \text{ times } 8 + 0 \text{ times } 4 + 1 \text{ times } 2 + 1 \text{ times } 1 + 1 \text{ times } \tfrac{1}{2} + 1 \text{ times } \tfrac{1}{4}$$

which can be simplified to:

$$11011.11 = 16 + 8 + 2 + 1 + \tfrac{1}{2} + \tfrac{1}{4} = 27\tfrac{3}{4} \text{ to the base } 10$$

Operations with numbers

There are four basic operations between numbers, each of which has its own notation:

Addition	$7 + 34 = 41$
Subtraction	$34 - 7 = 27$
Multiplication	$21 \times 3 = 63$, or $21*3 = 63$
Division	$21 \div 3 = 7$, or $21/3 = 7$

When several operations are combined, the order in which they are done is important. For example, $12 + 21 \times 3$ can be calculated in two different ways:

- Add 12 to 21 and then multiply the result by 3.
- Multiply 21 by 3 and then add the result to 12.

The first way gives a result of 99 and the second a result of 75. We need some notation that avoids possible ambiguities of interpretation such as this. What we do is to introduce brackets into the notation. Brackets are used to separate a complicated sequence of operations into smaller, unambiguous parts and at the same time they indicate the order in which the operations should be performed.

So, in our example, we could write, without any ambiguity:

(12 + 21) × 3 = 99

We could also write, without any ambiguity, a different expression:

12 + (21 × 3) = 75

Note that we calculate the parts of the expression inside the brackets first and then complete the remainder of the calculation.

The use of brackets to separate out every stage in a calculation can lead to very cumbersome-looking expressions. Brackets may be left out where the meaning is clear and, under this convention, we give priority to multiplication or division over addition or subtraction. Thus, the expression 12 + 21 × 3 can have only one interpretation with multiplication taking precedence over addition, namely 12 + (21 × 3) or 75.

Finally, note that the convention does not cover cases where multiplication and division both occur in a complicated sequence of number operations; and we need to use brackets if the meaning is to be clear and unambiguous.

You will usually see this written without a multiplication symbol outside the bracket – it is just implied, as in (12 + 21)3 = 99 *but* when using a computer spreadsheet, you *have* to include all the operators as in = (12 + 21)*3. Most computers use '*' instead of '×' and the equals sign informs the spreadsheet that what follows is a formula and not just text.

Rounding and truncating

For most business and commercial purposes, the degree of precision necessary when calculating with numbers is quite limited. While engineering can require accuracy to thousandths of a centimetre, for most other purposes tenths will do. When dealing with money, the minimum legal tender in the UK is one penny, or £00.01.

However, if we use a calculator to divide £10 by 3, we obtain £3.3333333, or as many '3's after the decimal point as the calculator will display. We can usually forget about most of these '3's and write the result as £3.33 to the nearest penny. This is a typical example of *rounding*, where we only look at the parts of the calculation significant for the purposes in hand.

In the early days of computing there were reports of systems analysts who made themselves rich by siphoning off fractional pennies from each of millions of banking transactions and accumulating the spoils in a personal account.

Consider the following examples of rounding to two decimal places:

1.344	rounds to	1.34
2.546	rounds to	2.55
3.208	rounds to	3.21
4.722	rounds to	4.72
5.555	rounds to	5.56
6.5445	rounds to	6.54
7.7754	rounds to	7.78

We get the rounded number by looking at the part of the decimal from the third place after the decimal point and beyond. If this part of the number is greater than or equal to 0.005, we add 0.01 to the second decimal place. If the part of the number is strictly less than 0.05, the rounded number consists of just the number up to the second decimal place. For example, let us look at the process of rounding 7.7754. Because the part of 7.7754 from the third decimal place onwards is 0.0054, which is greater than 0.005, we have to add 0.01 to 7.77 to get the final result 7.78.

Rounding to a given number of decimal places is not the only form of rounding that we need. There will be situations when we shall have to round to a specified number of significant figures. In this form of rounding, 7.7754 will round to 7.8 to two significant figures, 1472.9684 will round to 1470 to three significant figures, 0.00467 will round to 0.0047 to two significant figures, and 1.26385 will round to 1.264 to four significant figures.

The rule for rounding up or down is the same as in the earlier case of rounding to a certain number of decimal places, the significant figures part of the rounding process telling us how many places to use after any zeros before comparing what is left with a 5 in the next place to the right.

Truncating a number is much more straightforward and means just what it says. Truncating a number to so many significant figures, or to so many decimal places, means taking the number and ignoring the insignificant figures, or additional decimal places, respectively. For example:

12.75 truncates to 12.7 to three significant figures

1.9694 truncates to 1.96 to two decimal places.

While truncating is easy to do, it can introduce serious errors in lengthy calculations. Rounding can also introduce errors, but usually not on quite the same scale as truncation errors.

Fractions

So far we have thought of numbers such as 4.567 in terms of their decimal expansion, but this is not the only way of representing numbers.

A fraction represents a part of something. If you decide to share out something equally to two people then each receives a half of the total, and this is represented by the symbol $\frac{1}{2}$. For instance, in the UK a ruler used to be divided into inches and then subdivided into halves, quarters, eighths, tenths, and sixteenths of an inch. A measure of, say, $3\frac{15}{16}$ inches is approximately equal to 100 mm.

A fraction is just the quotient, or ratio, of two numbers, $\frac{1}{2}$, $\frac{3}{5}$, $\frac{12}{8}$, and so on, and we obtain the corresponding decimal forms 0.5, 0.6 and 1.5 respectively by performing division. The top half of a fraction is called the numerator and the bottom half the denominator. We divide the denominator into the numerator to get the decimal form.

A fraction can have many different representations. For example, $\frac{1}{4}$, $\frac{2}{8}$, $\frac{4}{16}$ and so on all represent the same fraction of one quarter, or 0.25. It is customary to write a fraction in the lowest terms, that is to divide out as many common factors as possible between the numerator and denominator so that one half is shown as $\frac{1}{2}$ and one quarter is shown as $\frac{1}{4}$.

We can perform the basic numerical operations on fractions directly. For example, if we wish to multiply $\frac{3}{5}$ by $\frac{2}{7}$ then what we are trying to do is to take $\frac{3}{5}$ of $\frac{2}{7}$, so we form the new fraction $\frac{3\times 2}{5\times 7}$ or $\frac{6}{35}$. In general, we multiply two fractions by forming a new fraction where the new numerator is the product of the two numerators, and the new denominator is the product of the two denominators.

Addition of fractions is more complicated than multiplication as we can see if we try to calculate the sum of $\frac{3}{5}$ and $\frac{2}{7}$. The first step is to represent each fraction as the ratio of a pair of numbers with a common denominator. To do this in this specific case we multiply the top and bottom of $\frac{3}{5}$ by 7, and the top and bottom of $\frac{2}{7}$ by 5. The fractions now look like $\frac{21}{35}$ and $\frac{10}{35}$ which have the same, or common, denominator of 35. In this new form we just add the two numerators. Thus:

$$\left(\frac{3}{5}\right)+\left(\frac{2}{7}\right)=\left(\frac{21}{35}\right)+\left(\frac{10}{35}\right)=\frac{(21+10)}{35}=\frac{31}{35}$$

Basic algebra

So far we have discussed numbers and their basic operations – addition, subtraction, multiplication and division – together with the interaction of these operations with concepts such as fractions, order and rounding. Throughout, we have used specific numbers by way of example, but in order to go further into more complicated manipulations and number concepts we need some simplifying notation. What we do is to introduce the idea of symbols for numbers, manipulate the symbols as though they were numbers, and hence make general statements which hold for all numbers.

The symbols for numbers that are most commonly used are the lower-case letters of the alphabet, often in italic type, *a, b, c ... x, y, z,* but occasionally we use parts of the Greek alphabet as well. It is obviously a good idea not to mix the symbol to represent a number, x, and the symbol $\times$, and the symbol * in order to denote multiplication in the same expression. As a simple example of how this notation works, consider the expression $x = 2a$, which tells us that x is an even number. An even number is one that is divisible by 2, so the equation above can be read as saying that the number represented by x can be written as the product of 2 and some other number represented by a. We can write similar equations that describe, for example, the fact that a number is divisible by 3, or that it is an odd number. The relevant equations are:

$x = 3a$

$x = 2b + 1$

We have said that we manipulate the symbols representing numbers in precisely the same way as if they were numbers. Some of the rules for calculating with numbers, which we can often take for granted when we are actually using numbers, can look a little strange at first, but they are all essential.

$a*0 = 0$

$a*1 = a$

$a + b = b + a$

$a*b = b*a$

$a \times (b + c) = ab + ac$ or $a*(b + c) = a*b + a*c$

$a + (b + c) = (a + b) + c = a + b + c$

$a*(b*c) = (a*b)*c = a*b*c$

How can we use this symbolism? A typical use is shown by the following example.

Example

A sum of money is borrowed to be repaid in four instalments, the first repayment being $\frac{1}{3}$ of the loan, the second $\frac{2}{5}$ of the loan, the third $\frac{1}{4}$ of the loan and the final repayment £13. How much was borrowed?

We can use the symbol notation and let £x stand for the sum borrowed. Then the sequence of repayments is:

$$\frac{£x}{3} + \frac{£2x}{5} + \frac{£x}{4} + £13$$

The sum of these repayments must equal the sum borrowed, so omitting the £ sign for the moment:

$$x = \frac{x}{3} + \frac{2x}{5} + \frac{x}{4} + 13$$

This equation can now be rearranged by bringing the fractions to a common denominator of 60:

$$x = \frac{(20x + 24x + 15x)}{60} + 13$$

or

$$x = \frac{59x}{60} + 13$$

If we subtract $59x/60$ from the left-hand side of the equation, and then subtract it from the right-hand side, the equality is unaffected. But numerically we find that:

$$\frac{60x}{60} - \frac{59x}{60} = \frac{59x}{60} - \frac{59x}{60} + 13$$

This is equivalent to:

$$\frac{x}{60} = 13$$

or, multiplying both sides by 60, $x = 13*60$ and so $x = 780$.

Hence the original sum borrowed was £780.

In this example we were solving an equation for an unknown quantity represented by the letter x and, for the moment, we will concentrate on the general rules for solving such equations.

Consider the equation:

$$3x - 5 = 4$$

To solve this equation, we wish to find a value for x that makes the equation a valid statement. What we do is manipulate the equation into a form in which the unknown quantity x is isolated on one side of the equation only, say the left-hand side. If we reach such a position, then what is in the right-hand side of the equation is the required solution.

So, for $3x - 5 = 4$

we add 5 to both sides of the equation to get $3x - 5 + 5 = 4 + 5$

therefore $3x = 9$.

If we divide both sides of the equation by 3, then $x = 3$.

The required solution is the number 3.

A1.2 Indices

Numbers and powers

The number 25 is the product of the number 5 with itself:

$$25 = 5 \times 5$$

and the number 125 is the product of three 5s:

$$125 = 5 \times 5 \times 5$$

There is a convenient and descriptive notation for writing down numbers of this special form, the *index* notation. What we do is to write 25 and 125 in the following way:

$$25 = 5^2$$

and

$$25 = 5^3$$

In general, the index notation x^y represents the product of y copies of the number x, at least for positive integer (i.e. whole number) values of y. This idea of the product of multiple copies of a number leads to some rules for indices. Suppose we calculate the number 5^6, then we have the product of six copies of the number 5:

In computer spreadsheets this system of superscripting is normally represented by the '∧' symbol, so x^y would be typed as *x*∧*y*.

$$5^6 = 5 \times 5 \times 5 \times 5 \times 5 \times 5$$

We can bracket the right-hand side of this equation in several ways:

$$5^6 = (5 \times 5) \times (5 \times 5) \times (5 \times 5) = 5^2 \times 5^2 \times 5^2 = (5^2)^3$$

or

$$5^6 = (5 \times 5 \times 5) \times (5 \times 5 \times 5) = (5^3)^2$$

or

$$5^6 = 5 \times (5 \times 5 \times 5) \times (5 \times 5) = 5^1 \times 5^3 \times 5^2 = 5^{1+3+2}$$

It is a straightforward consequence of this kind of analysis to show that if a and b are positive whole numbers, then for any number x:

$$x^{a+b} = x^a x^b$$

and

$$(x^a)^b = x^{ab}$$

The requirement for a and b to be positive whole numbers can be unnecessarily restrictive so how can we give some meaning to x^y when y is not a positive integer? We progress in stages. What we would like is an interpretation for x^y such that for any values of a and b:

$$x^{a+b} = x^a x^b$$

and

$$(x^a)^b = x^{a*b}$$

First, $x^1 = x$, because the product of just one copy of x must be x itself. Now consider x^0. If we want our formulae to hold for any value of y, we must have:

$$x^{a+0} = x^a x^0$$

and

$$(x^0)^a = x^{0*a} = x^0$$

and hence x^0 must be a number such that when any other number is multiplied by x^0 the number is left unchanged, and the product of any number of copies of x^0 is just x^0. There is only one possible value for x^0.

$$x^0 = 1$$

Next, we observe that:

$$x^{a-a} = x^0 = 1$$

so that:

$$(x^a)(x^{-a}) = 1$$

and x^{-a} must be the reciprocal of x^a, that is:

$$x^{-a} = \frac{1}{(x^a)}$$

A reciprocal is a mathematical function or expression which is so related to another that their product is unity.

We now have interpretations of x^y when y is a positive or negative integer, including $y=0$, and $y=1$, as well as when y has the fractional form $1/a$ for some integer a.

There is a special notation for fractional indices of this type, $1/a$, the root notation.

$$x^{\frac{1}{2}} = \sqrt{x}\text{, or } \sqrt[2]{x}$$

$$x^{\frac{1}{3}} = \sqrt[3]{x}$$

and, in general, if n is a positive integer:

$$x^{\frac{1}{n}} = \sqrt[n]{x}$$

This root notation is only used with small values for the integer n, but you will find it on many calculators and in many textbooks. It is straightforward, now, to extend the interpretation of x^y for all fractional values of y. All we need to do is to recall that if y is a fraction, then it takes the form $y = a/b$ where a and b are integers, and our formula tells us that:

$$x^{\frac{a}{b}} = \left(x^{\frac{1}{b}}\right)^a$$

That is, to calculate $x^{a/b}$ we first calculate $x^{1/b}$ and then raise the number we get to the power a. It is difficult to calculate actual values of the form $125^{1/3}$ or 7^9 without using a calculator. In the days before calculators – only the mid-1970s – we had to use logarithm tables and such calculations were tedious in the extreme. Nowadays we use the x^y key on a calculator and life is simple. For example, to calculate 7^9, enter 7, press the x^y key, enter 9 and press the = key, and the answer 40,353,607 appears.

Exponential form

We can use the power notation to provide an alternative representation for numbers which is particularly useful when dealing with very large or very small numbers. For example, we can calculate the number of seconds in a year by doing a sequence of multiplications on a calculator:

60*60*24*365 = 31,536,000

Apart from any intrinsic curiosity as to what this number actually is, it is easier to remember if we round it to three significant figures: 31,500,000. We can also write this number more neatly if we recognize that:

$31{,}500{,}000 = 315 \times 100{,}000$

and then use the index notation to write 100,000 as 10^5, so that:

$31{,}500{,}000 = 315 \times 10^5$

Alternatively, we could have written:

$$31{,}500{,}000 = 31.5 \times 10^6$$

or

$$31{,}500{,}000 = 3.15 \times 10^7$$

The number is now said to be in exponential form, that is, it has been written in the form $a \times 10^b$, where the magnitude of a lies between 1 and strictly less than 10. In order to store a number in exponential form, all we have to do is to record the values of a and b. This is precisely what some calculators will do with numbers larger than the number of digits in the calculator display. For example, if we go back to the number of seconds in a year and try to calculate the number of seconds left before the turn of the century from the year of writing this text (1994) at some stage we will need to do a sum of the form:

$$60 \times 60 \times 24 \times 365 \times 6$$

which, on my calculator display of no more than 10 characters, comes out as 1.89216^{08}, which represents the number 1.89216×10^8. That is nearly one hundred and ninety million!

Finally for this section, multiplying numbers in exponential form is quite straightforward. Suppose that we wish to calculate:

$$(a \times 10^b)(c \times 10^d)$$

This is the same calculation as:

$$(a \times c)(10^b \times 10^d) = (a \times c)10^{b+d}$$

So, to multiply two numbers in exponential form, we multiply the numbers, represented by $a \times c$, and add the indices, represented by $b + d$, to get the appropriate power of 10. We then check that what we have is in exponential form, which it will be if the product ac is less than 10. But if the magnitude of ac is greater than or equal to 10, then we divide ac by 10 and change the index for the power of 10 to $b + d + 1$.

Example

Multiply 2.46×10^7 by 5.32×10^{11}.

This is a situation in which $a = 2.46$, $b = 7$, $c = 5.32$, $d = 11$.

Our rule for multiplying such numbers requires first to calculate:

$$ac = 13.0872 \text{ and } b + d = 18$$

so that the product is 13.0872×10^{18}.

Now ac is greater than 10 in magnitude, so the product is not quite in exponential form. We need to make the final adjustment of dividing 13.0872 by 10 and increasing 18 to 19. The final form is 1.30872×10^{19}.

A1.3 Probabilities

A large part of a manager's job concerns decision making under conditions of uncertainty. If we always had perfect information at our fingertips, the quality of our decisions would probably improve dramatically. (But note the 'probably'; how certain are we that this would happen?) One way to address the problems of uncertainty is to replace words such as 'likely', 'probably' and 'almost certainly' with something more precise. (And yes, that means using numbers …)

Simple probability

There are two problems with probability. First, for whatever reason, many people, managers included, have something of a phobia about numbers in general and statistics in particular. Second, when we do start to apply numbers to probability, we may get results that run counter to our intuition.

The classic example for illustrating probability is the issue of children. For example, if a couple decide to plan for two children, what is the chance they will end up with a boy and a girl? (For the sake of our discussion, we will assume that there is an equal likelihood of boys and girls being born and ignore the possibility of multiple births.)

As in all such cases, the easiest and most effective technique is to enumerate the possibilities, but herein lies the problem; great care must be taken to identify every possible case. The trap, which is remarkably easy to fall into even in simple cases such as this, is to ignore the different ways in which the results can be achieved.

Thus, the cursory (and wrong) analysis says that there are three possibilities – boy-boy, girl-girl, and one of each – and hence the probability of the latter is one in three.

Enumerating the possibilities requires a great deal more rigour. The possibilities start with the arrival of the first-born: either a boy or a girl. This divides our universe of possibilities into two, and we need to evaluate both cases. Given a boy first, the options are boy-boy and boy-girl; given a girl first, the options are girl-girl and girl-boy. There are thus not three but four different possibilities. If we now examine these possibilities, we can see that 'one of each' is satisfied by both girl-boy and boy-girl, that is two of the total of four. The chance is therefore one in two or 50%.

At this juncture, it is worth looking at the different ways of expressing probabilities. The idea of 'one in two' is to express the probability as a simple fraction: the number of (*favourable*) outcomes divided by the *total* number of outcomes. This fraction could also be expressed as a percentage, i.e. one divided by two equals 50%.

Another legitimate expression is the term 50:50 which is a ratio of the number of favourable outcomes to the number of *unfavourable* outcomes. In the example above, the chance of two children of the same sex (i.e. two boys or two girls) is 50:50, but the chance of, say, two girls is 25:75, i.e. 25%, or one chance in four. It is important that you should be able to convert freely between these different modes of expressing the same thing.

Unfortunately, the relative clarity of the expressions above is complicated by some people (most notably bookmakers) insisting on quoting the 'odds'. This scheme of things uses phrases such as '3 to 1 against' as a way of comparing the number of unfavourable outcomes with the number of favourable outcomes. In the case used above, 'three to one against' is indeed the chance of producing two girls, and says the same thing as 'one in four', '25%' or '25:75'.

Let us return for the moment to the question of children, and assume that our hypothetical couple have ambitions for a larger family, say of four children. What is the probability of two boys and two girls?

An enumeration of the possibilities is:

BBBB

all four are boys;

GBBB BGBB BBGB BBBG

three boys and a girl, showing the girl as first-, second-, third- or last-born;

BBGG BGBG BGGB GGBB GBGB GBBG

two boys and two girls, first when the first-born is a boy (three possibilities), followed by the three possibilities after a first-born girl;

BGGG GBGG GGBG GGGB

three girls and a boy, showing the boy as first-, second-, third-, or last-born. Note that this is a reversal of the second row;

GGGG

all four are girls – a reversal of the first row.

Thus six out of 16 give two of each!

You may or may not feel this to be counter-intuitive; one of the problems with introductory statistics is that it often highlights areas where our 'intuition' is misleading.

As the numbers increase, the method of enumerating the possibilities becomes increasingly cumbersome, so a little mathematics can simplify things. Let us try tossing the proverbial 'fair coin'. The chances of throwing 'heads' is one in two. Parallel with the case of boy/girl above, the chance of two successive heads may be deduced as one in four ($\frac{1}{2} \times \frac{1}{2}$), three successive heads is one chance in eight ($\frac{1}{2} \times \frac{1}{2} \times \frac{1}{2}$), and the chance of four successive heads is one in sixteen ($\frac{1}{2} \times \frac{1}{2} \times \frac{1}{2} \times \frac{1}{2}$). The rule in this case is that our two possibilities, if repeated four times, give 2^4 (= 16) possible outcomes. The general rule is that the total number of outcomes of x tosses of our fair coin is two to the power of x, and hence the probability of *any* particular sequence is $\frac{1}{2}^x$.

We can extend the general rule to the case of the 'fair die', where each of the six faces is equally likely to be thrown. The chances of throwing four consecutive 'sixes' (or throwing four dice to be all sixes, which is statistically the same thing) is one in six to the power of four ($6^4 = 1296$). Thus, where we make X attempts at an experiment with Y equally possible outcomes, we generate a total of Y^X possible outcomes.

The key factor regarding such things as a 'fair coin' is that they have no memory. No matter how many heads are revealed in succession, the chances at the next throw are *still* 50:50!

Conditional probability

The discussion of coins and dice, etc. covers the situation where the first result has no influence on the next, i.e. the successive events are *independent*. Let us briefly turn to a normal pack of 52 playing cards. If you were to draw a single card, the probability of it being an ace is 4 in 52, or 1 in 13. If you were to replace the card, shuffle, and try again, the chances would still be 1/13. Thus, by the argument outlined previously, the chance of drawing an ace on two consecutive attempts is $1/13 \times 1/13 = 1/169$.

But what is the chance of drawing two aces if we had not replaced the card on the first attempt? The first draw is unaffected; the original quota of four aces is present and we have a 4 in 52 chance of finding one (or, to put it a different way, 48 chances out of 52 that we would not find one). Should the first draw indeed be our ace, then we are still in with a chance! Of the remaining 51 cards there are now but three aces; our chance of finding one on this second draw is therefore 3/51. The basic rule remains unchanged, that is, we need to multiply the two probabilities to find the chance of them both occurring, and so the combined probability is $4/52 \times 3/51$, which gives 1/221.

As we noted earlier, the literature of probability is full of phrases such as 'a fair die' (i.e. one where there is an equal probability of any of the six faces being thrown) or 'a perfect coin' (equal chances of heads and tails). These devices (which include 'we will assume that there is an equal likelihood of boys and girls being born, and we will also ignore the possibility of multiple births') are ways of postulating events of equal probability.

As you may know, the numbers of male and female children born are not equal, but numbers such as 48.9% would have cluttered the example with unnecessary arithmetic. In addition, people who are planning to start a family are not especially interested in the statistics for the population at large, they are interested in the probabilities *in their case*. There is evidence to suggest that, *for a given person*, there may indeed be valid reasons why they are more likely to have girls rather than boys or vice versa.

There is a refinement to simple probability theory, based upon Bayes Theorem, which can take account of new information to revise the probabilities. Fortunately or unfortunately, Bayesian statistics is beyond the scope of this course, but there is one related issue which merits our attention. 'Of equal probability' is often an assumption which merely conceals our lack of knowledge about a particular situation. If we have no information to the contrary, the assumption that boys and girls are equally likely to be born *for any particular person* is perfectly reasonable, but how long will we insist on this being the case in the face of mounting evidence to the contrary?

STATISTICAL FORMULAE

Mean

The mean, $\bar{x}$, of a distribution of readings x is given by:

$\bar{x} = \frac{\sum x}{n}$ where n = the number of readings of x.

Mode

The mode of a distribution is the reading x that occurs most frequently, the commonest result, i.e. if n_x = the number of times the reading x occurs then Mode = Z where n_z is the maximum of the n_xs.

NB: There can be more than one mode if two or more readings all have the same value as the maximum of the n_xs.

Median

The median is the middle reading of a distribution. If there are n readings, then:

(i) If n is *odd*, the median is the $\frac{(n+1)}{2}$th reading.

(ii) If n is *even*, the median is the average of the $\frac{(n-1)}{2}$th and $\frac{(n+1)}{2}$th readings.

Range

The true statistical range is the difference between the highest and lowest reading, i.e.:

Range = $x_{max} - x_{min}$

Alternatively, we could actually state x_{max} and x_{min}. If we had a distribution with the highest reading being 95 and the lowest 27 then:

a *statistician* would say the range was '68', i.e. 95 – 27 whereas

a *manager* might say the range was '27 to 95'.

Inter-quartile range

The IQR is the range that covers the *middle half of the readings*.

Again, a statistician would give a single number for IQR, whereas a manager would be more likely to state the start and end points.

Standard deviation

The standard deviation, s, of a distribution is given by:

$$s = \sqrt{\frac{\sum (x - \bar{x})^2}{n}}$$

where $\bar{x}$ is the mean as defined above.

Correlation coefficient

The correlation coefficient, r, of a distribution of paired readings (x, y) is given by:

$$r = \frac{n\sum xy - \sum x \sum y}{\sqrt{[n\sum x^2 - (\sum x)^2][n\sum y^2 - (\sum y)^2]}}$$

Note that r should be a number between –1 and +1.

Linear regression

A 'least squares' best fit linear regression line of 'y on x' for a set of paired data (x, y) is given by:

$$y = a + bx$$

where

$$b = \frac{n\sum xy - \sum x \sum y}{[n\sum x^2 - (\sum x)^2]}$$

$$a = \frac{\sum y}{n} - \frac{b\sum x}{n} = \bar{y} - b\bar{x}$$

Note the similarity between the equation for 'b' and that for 'r', the correlation coefficient.